Modern Scottish Short Stories

Modern Scottish Short Stories

EDITED BY

Fred Urquhart and Giles Gordon

HAMISH HAMILTON
LONDON

First published in Great Britain 1978
by Hamish Hamilton Limited
90 Great Russell Street London WC1B 3PT

British Library Cataloguing in Publication Data

Modern Scottish short stories
    1. Short stories, Scottish   2. English fiction –
Scottish authors
I. Urquhart, Fred II. Gordon, Giles
823' .9' IFS   PR8676
    ISBN 0-241-10058-5

Printed in Great Britain by
Bristol Typesetting Co. Ltd, Barton Manor, St Philips, Bristol

Contents

		page
Introduction by Fred Urquhart		vii
Acknowledgements		xi
Neil M. Gunn	THE GHOST'S STORY	I
Muriel Spark	'A SAD TALE'S BEST FOR WINTER'	7
George Friel	A COUPLE OF OLD BIGOTS	12
James Kennaway	THE COMPLEXION OF THE COLONEL	18
Naomi Mitchison	THE SEA HORSE	25
Neil McCallum	ONE MAN ALONE	32
Giles Gordon	LIBERATED PEOPLE	35
J. F. Hendry	PEEPSHOW	42
Eric Linklater	JOY AS IT FLIES	48
Margaret Hamilton	BUNG	58
Angus Wolfe Murray	I WANT TO GO NOW	65
Eona Macnicol	THE MAN IN THE LOCHAN	70
Edward Gaitens	GROWING UP	79
George Mackay Brown	FIVE GREEN WAVES	88
Janet Caird	DESTINY OBSCURE	100
Alan Jackson	THE CONSPIRACY FOR ARTHUR	108
Ian Hamilton Finlay	THE OLD MAN AND THE TROUT	III
James Allan Ford	THE MOURNERS FROM 19D	116
Fred Urquhart	MAGGIE LOGIE AND THE NATIONAL HEALTH	126
Elspeth Davie	ALLERGY	134

Robin Jenkins	EXILE	140
Alan Spence	SAILMAKER	145
Dorothy K. Haynes	CHANGELING	151
Morley Jamieson	MOON AND THE MERRY WIDOW	159
Jeremy Bruce-Watt	FATHER TO A MONSTER	171
Douglas Dunn	THE BLUE GALLERY	178
Iain Crichton Smith	TIMOSHENKO	180
Allan Massie	IN THE BARE LANDS	185
Deirdre Chapman	INTO EUROPE	190
Biographical and Bibliographical Notes		199

Introduction by Fred Urquhart

Scots have been pioneers in many fields. They have been in the vanguard in medicine, education, engineering and shipbuilding, as settlers in Canada and New Zealand, and as mercenaries in the armies of Europe from the Middle Ages onwards. In these and many other adventurous enterprises they have received due recognition and have been either praised or blamed for their spirit, bravery, toughness or sang-froid. Yet there is one field in which scant recognition has been given them. And that is the art of the short story.

The best stories spring from unbridled imagination. The Scots have always had that. They have always lied with panache. Early signs of the scope of Scottish imagination are to be found in the legends of the Highlands and Islands, told once upon a time around the peat fires, and in the stirring, romantic cadences of the Border Ballads. 'Art—and the ballads are often great art—does not come into being from popular excitement, but from the inspiration of a particular gifted individual: it cannot be syndicated and socialized,' wrote E. W. Edmunds in *A History of English Literature* edited by John Buchan, published in 1923. 'The doctrine of the extreme antiquity of the original minstrel seems to be contradicted by the facts before us. . . . The probability is that most of the ballads were fashioned in the sixteenth century by minstrels who summed up a long ancestry of popular poetry, as in Burns culminated a long tradition of Scottish vernacular song.'

Whether ballads like *Otterburn*, *The Bonnie Earl o' Moray* and *The Wife of Usher's Well* were composed by one hand or several, they have had an important influence not only on Scottish literature but on the culture of the entire English speaking people. From this source the imaginative stream of Scottish fiction eventually flowed; it took some time to start because the Scots, a dogmatic and complacent race, were keener to glorify themselves in philosophy and theology, feeling that any kind of fiction or poetry was the work of the Devil. Their canting covenanting is responsible for much Scottish fiction, when at last it was allowed to emerge into the open, after disentangling itself from the clammy clutches of the Kirk, being concerned with the supernatural.

Early in the nineteenth century readers were able to turn thankfully from theological catechisms and rantings to the long-short stories of Walter Scott, John Galt and James Hogg, whom Douglas Gifford calls 'the last representative of the ballad tradition'. Then, early in Victoria's reign, came the popular series of Wilson's *Tales of the Borders*. From that time the long-short story developed in different ways in the work of George Macdonald, William Black, W. E. Aytoun, Margaret Oliphant, S. R. Crockett, Neil Munro, Robert Louis Stevenson, J. M. Barrie, R. B. Cunninghame Graham and John Buchan until by the beginning of the twentieth century there was what might be called a thriving industry of Scottish storytellers whose work was read and enjoyed by a great number of readers far beyond the Scottish borders.

The industry still thrives. Twentieth-century practitioners of the art include people as contrasting in style, outlook and subject matter as Neil M. Gunn, Eric Linklater, Naomi Mitchison, Edward Gaitens, Muriel Spark, George Friel and George Mackay Brown. And we must not forget that Arthur Conan Doyle, member of an Irish Roman Catholic family, born in Edinburgh and educated at its university, was the author of the Sherlock Holmes stories, which have probably had a greater number of readers than most short stories published in the past one hundred years.

Nor should we forget the Scottish influence on the literature of other countries. Pauline Smith, who wrote *The Little Karoo* and other marvellous stories of the South African veld, was the daughter of an Aberdeenshire woman and she published her first work, which dealt with Scottish life, in *The Aberdeen Free Press*. Margaret Laurence, Canada's best writer of short stories and novels, is of Scottish stock. Scots words and phrases crop up in the stories of William Faulkner and Eudora Welty of the American Deep South. And Whit Burnett, founder and publisher and editor of the internationally famous American magazine *Story*, devoted to what Frank O'Connor, a great storyteller himself, has called 'the lonely voice of the short story writer', was so proud of his Scottish forebears that he wrote a novella about Robert Burns (who may have been an ancestor) which took up one whole issue of his magazine.

At the risk of being accused of chauvinism—and this would be funny seeing that I have lived for more than half my life in England and am by no means a thistle-wielding Scots Nationalist—I must say that I believe many Scottish short story writers of today display infinitely more gusto, passion, rumbustiousness and vigour than some of their English contemporaries.

Yet, despite this vigour and its possible influence on other cultures, the Scots themselves are neglected in most modern studies of the short story. Although invariably there are copious references to their

Irish and Welsh contemporaries, few Scots are obviously judged to be worthy of inclusion. In three studies of the short story on my desk, only around half a dozen Scottish names appear, and two of these, Scott and Stevenson, are not signalled out for their Scottishness but for their influence on English literature. The name of Lewis Grassic Gibbon does not appear; indeed, few English literary text-books mention him. Grassic Gibbon wrote only a handful of short stories, but his novels, especially his Howe o' the Mearns trilogy, *A Scots Quair*, have had tremendous influence on the generations that followed his. Saki (Hector Hugh Munro) is mentioned in all these studies, but briefly, and none of the authors take the trouble to say (perhaps they didn't know) that Saki belonged to a Scottish family with long Anglo-Indian military connections, and that once, when visiting Edinburgh with his aunt, she complained of the absence of baps on the breakfast table in much the same bewildered way as I now complain of the absence of Scottish names in the indexes of studies of the short story.

Giles Gordon and I hope that this anthology of twenty-nine Scottish stories will remedy such a sorry state of affairs and encourage authors of future studies of 'the lonely voice' to take a broader view. All these stories were written and published in the past forty years, so they are reasonably representative of what is being written in Scotland today. Six of the authors are dead. The twenty-three still alive are capable of defending their own work. I will say only a few words about the ones who are gone.

Margaret Hamilton's story gives one side of shipbuilding life on the Clyde, Edward Gaitens's gives another. Each died without receiving proper recognition for their contribution to Scottish letters. Besides short stories, each published a novel. Margaret Hamilton's *Bull's Penny* spans a man's life from childhood on the Island of Arran to his death in the poorshouse. It is remarkable for the raciness of its language; she had a wonderful command of dialect, especially the old half-forgotten words. Edward Gaitens's *Dance of the Apprentices* is about the Macdonnel family who live in a Gorbals tenement from before the 1914-18 war to its aftermath. Gaitens too wrote realistic dialogue, and his characters are bursting with vitality and Glasgow 'gallusness'.

The stories and novels of another Glasgow author, George Friel, were admired by many people, but his work never achieved the wider acclaim it deserved. His short stories should be collected in one volume by an enterprising publisher.

Neil M. Gunn, Eric Linklater and James Kennaway all became famous in their lifetime. Gunn and Linklater were primarily novelists, but each also wrote many first class short stories. James Kennaway, killed in a car accident at the height of his success, wrote only a few

A*

short stories in his early days. For various reasons, none of these
seemed right for this book. But I gathered from a conversation I had
with him several years before his death that *The Complexion of The
Colonel* was conceived first as a short story. That he turned it eventually into the first chapter of the novel *Tunes of Glory* is neither
here nor there, and we make no apologies for including it. It is a
perfect short story, and it depicts a side of Scottish life that we
wanted to show.

Before leaving the book to the reader's own judgement, I want to
say that there is a passage in H. E. Bates's *The Modern Short Story*
which has some bearing on what I've said about Scottish influence.
Bates pays tribute to Constance Garnett's 'sensibility gently tempered
with Scots caution' when she started her translations from the
Russian, and adds: 'Without Constance Garnett's genius and astonish-
ing industry in translating Turgenev, Tolstoy, Gogol, Dostoevsky,
Gorki and Tchehov, the history of twentieth-century English literature, notably that of the short story and the drama, must inevitably
have been a different thing.'

Acknowledgements

Acknowledgements are due to the following for permission to include the stories which appear in this book:

the author and the Hogarth Press for 'Five Green Waves' from *A Calendar of Love* by George Mackay Brown;

the author for 'Father to a Monster' by Jeremy Bruce-Watt, first published in the *Scotsman* in a somewhat different form;

the author for 'Destiny Obscure' by Janet Caird;

the author and Messrs William Collins for 'Into Europe' by Deirdre Chapman, first published in *Scottish Short Stories 1974*;

the author and Messrs Anthony Sheil for 'Allergy' from *The High Tide Talker* by Elspeth Davie (Hamish Hamilton);

the author and Messrs A. D. Peters for 'The Blue Gallery' by Douglas Dunn, first published in *Vogue*, June 1974;

the author for 'The Old Man and The Trout' from *The Sea-Bed and Other Stories* (Castle Wynd Printers) by Ian Hamilton Finlay;

the author and Messrs William Collins for 'The Mourners from 19D' by James Allan Ford, first published in *Scottish Short Stories 1975*;

Mrs Isobel Friel for 'A Couple of Old Bigots' by George Friel, first published in *Chapman*, No. 17, Autumn 1976;

Mr Charles Turner, literary executor of the author, for 'Growing Up' from *Growing Up* by Edward Gaitens (Jonathan Cape);

the author for 'Liberated People' by Giles Gordon, first published in the *Scotsman*;

A. C. Gunn for 'The Ghost's Story' from *The White Hour and other stories* by Neil M. Gunn (Faber & Faber);

Mrs Nora Hunter, the author's daughter, and Mrs Bette Stevenson for 'Bung' by Margaret Hamilton;

the author for 'Changeling' from *Thou Shalt Not Suffer a Witch and other stories* by Dorothy K. Haynes (Methuen);

the author for 'Peepshow' by J. F. Hendry from *No Scottish Twilight* (William Maclellan, 1947);

the author and Messrs William Collins for 'The Conspiracy for Arthur' by Alan Jackson, first published in *Scottish Short Stories* 1976;

the author for 'Moon and the Merry Widow' by Morley Jamieson, first published in *New Saltire*, No. 1, Summer 1961;

the author for 'Exile' by Robin Jenkins, first published in *The Scottish Review*, No. 5, Winter 1976;

Mrs Susan Kennaway and Messrs Douglas Rae for 'The Complexion of the Colonel' from *Tunes of Glory* by James Kennaway (Putnam);

Mrs Marjorie Linklater and Mr Andro Linklater for 'Joy As It Flies' from *Sealskin Trousers and other stories* by Eric Linklater (Rupert Hart-Davis);

the author for 'One Man Alone' from *My Enemies Have Sweet Voices* by Neil McCallum (Cassell);

the author and Messrs William Blackwood for 'The Man in the Lochan' from *The Hallowe'en Hero and other stories* by Eona Macnicol;

the author for 'In the Bare Lands' by Allan Massie, first published in the *London Magazine*, 1978;

the author for 'The Sea Horse' by Naomi Mitchison, first published in *The Scottish Review*, No. 6, Spring 1977;

the author for 'I Want To Go Now' by Angus Wolfe Murray;

the author and Messrs Victor Gollancz for 'Timoshenko' from *The Hermit and other stories* by Iain Crichton Smith;

the author and Harold Ober Associates Incorporated for ' "A Sad Tale's Best For Winter" ' from *The Go-Away Bird and other stories* by Muriel Spark (Macmillan):

the author and Messrs William Collins for 'Sailmaker' by Alan Spence, first published in *Scottish Short Stories* 1977;

the author for 'Maggie Logie and the National Health' from *The Dying Stallion* by Fred Urquhart (Rupert Hart-Davis).

NEIL M. GUNN

The Ghost's Story

I WAS NEVER a fighting man, said the ghost; yet for seventeen years I fought in the wars over the broad back of Scotland, from the glens and the moors to the low lands that spread themselves out far south of the waters of the Forth. But in all that great country there was no land so bonnie to me as my own land, the Laigh of Moray. My fore-fathers had been on that land for generations going far back beyond the coming of the Danes, and sometimes indeed my blood told me that they had been there for ever.

It was the year 1297, for that was the year I got married. The name of the girl I married was Janet Gordon, and she could have married anyone in all that countryside, but for some reason of her own she married me. We had our cottage and our bit of land, our small head of stock, and the outrun on the moor. She was nineteen and I was twenty-two. It was like being at the beginning of the world.

Now often enough there were wars, and chiefs would raise their men and march away with them on some wild foray. There were lads in my land who were fond of adventure. But the great bulk of us did not care for fighting. That's the way it always was. But now something strange began to happen to that land, and because it hap-pened to that land it happened to us.

Our country had been conquered by the English. They had marched through the length and breadth of it, through all the bonnie lands of Moray, and had put garrisons in the strong castles and fortified places. Sir Andrew de Moray, who was the overlord of our land, was shut up in an English prison.

Well—so it was. But what, at the end of the day, had that to do with us? Some of our cattle had been lifted and some damage done; but far more damage had been done many a time in a clan fight, as the tales told. The lords of the castles fought, and their fighting always boded ill for us. Let them fight.

But now, as I say, something strange began to happen in that land. The name of Sir Andrew's son, young Andrew, was whispered from one mouth to another, from one tree to another; you heard it in the sound of the river water, it lay in the throat like a salmon in the throat of a pool. I fell silent, thinking of that name. And all the time like a voice in the night it called: Come!

It was not the beauty of my wife Janet that had troubled the minds of men, it was her spirit, the way she bore herself under her bracken-bronze hair: it was her eyes. And she hated war.

'This is different,' I said to her.

'Ay, it's always different,' she answered. 'And it's always the same. The great lairds call you to their private tulzies and you go like sheep, and like sheep are killed.'

'No,' I said, 'it's not the same. The greatest lairds in Scotland, the highest nobles, side with the English and sit fast in their lands. Moray could do the same. By rising now against the English, he is risking everything, including his own father's life. Like you and me, he is newly wed; and maybe he loves his wife as I love mine.'

At that her anger against me increased. She drew her own picture of the state of Scotland in the grip of the English, with Scottish war lords supporting the English rule, and, behind that, the whole might of England herself. What chance did we think we had—we, a handful of simple Moray loons, against such powers? But though the flame of her scorn irked me a little, I replied as truthfully as I could, saying, 'I think we have nearly as good a chance as the snowflake has in hell.'

After that, for two days we hardly spoke a word. During the seventeen years that followed I never again experienced so hard a time as that time. Moray's voice spoke now not from the trees and the river and the wind, but up out of the land I walked on, until I knew it was no longer Moray's voice that called me, but the voice of the land itself. I looked at the land, this land of ours, this land. Then . . . I found . . . I could not look at it.

That night suddenly, and for no reason I could see, Janet gave way, and buried her face against me, and wept.

'You will go,' she said at last, 'you will go, and I will go with you.'

All through the night we talked of it and I tried to persuade her to wait for me, to wait at home. But now that the hard wall of her anger had been swept away, she was full of a light fun, and teased me, and mocked me, and did many a queer thing besides. It was no unusual thing for women to follow their men to war. Women were the camp-makers. They cooked the food and attended to the wounded, and left the men free to forage and to fight. And Janet had always been curious about herbs and growing things, for her grandmother had great skill amongst them.

So it came about that one fine evening in the middle of May, Janet and I walked into the camp of the men of Moray. I smile sometimes to myself when I think of that odd gathering of country lads with little but a bow and a bunch of arrows to their back, and the handful of women who were sometimes with them and sometimes not. For their aim was not to defend their simple homes against a gang of freebooters, but to go forth and take great castles and reduce strong garrisons, to turn aside thundering cavalry charges, to defeat armies, and finally to smash the mail-clad chivalry of all England and drive the English from our Scottish lands. One might well say, looking at the matter calmly, that the snowflake had the better chance.

Yet one new thing there was in that little camp, perhaps, for the first time in all Europe. And it was this: it was a meeting of the common people, a rising of the folk themselves, determined to win back freedom from the hand of the conqueror, to win back the freedom, not of Moray, not of Galloway, not of any one place, but of all Scotland—of Scotland, their own native land. It was a strange, fitful thing, this spirit, but it would not let us rest; a haunting, powerless thing that drove us on. Yet nameless as it was, time proved that in the end only one force could defeat it, and that force was death.

Now, because of this spirit among us, we in that company were often a happy band. In fighting for the freedom of our own land we found freedom in ourselves. From Moray we passed to Inverness. Our band grew. Young Andrew raised the standard at Avoch. The English nobles met in the castle of Inverness to see how best to destroy us. With Andrew at our head, and an Inverness burgess as next in command, we ambushed Fitzwarine of Castle Urquhart on his way home from the meeting with his escort of troops. It was my first fight. In Inverness I had gotten a long spear. Never before had I encountered a mail-clad man, but many a horse had I ridden. I made the horse rear so suddenly on that broken ground that he heaved right over and pinned his rider to the ground. Fitzwarine and a few of his escort were lucky to get away. It was our first fight, and we had won! We laid siege to the castle itself. In the dark we tackled its walls. But it was too strong for us. The Countess of Ross, who was on the side of the English, managed to send provisions to the garrison. We lifted the siege and turned our attentions to the Countess. And so the war for freedom started.

If I harp on this word freedom, it was because we soon found that the spirit that had moved us was everywhere wakening in Scotland. In July we were back in Moray, but not yet strong enough to meet an armed force sent against us from Aberdeen. We let it pass. But now, behind it, Aberdeen rose. And down in the forests of Selkirk, Wallace was waiting with his men. There were risings and there were capitulations. But ever and always Moray in the north and Wallace in the south held on. Their power grew. Castles fell before them. Within six weeks from that same July the men of Moray looked down from the Rock of Stirling upon an English army that was ten thousand strong. The moment had come at last. The fights and the skirmishes were over.

You know how the battle went: how the Scots won, and how Wallace followed the fleeing enemy to the border. But not Andrew of Moray, for he had led the way into the heart of the battle. I had seen him go down. Oh, desperately we fought, a little ring of us, over his body. Janet, running, met us as we bore him from the field. She said he was not dead, and she made us lay him down, and there and then she dealt with him according to her skill.

He lived long enough to know that Scotland was free. His name first, and Wallace's next, were put in documents of State; and then he died.

Back in the Laigh of Moray, we thought the wars were over. They had hardly yet begun. England gathered all her strength, set her intrigues going at home and abroad, and marched her forces north once more. Wallace was defeated at Falkirk and became a fugitive, hiding in his woods of the south.

Edward came again, and came to Moray, and near and far he laid our bonnie lands waste. For six weeks he sat between Kinloss and Lochindorb when the birches were turning yellow, and from there sent his armies to the taking of all the great castles in the north.

For seven bloody years after our victory at Stirling Bridge, Scotland suffered as surely she had never suffered before. She was so beaten down, with all her great lords Edward's men once more, so trampled upon and overcome, that it seemed never in the history of the world could she breathe the word freedom again. I looked at Janet and wondered, but she said no word. Our first son was now six years old, and our second son was three. She had won back from the hunted woods to our little place, and I had joined her there. Was it the end of fighting now for me? She said no word. That was in the month of September in the year 1305. I can remember the evening, for a lovely quiet evening it was. My care for Janet had grown with the years. I should stay with her, for a new birth was near to her; and the bonnie woods and the land. . . . It was in the quiet of the evening the man came to our door. I looked at his desperate face. 'Wallace,' he said, 'Wallace—has been beheaded in London town as a traitor— and his body torn asunder.'

The news froze our hearts and all the outside world, so that for a time everything was still as death. So still the birch trees were, you would think they grew in eternity. Never in my mortal life did I know so stricken a moment as that moment.

We spoke little. The man went on his way. And that night, out of a great quietness, Janet said to me: 'Tomorrow you will go, but this time I cannot go with you.'

And on the morrow I went, slipping through the woods to join with the hunted men. And as I went I knew why Edward had murdered Wallace and torn his body apart with the bloody hatred that no wolf knows. He had done it because of this thing, this new thing, which had been in Wallace's heart, which was in the hearts of all the hunted men and women of Scotland. Great lords he could buy and sell according to the rules of that chivalry of which he was the head. But this new thing, this love of our land, this love in the heart of the common folk, this love of freedom, this thing he could neither buy nor sell, and so he feared it.

As I went on my way, I saw Wallace again as I saw him before Stirling, and I called his name, and I wept. There in that wood I made my vow to myself—to hold by the struggle till Scotland's freedom was won, or to die.

There followed years of such adventure that the telling would take nights without end. You will have heard how Bruce was hunted by man and by beast, and how often his escape seemed half a miracle. His wife and daughter were torn from holy sanctuary at Tain by the Earl of Ross and sent prisoners to Edward; just as the son that had been born to the widow of young Andrew of Moray, a few months after his death at Stirling, had been caught and sent to England, too.

But through all these terrible years the thing that Edward feared did not die. Watered by tears and blood, it grew. It grew, and grew stronger; and at last, seventeen long years after the battle of Stirling Bridge, I was once again a spearman in an army, gazing down on the might of England, this time at that place where the Bannock Burn runs into the Forth.

In men they outnumbered us by three to one, and in war-arms they outdid us still more. On the first day I was one of Randolph's men, one of that schiltrom of spears against which the cavalry of Clifford and Beaumont broke as great waves break on rocks. The spears that could not be broken, until the schiltrom broke of itself to pursue the flying horsemen.

But the main armies did not engage that day, and at night Bruce left it with our leaders whether we should fight on the morrow or, against such desperate odds, more prudently retire. But all the leaders and all the army cried out to fight, and fight they did.

It was a sunny daybreak in the middle of June in the year 1314 when the Scots went forward to the attack. Before we reached the English lines, we kneeled for a moment. At that, there was a shout from the English, who thought we were kneeling to them. I was in the centre, under Randolph, and after our right had been engaged under Edward Bruce, we held steadily against the main body.

It was a desperate battle, that battle, and we fought on grimly without a word, without a cry. But what drove the battle in our favour, rising like a slow tide, was just that simple thing which we had and which they had not, the thing which I have called the love of freedom. And it beat them in the end. It broke them. As we saw them break, the warm flood of emotion at last mounted in us, and from our ranks rose the great cry: 'On them! On them! They fail!'

At that immortal moment, as they broke in rout and victory was certain, a horseman leaned over towards me. There was a soft, sickly movement in my body and I lay down for ease; and then over me came a great desire for sleep. As I fell asleep, I cried on Janet in a loud voice. . . .

My boy, Andrew, who was named after me, was cleaning a piece of ground in front of our cottage as I drew near. I went up to him with a strange excitement for there had always been an affection between us. He was a fine lad of sixteen years and working in my absence as head of the house. I stood before him and waited for his cry of welcome, but no cry came. It was as though he could not see me.

Then Janet was in the door. Her face looked scared. She took a step or two towards us and stopped. 'Andrew,' she said to her son, 'did you hear anyone crying?'

'No, Mother,' answered my son and as he glanced about him his eyes went through me.

'I thought,' she said, 'I heard your father crying my name.'

'Nonsense, Mother,' he said, but gently. She went inside. After a moment he heard her weeping, and took a step or two towards the door, but thought better of it and came back to his work.

MURIEL SPARK

'A Sad Tale's Best For Winter'

There was a man lived by a graveyard. His name was Selwyn
Macgregor, the nicest boy who ever committed the sin of whisky.

'Selwyn, what a place to live!'

'Have a tot for the road, dear.'

'Oh, Selwyn!'

'I get my letter tomorrow. Tomorrow I get the letter.'

'Now, Selwyn Macgregor!'

'It always arrives the first of the month. The first it always comes.'

'Macgregor, you're a case. Make it a small one.'

'For the road, mind.'

'Mac, I'm on my way. What a place to live, what a graveyard and
the mucky old church with the barbed wire round it, who'd ever
want to trespass within yon?'

'Cheerio, cheers!'

'Here's to you, Mr Macgregor. I would have to be a sore old tramp
to shelter in yon for the night. The barbed wire I cannot understand,
I can not.'

'The money comes on the first.'

'I'm away, Selwyn, the night's begun to rise.'

So it continued for thirteen years, with Selwyn increasing in age
from twenty-five to thirty-eight. At twenty-five he was invalided out
of the army, at thirty-eight was still living in the shack in the garden
of the fallen manse. There by the graveyard he was still getting his
letter from Edinburgh every month on the first, when he would cash
the cheque.

'Good evening, Mr Macgregor.'

'Just a tot, the both of you, come on now.'

'Mr Macgregor, we beg to enquire, will you play the piano at the
concert?'

'Aw, but that's to be the middle of the month.'

'Mac, you will play us a piece.'

'Mid-month I'll be in contemplation.'

'No more for me—well, a small . . . that's enough, Mr M.'

'Cheerio!'

'We'll put you down for a tune then, Selwyn.'

'Aw no,' I said.

'Mr Selwyn, you'll go melancholy mad. What a place to dwell by!'

'Here's luck t'you both.'

Always, about the middle of the month, Selwyn's money ran dry. Then he would go thirsty; he wouldn't open the door to anyone even if they had a plate of dinner in their hands. He lived on what he could get, turnips and sometimes the loaves and dinners which they left on the doorstep. The 25th of the month he opened his doors again, borrowed a bit till the first, received visitors, brought out the bottle.

But in those ten silent days between the middle of the month and the twenty-fifth Selwyn Macgregor would sit by his window and contemplate the graves of the dead.

*

Selwyn's aunt lived in a tenement flat in the Warrender district of Edinburgh. Those flats were once occupied by people of good substance and still here and there contain a whole lot of wealth behind the lack of show.

'The district's going down,' Selwyn's aunt was saying for twenty years. But let anyone come and tell her, 'This quarter's going down':

'Not in my consideration, it isn't,' she would say.

It was Selwyn's Aunt Macgregor who, in view of the fact that his Mother had been Welsh, sent him his monthly cheque, for it wasn't Selwyn's fault that his mother had been Welsh and mad or at least bone lazy. What's bred in the bone comes out.

There wouldn't be much point in going into many details about Aunt Macgregor, what she looked like in her navy blue and how her eyes, nose and mouth were disposed among the broken veins of her fine severe old face, because her features went, as Selwyn said, under the earth where corruption is, and her navy blue went to the nurse.

Well, she died. Some months before, you must know, she visited Selwyn up there in that shack by the graveyard. She wore her brown, for she was careful with the navy. So up she went on the excursion to Selwyn Macgregor. He wasn't contemplating just then, so the doors were open.

'Auntie Macgregor! A little drop, Auntie, oh come on, a bit of a drop. That's the girl.'

'Selwyn,' she said, 'you're the worse.'

'Worse than what?' Although Selwyn knew she meant for the drink.

'Worse than what? Worse than who? Than who-oo-ooo?' Selwyn kept on chanting, and she started to laugh. She had a soft spot really for Selwyn.

Well, she died and left him a packet. Selwyn travelled to the funeral, a bitter cold day. Bitter cold, and naturally he had his flask in his pocket. For you must know Selwyn entertained a lively faith in the Resurrection; work it out, there was no dishonour meant to Aunt Macgregor by Selwyn's taking precautions against the cold at the graveside, though he tottered and there was talk.

'Dust to dust. . . .'

'That's never Miss Macgregor's nephew! Surely yon's never!'

'That's the chief mourner, her brother's boy. What's he up to for the Lord's sake?'

Selwyn lifted a handful of earth. But then, then, he stood looking at it with his smile. There was the coffin waiting and all the people waiting. So when the minister nodded as if to say, 'All right, toss it on the coffin,' Selwyn flung the earth over his left shoulder out of force of habit, as he did at home with the salt. After that he beamed round at the mourners as much as to say, 'Here's health!' or 'Cheerio!' or some similar saying.

'Poor Miss Macgregor. The only relative, poor soul.'

*

Shortly afterwards Selwyn received a letter about his aunt's will from one of the trustees. It was rather complicated, and so Selwyn wrote, 'Come and see me after the twenty-fifth.' And he busied himself with contemplation until that date. On the twenty-sixth the trustee arrived at Selwyn's door with his healthy face and dark overcoat. Selwyn thought, what a nice wee trustee, here's hoping he's brought some ready.

'Make yourself at home,' said Selwyn, getting out another glass.

'Ta,' said the man.

'Here's hoping,' Selwyn said.

And eventually this trustee said to Selwyn. 'You know the provision in Miss Macgregor's will?'

'I did notice something,' Selwyn declared, 'in that letter you sent me but I was busy at the time.'

So the man read out the will, and when he came to the bit '. . . to my nephew Selwyn Macgregor . . .' he stopped and looked at Selwyn, '. . . providing,' he continued, 'he looks after his health.'

'My auntie all over,' Selwyn said and filled up the glasses. 'A very fine woman, Mr—?'

'Brown,' said the man. 'My partner Mr Harper is the other trustee. You'll get on fine with him. When will you be moving from here?'

'Aw when I'm dead,' said Selwyn.

'Now, Mr Macgregor, this is not a healthy spot. The will says—'

'To hell with the will,' said Selwyn, and patted Mr Brown on the shoulder, so that Mr Brown couldn't help warming to him, what with the whisky-tingle inside him, and the pleasant Welsh lilt of the 'L's' when Selwyn had said, 'To hell with the will.'

'My work keeps me here,' Selwyn added.

'What is your work, Mr Macgregor?'

'The contemplation of corruption.'

'Now, Mr Macgregor, that is not a healthy occupation. I don't wish to be difficult but my partner Mr Harper takes his duty as a trustee very much to heart. Miss Macgregor was an old client of ours and she always worried about your health.'

'Bung ho, press on!' said Selwyn.

'Same to you, Mr Mac. Here's to you, sir.'

'You can tell Harper,' Selwyn pointed out, 'that you found me in good health and busy working.'

'You look a bit thin, Mr Macgregor. This doesn't look a healthy spot to me.'

Selwyn played him a tune and sang him a song. 'O mother, mother,' he sang, 'make my bed. O make it soft and narrow. . . .'

'Very nice,' said the trustee when he'd finished. 'That was rare.'

'I'm a musician,' said Selwyn. 'You needn't mention my other work to Harper.'

'Here, you're trying to corrupt me, that'll never do. Didn't you say corruption was your line?'

'No, no. I do contemplation of corruption,' Selwyn explained. 'A very different thing, very high. Drink up.'

'Here's wishing you all you wish yourself,' said Mr Brown. 'You don't corrupt me, mind!'

'It's either I corrupt you or you corrupt me,' Selwyn stated, and he went on to explain himself, and they argued the point while the time became timeless and they got muddled over the word corrupt, calling it cupped.

'Who's cupping who?' said Mr Brown. 'Who's cups?'

Eventually Selwyn couldn't laugh for coughing, and again, he couldn't cough for laughing. When he recovered he passed the bottle and went deep into the question of cups being a corrupt form of corrupt.

He sang out, 'Ha, ha, ha. Hee, hee, hee. I'll cup you or you'll cup me.'

'Here's a short life and a merry one!' said Mr Brown.

*

Well, it was Selwyn corrupted the trustee. His monthly cheque, bigger than before, continued to come in. All through the winter he carried on his routine, doors open for company on the twenty-fifth, and on the fifteenth doors shut, and Selwyn at his window contemplating the dead graves.

He died the following spring. There had been an X-ray two years back, when Selwyn had said; 'Aw to hell with my chest, I've work to do. Here's a health!'

Mr Brown said to his partner, 'He never told me of his chest. If I'd known of it I would have seen him into a warm house and a new suit. I would have seen him with a housekeeper and I would have seen him into medical hands.'

'These musicians,' said Mr Harper. 'Too dedicated. One must admire them, though.'

'Oh, must one? Oh, must one?' said Mr Brown irritably, for he couldn't himself think highly of Selwyn who had been so shabby as to actually die when he had more or less agreed only to contemplate.

'A sad tale,' said Mr Harper dreamily. 'Macgregor was a hero in his way.'

'Oh, was he? Oh, was he?' At that moment Mr Brown despised his stupid partner almost more than he resented the dead man. Though lately, chancing to be in those parts where Selwyn had lived, even Mr Brown couldn't help the thought, 'Oh, Selwyn Macgregor, what a manner you had!' And when he saw that they have levelled out the old graveyard to make a playground for the children, he contemplated Selwyn's corruption for a long time.

GEORGE FRIEL

A Couple of Old Bigots

The two miners reached the place together and Geddes lay down on the pavement. He grunted, resigned to his daily darg. Crouched on his side in an inch of water he prepared to start hewing.

'How now,' he declaimed, 'which of your hips has the most profound sciatica?'

He wriggled from his hip to his back, the pick under his right hand. Self-educated beyond his station, he liked to come out with the odd bits of Shakespeare he had learnt by heart and he got a kick out of throwing to Liam Rooney, his neighbour at the coal-face, the scraps of his unguided reading. Sometimes he did it from simple generosity, sometimes from malice aforethought. He was a quarrelsome atheist, and baiting Rooney, a practising Catholic, kept him happy. They were the best of friends.

'Tell me this, Liam,' he heaved through his toiling. 'Do you believe in free will?'

'I wish you'd give your tongue a wee rest,' Rooney complained, pushing the hutch nearer. 'You're aye blethering a lot of bloody nonsense.'

'No, but do you?' Geddes persisted. 'Damn it all, man, you surely ken what you're supposed to believe.'

'Ay, all right then, I believe in free will,' Rooney conceded. He thought the best policy was to humour Geddes, to be a willing victim and let him have his joke and his triumph. But sometimes he wished he could find an answer that Geddes couldn't use. When that ambition came to him he would make up his mind to read a book, but he never found the time and he never found the book.

'And do you believe God's almighty?' Geddes pursued him with a negroid grin.

'Of course He is,' Rooney answered impatiently. He knew there was a trap being sprung, but he couldn't see how to avoid it. 'How could He be God if He's no'?'

'But he canny be, no' if every man's got free will,' Geddes gloated up at him. 'Ye canny have it baith ways.'

'Whit way can I no'?' Rooney demanded.

Geddes kept it up, but it led nowhere. At the end of the shift they left the place together and walked one behind the other the couple of miles to the cage. They were working at the furthest point from the main road and lagged a fair distance behind the other miners. Then Geddes stopped suddenly, his hand out to stop Rooney too. They heard a creaking in the pine props, but they weren't sure where it came from.

'Go on!' Rooney screamed, pushing Geddes forward.

'No, get back,' Geddes shouted, shoving Rooney the other way.

The speed of his turn threw him off balance and he finished up sprawling across Rooney just as the first of the fall came down. It cut them off from the rest of the shift, and it was all over in less than a minute. The tumult was like a tenement collapsing, like thunder directly overhead.

'Jesus, Mary and Joseph!' Rooney panted, blessing himself. He gawked up at the threatening roof. The roar of its anger stopped, and there was only an occasional belch as some fragments shifted, a mild pattering as the soil filtered through.

'I wonder how long that's been pickling,' Geddes muttered resentfully. 'They ought to have kent aboot that.'

Rooney squatted on his hunkers, gulping and mouthing. He wanted to speak, to ask questions that Geddes would answer encouragingly since Geddes was the clever one with an answer to everything, but he couldn't get a word out.

'How much of it fell do you think?' Geddes asked him.

'A hell of a lot by the sound of it,' Rooney whispered, really frightened.

They were three and a half days in there together and stuck it out well because they were old friends, though Rooney lost his temper twice. The first time was when Geddes laughed at him for taking out his rosary and saying Our Fathers and Hail Marys on and on, mysteriously.

'Christ, dae ye aye carry thae beads wi' ye?' he scoffed.

'Ye ken damn fine I aye have my rosary in my pocket,' Rooney snapped. 'And ye could do worse than say a wee prayer yourself.'

The second time he lost his temper was half-way through the second day when Geddes was seized with a sudden spasm of vigour and hammed too near the bone.

'Ay, but to die, and go we know not where,
To lie in cold obstruction and to rot.'

'Ach, shut yer face,' Rooney growled. 'We're no' a' that deid yet.'

To begin with they did what they could to clear away the rubble, cheering each other, keeping their spirits up with guessing-games, football quizzes and songs. Geddes sang 'The Star o' Rabbie Burns' and Rooney taught him 'Faith of Our Fathers'. They drank the moisture that dripped from the roof, but long before they were rescued they were too weak to move. They were silent for hours at a stretch, past singing and arguing. The knocking they had answered over the nightmare term of darkness came slowly nearer and they sat against the wall and waited.

'Are ye all right, Liam?' Geddes croaked.

'Ay, I'm grand, Willie,' Rooney breathed faintly.

'It'll no be lang noo,' Geddes comforted him. 'Ay, we'll be having a pint in Sloan's the morrow night, you and me, so we will.'

The first small gap appeared. They heard the voices come through loud and clear. They got a glimpse of Lumsden, the brusher, and the wall-eye of Grant the drawer. Then a large anonymous hand came to them with food and drink.

It wasn't the first accident they were in, and it wasn't the last, but it was the only time they were alone together. It was one more bond between them. They went back to work on the same day, still neighbours on the same shift, and their dialogue went on as before.

'Willie Geddes has got some terrible stories about the Popes,' Rooney told his wife. 'I don't know where he gets the half of them. But if he's right there's been some quare old birds in the Vatican.'

'Sure everybody knows there's been bad Popes,' Mrs Rooney shrugged it off, ladling out his soup. 'You don't need Willie Geddes to tell you that.'

'Well, he's told me one or two things I never knew,' Rooney said grudgingly. 'Then he says, Ay, and you believe the Pope's infallible!'

His daughter looked up perkily from her secondary school homework spread out at the other end of the kitchen table and gave him advice.

'Just you tell him the Church doesn't say the Pope's impeccable.'

Her father glowered at her, ready to be embarrassed by the implications of the strange word. She explained it.

'Jees, I'll catch him with that one tomorrow,' he laughed. 'That's a rare word that is.'

The next time Geddes got on to the lives of the Popes Rooney carefully repeated what his daughter told him.

'Have you been reading a book?' Geddes asked sourly.

'Och, I don't need to be reading books,' Rooney joked. 'I learned a thing or two at school. Of course an Orangeman like you canny understand Catholic doctrine.'

'I'm no' an Orangeman,' Geddes shouted, angry at the name. 'I read the Freethinker every week, as you damn well know.'

'Well you ought to be,' Rooney cut back at him. 'Sure your father was, and his father afore him.'

'Keep my father out of it,' Geddes huffed. 'I know a lot mair aboot religion than a bigot like you.'

'I'm no' a bigot,' Rooney protested. 'It's you that's the bigot.'

'It's no', it's you,' Geddes insisted. 'You'll never admit you're in the wrong.'

'I will so, if I am,' Rooney retorted. It's you that's always sure you're right.'

It went on like that for years, and as they spent their days in familiar disputation old age came along and joined them, making in their company a third of whose presence they were only slowly aware. They became old grey men, they qualified for their pension, they stopped working, they mooned about the dying mining village, they drank together in Sloan's, and Geddes always got on to religion. The retreating years were making Rooney more devout, and more touchy in his piety, but they were making Geddes more aggressive, as if he had to prove his case to Rooney before it was too late and death proved everything.

They were two dottering old men, two local worthies, and the village smiled on their crabbit friendship and loved them equally. They might have gone to their common end still friends if Geddes hadn't said too much in Sloan's one Saturday night with a good drink on him. He dragged in the Virgin Mary and spoke of her with a coarseness he had never used before. He had been clever and sarcastic, he had been jocular and irreverent, but never coarse. Rooney was shocked. He was hurt. He looked into his pint and shook his head over it.

'That's enough, Willie,' he said. 'Maybe you're my best friend, but that's just wicked blasphemy. You've went too far this time. You're just an old bigot, so you are. I'm finished wi' ye!'

He emptied his glass and left the bar without another word, neither hurriedly nor slowly, walking out quite calmly.

'Christ almighty, some people!' Geddes complained to the barman. 'Canny take a joke.'

He had another drink to cover his vexation.

'He's no' getting me to go running after him,' he told the neutral barman. 'Him and his Virgin Mary! I don't believe a word of it.'

He waited for Rooney to come back and be teased into conversation again. He waited till the bar closed, and then he had to plod home alone. Over the next few days he tried to find Rooney. He went to all the usual places at the usual times, but he never saw him. His wife, coming in from her shopping, would tell him she had just seen Rooney here or there, all by himself, and he acknowledged the information with a grunt. He didn't want to tell her Rooney was deliberately avoiding him. He brooded, sour in his loneliness.

He didn't have to brood long. Rooney died in his sleep a week later, when a January wind was bringing a sleet across the village. He was in his chair at the fireside when his wife bustled in with the news.

'I just met Mrs Lumsden in the grocer's there,' she said. 'She was telling me Liam Rooney passed away during the night.'

'Och ay,' he nodded with Scottish brevity, showing no emotion.

He sat forward in his chair, staring into the fire, and as he looked at the living coals he thought of the pit. Nearly sixty years of working with Rooney jumbled through his mind, and the fire was refracted through his unfallen tears. When he went for his afternoon walk memories of Rooney kept him company. He was passing Sloan's when a young woman crossed the street to speak to him. It was Miss Rooney, teacher of modern languages in the local Catholic secondary school.

'Oh, Willie,' she said, very grave, 'You'll have heard about my father?'

'Oh ay,' he said solemnly, and waited.

'I was on my way round to see you.' Rooney's daughter spoke to him softly. 'My mother sent me. She wants you to take a cord.'

'But that's no' my place, that's for the nearest,' Geddes said, his scalp prickling at the very thought of going to a Catholic funeral. 'And there's all your uncles.'

'Oh, you come before any of them,' she warmed him with a wee smile. 'Some of them have never put a foot across the door for years. You were the first my mother mentioned when she was asked who was all taking a cord.'

'Your mother's very kind,' he said.

He went to see the widow. He guessed at once Rooney had never told her of their last night at the bar. She had no idea her husband's last days on earth were spent avoiding his old butty. He said what he could to show his sympathy, and she gave him hers.

'It was that sudden, Willie,' she whimpered. 'And you'll miss him yourself. After all these years. You and him were through the General Strike thegither and on till that November, and that wasn't yesterday. And he thought the world of you. Every time he came off a shift it was Willie Geddes says this and Willie Geddes says that. Just the night before he died he was talking about you.'

'But how can I go to the funeral?' he asked, screwing up his eyes. 'Me in a Catholic church! They wouldn't let me in, would they? You know what I am.'

'Now you've no call to be worrying about that,' Mrs Rooney smacked his hand lightly. 'God knows best what we all are. If you think you'd feel strange coming into the church just you meet the party at the door when they bring the body out. All I want you to do is take a cord when they lower the coffin—'

She started to cry again, her own words too blunt for her, and his huge hand patted her shoulder.

'I know Liam would have wanted you there,' she sniffled.

He put on a black tie and his good suit and his dark coat and he went to the funeral. He stood beside the grave while a chubby priest, talking Latin with a Donegal accent, said a lot of prayers he couldn't follow, and when he had taken the cord assigned to him and helped to lower the coffin deep into the damp clay he saw the priest sprinkle water on the lid with a little feather duster. Stuck at the edge of the dismal pit, he felt he was a white man taking part in the rites of a black tribe. On the other side of the grave four of Rooney's unknown brothers, big men with heavy coats and dull faces, huddled together and their lips moved knowingly to the priest's last prayer. When they stopped praying they made the sign of the cross, and determined to be just as much Liam Rooney's mourner as any of them, old Geddes too made the sign of the cross. At that moment he remembered a phrase he had often heard Rooney use, and he repeated it deliberately in a willing suspension of his disbelief.

'God rest him,' he mumbled.

The wind across the cemetery crested his white hair, slapped at the tails of his coat and chilled his old bones.

JAMES KENNAWAY

The Complexion of the Colonel

There is a high wall that surrounds Campbell Barracks, and in the winter there is often a layer of crusted snow on top of it. No civilian rightly knows what happens behind that grey wall but everybody is always curious, and people were more than ever curious one January a year or two ago.

The north wind had blown most of the snow to the side of the barrack square, and not a soul walked there; not a canteen cat. In the guardroom the corporal commanding the picket was warming his fingers on a mug of hot tea, and the metal-work on the sentry's rifle was sticky with frost. In the bath-house the Battalion plumber was using a blow-lamp on the pipes, and he had reached the stage of swearing with enjoyment. The sergeants were in their Mess, singing to keep themselves warm, and drinking to keep themselves singing. National Servicemen wished they were home in their villas, and horn-nailed Regulars talked of Suez; even the bandboys wished they were back at borstal. In the Married Quarters, the Regimental Sergeant-Major, Mr Riddick, was sandwiched between his fire and his television set.

But it was warm in the Officers' Mess. Dinner was over, and the Queen had had her due. The long dining-room with the low ceiling was thick with tobacco smoke. The regimental silver cups, bowls and goblets shone in the blaze of the lights above the table, and from the shadows past colonels, portrayed in black and white, looked down at the table with glassy eyes. Two pipers, splendid in their scarlet, marched round and round the table playing the tunes of glory. The noise of the music was deafening, but on a dinner night this was to be expected.

The officers who owned 'Number Ones' were in their blue tunics and tartan trews. Sitting back from the table they crossed their legs and admired their thighs and calves. They moved their feet and felt the comfort of the leather Wellingtons that fitted closely to the ankle. Only one or two of the subalterns who could not rise to Number Ones were wearing khaki tunics and kilts. But, drunk to the stage of excited physical consciousness, they too crossed their legs and glanced with anxious pride at their knees. They had folded their stockings to make the most of the muscles of their legs, and they wore nothing under their kilts. Some were anxious that the dinner should finish early giving them time to visit their women. Others of a more philosophic turn of mind had resigned themselves by now. They had ruled out the idea of visiting a woman and they were now falling into a slow stupor. Both sets of officers would in the end return to their bunks, thoroughly dispirited, and breathless with the cold of three o'clock in the morning. The lover as likely as not, if he were still a subaltern, would be disappointed to the point of pain, and the philosopher, bowing patiently and bowing low to the inevitable, would be sick. And both would live to fight another day.

But it was at this point in the evening, when the pipers played, that the officers could see most clearly how the night would end. Their fate lay in the hands of the man sitting half way up the table, and in spite of the Mess President at the head, nobody could deny that the table was commanded by the unforgettable figure of Acting Lieutenant-Colonel Jock Sinclair, D.S.O. (and bar).

The Colonel's face was big and smooth and red and thick. He had blue eyes—they were a little bloodshot now—and his voice was a sergeant's. His hair, which was thin, was brushed straight back with brilliantine. It was not a bit grey. The Colonel did not look broad because he was also deep, and had the buttons on his tunic been fastened there would have been little creases running across his chest and stomach. But at times such as this he was inclined to unfasten his buttons. He had even unfastened the top two buttons of his trews this evening and his striped shirt protruded through the gap in the tartan. His trews were skin tight and it looked as if he need only brace his muscles to tear the seams apart. In his lap he nursed a very large tumbler of whisky, and he tapped his foot on the ground as the pipers played. He did not seem to find the music too loud.

From time to time he glanced round the table, and other officers when they caught his eye quickly turned away while he continued to stare. The look in his eye was as flat as the sole of his polished boot.

He had already made the pipers play three extra tunes that night, and as they played 'The Green Hills' for the second time he hummed, and the music comforted him. He put his glass on the table when the room was silent again.

'Get away with you,' he said, surprisingly kindly, to the Corporal-Piper and as the pipers marched out of the room the officers applauded in their usual way: they banged their fists on the table and stamped their feet on the floor-boards. Jock sent orders that the pipers should be given double whiskies, then he leant back in his chair and groaned, while his officers talked. It was some minutes later when one of the younger subalterns at the far end of the table caught his attention. Jock tipped forward in his seat and put his clenched fists on the table. The flat eye grew narrow; the meat on his face quivered, and along the table conversation died on the lips. He made a suppressed sound which was still something of a shout:

'MacKinnon, boy!' Then he lowered his voice to a hiss. 'For Christ's sake smoke your cigarette like a man. Stop puffing at it like a bloody debutante.' He moved his hand as though he were chucking away a pebble, and he spoke loudly again. 'Get on with you; smoke, laddie, smoke. . . .'

There was silence in the room as the young subaltern put his cigarette to his lips. He held it rather stiffly between two fingers and he half closed his eyes as he drew in the tobacco smoke. There was still a hush. He looked nervously at his Colonel as he took the cigarette from his lips. Even the movement of his wrist as he brought the cigarette down to the plate had something inescapably feminine about it, and this made Jock shake his fist. The boy's mouth was now full of smoke and he sat very still, with his eyes wide open.

'Go on then, laddie; draw it in, draw it in.'

MacKinnon took a deep breath which made him feel a little dizzy and he was glad that the Colonel could not resist a joke at this point. The sound of his little cough was drowned by the laughter that greeted his Colonel's witticism. Jock looked from side to side.

'We've got laddies that've never put it in, I know,' he said with both a wink and a nod. 'What I didn't know is how we've one who can't even draw it in, eh?' When he laughed the veins on his temple stood out. Then the laugh, as usual, deteriorated into a thick cough, and he shook backwards and forwards in an attempt to control it.

The officers were a mixed collection. One or two of them, such as Major Macmillan, who was perpetually sunburnt, seemed very much gentlemen, although they too laughed at Jock's jokes. The others, if not gentlemen, were Scotsmen. The younger they were the larger were their jaws, the older they were the fatter were their necks, except of course for the Quartermaster, Dusty Millar, who had no neck at all.

At last Jock recovered himself. 'Aye,' he said, with a final cough, 'aye . . . Well gentlemen, I have news for you.'

Someone at the far end of the table was still talking.

'All of you, you ignorant men.' Jock raised his voice. 'News that'll affect you all.' He paused. 'Tomorrow there's a new colonel coming, and he'll be taking over the Battalion. D'you hear? D'you hear me now?'

All the officers hesitated. Their jaws dropped and they leant forward to look at Jock, who was looking at his tumbler.

Macmillan had a light-comedy voice. He touched his fair hair with his hand and he said, 'Come, Jock, you're pulling our legs.'

'Aye,' someone said uncertainly, disbelievingly. 'That's it, isn't it?'

'What I'm telling you is true.' Jock took a sip of his drink. 'Ask Jimmy Cairns. Jimmy knows right enough.'

Cairns, who was his Adjutant, did not know what to say but felt it was a time when something should be said. He moved his hands, and he frowned,

'That's the way of it,' he said.

'Och . . .' The Quartermaster moaned, and others echoed him.

'That's not right,' one said; and another, 'It can't be true.' The Battalion without Jock as C.O. seemed then an impossibility.

Jock raised his hand in the smoky air.

'We didn't ask for comments,' he said. Then, glancing at the younger officers at the far end of the table, some of whom did not seem so dismayed by the news, he added, 'One way or the other,' and he showed his teeth when he grinned. He grew solemn again and drew his hand down his face and wagged his head, as if to clear his vision. 'It's just a fact,' he said slowly, 'it's just a fact,' and he leant back in his chair again.

Major Charlie Scott, who sat next to Jock, had an afterdinner habit of stroking his large red moustache, but he dropped his hand to ask, 'What's his name, eh?'

'Basil Barrow.'

'Major Barrow?' a clear-voiced subaltern said at once. 'He lectured at Sandhurst. He's an expert on Special. . . .' Suddenly aware that he had sounded a little too enthusiastic, his voice trailed away. He looked around, brushed some ash from his trews, and continued in a nonchalant tone, 'Oh, he's really quite all right; they say he's frightfully bright upstairs.' The officers looked towards the Colonel again. They were gradually recovering.

'Aye,' Jock said. 'He went to Oxford, if that means anything. They say he was a great success as a lecturer or whatever he was. Quite a turn with the cadets.' He gave a malicious grin and another big wink. Then he belched and made a sour face. He took another drink of whisky.

'Colonel Barrow's a man about forty-four. Eton—aye, it's right, what I'm telling you—Eton and Oxford. He joined the Regiment in 1935 and he was only with it a year or two before being posted on special duties. He has some languages, so it seems. It's as young Simpson says. He's bright upstairs. He got the M.C. and he was taken prisoner pretty early on.' Jock swung his eyes around the table. 'I know all about him; you see that?'

'There was a fellow we used to call Barrow Boy. D'you remember him? A lightweight chap; good at fencing, if I recall.'

'I remember. Good Lord, yes.'

B

Jock spoke again. 'That's the same chum. That's him. He was well placed in the Pentathlon sometime just before the war.' He grew suddenly tired of the subject. 'Well, he's to command the Battalion and I'll have another tumbler of whisky.'

A Mess steward dashed forward and replaced the empty glass with a full one. On nights like this Jock's drinks were lined up on a shelf just inside the pantry door; lined up in close formation.

'And what about you, Jock?' Cairns asked.

'Aye. And what about me, china?'

'You staying on?'

'Unless you're going to get rid of me, Jimmy.'

Cairns knew just how far he could go with Jock.

'I thought there might be a chance of it.'

Jock was about to smile when the same subaltern who had known Barrow interrupted. 'Staying on as second-in-command, you mean?' and he was too young and a little too well spoken to get away with it. His seniors glanced immediately at the Colonel. Jock eyed the boy with real hatred, and there was a very long pause.

One of the stewards by the pantry door all but dropped his salver; his eyes grew wide, and he felt the hair rising at the back of his neck. Goblets and glasses poised in the air, whisky stayed in the mouth, unswallowed, and the swirly cloud of smoke above Jock's head for one instant seemed perfectly still.

Jock spoke very sourly, and quietly. 'So may it please you, Mr Simpson,' was what he said, looking back to his tumbler.

'Oh, I'm glad you're not leaving us, sir.' But the answer came too glibly. Jock shrugged and gave a little snigger. He spoke as if he did not care whether he was heard. 'You're away off net, laddie . . . and, Mr Simpson?'

It was fairly easy to see that Mr Simpson had been a prefect at school. He looked the Colonel straight in the eye and he never quite closed his mouth.

'Yes, sir?'

'No "Sirs" in the Mess. Christian names in the Mess except for me and I'm "Colonel". I call you just what I feel like. O.K.?'

'Yes, Colonel.'

'Yes, Colonel . . . Now, gentlemen; now then. This is Jock's last supper and there'll be a round of drinks on me. Even one for Mr Simpson. Corporal!'

'Sir.'

'Whisky. For the gentlemen that like it and for the gentlemen who don't like it, whisky.'

He turned apologetically to Charlie Scott, who was still stroking his moustache.

'I'm no good at talking at the best of times, Charlie, and tonight

I'm no coping at all. Will we have the pipers back? It fills in the gaps.'

'Whatever you say, Jock; it's your night.'

'Aye.' Jock opened his eyes very wide: this was one of his mannerisms. 'Aye,' he used to say, then with his eyes wide open he would add a little affirmative noise. It was an open mouthed 'mm'. Aye, and a-huh. 'Well I say we'll have the pipers.' He leant back in his chair and addressed one of the stewards who was hurrying by with a bottle. 'Laddie, call the pipers.'

'This minute, sir.'

'Just "Sir".' He made a gesture with his flat hand: a little steadying gesture. It was the same gesture that had steadied men in the desert, in Italy, France, Germany and Palestine. 'Just "Sir". That's all you need say.' Then he sighed, and he said, 'Aye, Charlie.' He dug the point of his knife into the table-cloth again and again as he talked. He first made a hole with the knife and gradually he widened it.

'. . . And you'll have a tune, and I'll have a tune, and Macmillan here'll have a tune, and I'll have another tune. Charlie, why the hell d'you grow that moustache so big?'

Major Charlie Scott continued to stroke it with his fingers. His great green eyes grew wide, under the shepherd's eyebrows. He could think of no explanation.

'Dunno; I'm sure. Just grew.'

Jock leant his chair back on two legs again and his arms fell down by his sides. 'And you're not the great talker yourself.'

' 'Fraid not.'

'No . . . Well, let's have the music. "Ho-ro, my Nut Brown Maiden" for me, and for you, Charlie?'

' "The Cock o' the North".' Jock tipped forward at that. The legs of the chair creaked as they pitched on the floor again.

'Yon's the Gordon's tune!'

'I still like it.'

Jock screwed up his face: he was genuinely worried.

'But yon's a cheesy tune, Charlie.'

Charlie Scott shrugged.

Jock leant forward to persuade him. 'Laddie, I was with them for a wee while. They didn't like me, you know; no. And Jock didn't care much for them, neither.'

'Really?'

'Can you no think of a better tune?'

'Myself, I like "The Cock o' the North".' Charlie Scott put another cigarette in his holder.

Jock laughed and the veins stood out again. He slapped his thigh and that made a big noise.

'And I love you, Charlie; you're a lovely man. You're no a great talker, right enough. But you've a mind of your own . . . Aye, pipers, and where have you been?'

'Pantry, sir.'

'Are you sober?'

'Sir.'

'You'd bloody well better be, and that's a fact. You're no here to get sick drunk the same as the rest of us are.'

The drones began as the bladders filled with air. The pipers marched round and round again. The room grew smokier, and the officers sat close into their chairs as the drink began to flow. The stewards never rested.

NAOMI MITCHISON

The Sea Horse

It was after the sea horse was killed that things began to go badly. It is not just that *he* was killed as well as the horse and he had been a good laird and a friendly man. But that was not the whole of it. Some people say it was all a lie but Neil and his wife went down to the strand early to catch the tide and he saw them both, the great white beast lying with the blood pouring from the gash in its throat and its hooves pawing and striking at the air and the man with his sword still in his left hand—he was *ciotach* you see, and a great bunch of the mane in his right hand. Neil and his woman both saw it as they rounded the rock—the rock we all know—and they let out a great screech and the woman dropped her basket and they ran for it, the two of them, back to the township and from house to house crying at us all to come. For who could face it alone?

But when we had got together and spoken about it and the priest had given his blessing to protect us and when we went down to the strand the tide was making and no sign of the sea horse, only a great dark patch on the sand—it was there yet—and he dead with a terrible bruise on his temple where the sea horse had struck with his hoof and broken the bone. We took him up among us and his hand still grasping the white lock; there was nothing to be done. Already by the time we had got him up and into the church and two of us had gone to the Tigh Mhor, for there was no telephone in those days, there were those to say that there was no sea horse. It had all been some kind of accident. Yet we had all seen the great hoof marks bigger than any Clydesdale and unshod.

You ask why he had taken the sword which had rested so long on the wooden brackets over the mantelpiece in the hall. He could have taken the service revolver which he had certainly used at the battle of Richebourg L'Avouée before he was wounded. He had the cartridges. Yes, but—he knew what was laid on him. He knew how it had to be done.

She was almost waiting for us. As soon as she saw us coming she sent the children off. Their nurse was a Lowland woman, who came and took them into the walled garden; we heard their voices playing

some game with her. She said 'I know, I know, don't tell me—he
was mad!'

'We are all deeply grieved,' we said, 'but it is as you think. The
priest will be coming.'

'It was on the sea's edge?' she asked.

'Yes,' we said, 'and a grip of the brute's mane in his right hand.'

'No,' she said, 'No! It was seaweed, it must have been seaweed!'

'It shall be what you say,' we answered her, for there were tears
streaming down her cheeks and her hands pulling, pulling at the scarf
she had round her neck as though she would wish to strangle herself.

She began to speak low, almost to herself and I remember every
word. 'It was after he was wounded—not the first time but the
second, when the Highland Division—you will remember—he spoke
to me about this. But I did not believe him. How could I? How could
anyone?'

'How could you indeed, Mistress Betty,' I answered, and thought
of them so newly married and all and she would have thought it was
some kind of shellshock maybe and would wear off. But it was not.
He knew it as his folk had known it far back. It was always there
underneath. There was his uncle that made the pictures of white
horses and every time they were on the point of death, whether it
was lions or dragons, or a fine manly hero with a golden helmet and
a great sword and always largely towering waves in the back of the
picture somewhere. But although the horse was always well painted,
it was not the same with the people or the lions and I have it in the
back of my mind that the pictures were gifted to some gallery, but in
some way they were never shown. Myself, I have a small picture he
did with the horse coming out of the water and some kind of a sea as
well. But it is an unchancey picture to have about the house so it is
put away at the back of the press.

So there was poor Mistress Betty, the soul, and her man dead and
the estate not doing too well as we all knew, and the wee ones would
need to be told. We were that sorry for her but little we could do or
say. The thing was fated. He had a good wake, that is one thing
certain. But after that she went back to her own folk in the Borders
and we saw little of any of the family except that they would come
once in a while during the summer. But there was no nanny and
Mistress Betty did the cooking herself and made jam and jelly out
of the fruit from the walled garden. It was going badly for there was
no gardener, only Neil went in once a week and scythed the long
grass and once in a while put out a few cabbage plants. The rhubarb
plants went on for all that the nettles were growing up round them
and so did the blackcurrants, making a tangle of long stems that only
a child could get through. The raspberries went on the way they
do, and a few of the big bush fruits with the brambles growing away

through them, but there was barely an apple bearing. Oh, it was sad that and we wished she'd had the money to keep things up as they were once.

For those were bad years all over. You'd hardly get the price of its rearing for a young stirk and MacBrayne forever putting up the fares. The lambing was bad everywhere; only the foxes flourished. Most young folk left the island but things were no better if they got to Glasgow with the unemployment and by and by talk of Hitler and that. Yes, a few went into the army but we had suffered and lost too much in the First War to be glad, we older ones, even if the money was better than it had been in our time. In those days you did not have the bed and breakfast folk coming to the Highlands, nor would we have been able to give them what they wanted for there were few of the croft houses with any conveniences. Some of us were half afraid that she might sell the estate or try to, and we kept a kind of watch in case some lawyer body might come over or anyone looking at the land and the house. And while she and the wee ones, though they were growing tall schoolchildren, were John and Ellen, stayed with her, we took care that one or another of us would bring her over a fish or a few scones fresh from the girdle. It was seldom enough that she had friends staying beyond her mother and the two grey haired ladies, his elder sisters.

But then came the summer when she had some younger ones, her own brother with his wife whose folk were from south Argyll; she had the Gaelic, anyway the songs, but she spoke it so that it sounded kind of queer to ourselves. They had a young family and it was fine to see the cousins at play together. Then one or two friends of theirs came, young folk, and there was laughing again and she had the silver out and opened bottles of wine that were thick with dust. I know this for was it not my own daughter Christina who went to help at the house; she got on fine with the young folk who were always friendly to her and it seemed to her that it might be that Mistress Betty was getting a small bit of consolation and not before time. He was someone a bit high up in an office in Edinburgh and brought his rod with him, not new but the best, a good sign that.

*

It was Ellen who was around fourteen at the time and she was at Christina for lumps of sugar. 'Will I make you some tablet when I've a moment?' Christina asked, for she was fond of the lassie.

'No, no,' said Ellen, 'it's not for me, it's for my horse.'

'What horse would that be?' Christina asked, for there was no horse and the children had never had ponies. Maybe, she said to herself, Ellen has a horse down on the borders.

'But you know,' said Ellen, 'surely?' Christina shook her head. 'The horse that comes always—since he was a foal when I tamed him. The horse that comes to the edge of the lawn in the evenings. You must have seen him.'

Now Christina took a swallow and said: 'What colour of a horse is it?'

'Why?' said Ellen, 'the white horse,' as though Christina was bound to know. And then: 'Sometimes I wonder whose horse is he really. You'd know that, wouldn't you?'

Christina must have given something away in her looks.

By a touch of grace the cousins came bouncing in so Christina could get safe away and down to ask me what should she say to the lassie, for it was bound to come up again. And this was a horse which only Ellen had seen. But how could a sea horse be tame and eating sugar lumps? But there was no other white horse on the island; it would have been thought unlucky for any of us. She knew that as well as I did.

'Find you out what went before this,' I said, 'and then we shall see. For maybe the luck might turn. Find out above all whether anyone told her even one thing about the death of her father.'

So back went Christina and nothing said until the next time the Ellen lassie asks for sugar lumps. Well then, while Christina is looking in the tin she begins to ask the questions which must be asked, but soft and light so that there is nothing to take hold of. And it seemed that when she was seven years old or thereabouts Ellen had run down to the beach, splashing through the rock pools, dodging her mother and the old nurse and there she had found a foal 'doubled up and wet and sandy' as she said. Now as luck would have it she had an apple with her and she picked a wisp of green grass and went over to the white foal, again as she said, 'on all fours' and maybe that has its importance since one is always best to swallow one's human pride when one has dealings with the other side. So after that whenever she came back in the summer the foal would be there but grown.

'Did you ever ride it, Miss Ellen?' Christina asked. But Ellen shook her head. She had never learned to ride. It seemed that her mother was against it and the girls at her school who went riding were not her friends. That also perhaps was as well. It is rare for a sea horse to be ridden; it might have thrown her.

It was later a bit that Christina spoke with her about her father's death, making out that she herself did not know and her father—myself—would not speak of it. Ellen said that her father had been drowned and his body washed up on the shore. But she and John were both good swimmers, she said. She hardly remembered her father though John did a little. So speaking it over with Christina it was clear enough that the Ellen lassie had no notion at all of what her horse might be. But could it hurt her? And should the thing be brought to the notice of her mother? That was something we were worried over, speaking about it in the evenings among ourselves.

So there was myself and Neil and two or three others with our minds almost made up to speak with Mistress Betty once we could find just the timeous moment when all of a sudden it came out that Sir Archie, the one with the fishing rod, had proposed to the lady of the house. Yes, just that and Mistress Betty had accepted him and there was a great flurry and rush of happiness and who were we to spoil the luck? So we did not speak and in a while they were all away and the wedding to be down in the Borders. They did what was right by the island and asked the senior folk down but said there would be an evening here with dancing later on. So just the three of us went and a good wedding it was though I cannot care for this champagne that most of them were drinking. Still and all there was a bottle of the real stuff opened now and again so that we were all in the best of spirits and the Ellen lassie whirling her new father around by his two hands and her hair flying behind her.

Now as luck would have it Christina herself got married the next year and I am half thinking it was on account of that dance they gave for the island that a fair few lads came across for it. I was spited not getting news from the house. They did some painting and papering and now there was another man working in the garden alongside Neil and the fences were mended and some young stirks brought in so that things began to take shape again. Young John was by now at university; he too was left handed but it makes no difference at all in the examinations so they say. But whatever may have gone better for the house and its folk things went yet more badly for the rest of the world, for the man Hitler came out against us and first the Dutch and the Belgians and the French gave way and all the old names from the last war that we had hoped were forgotten came back dreadfully into the news. And young John was in the army and then it was Dunkirk and the last days of May went by and no news of him but the Highland Division cut off at St Valery. A few, a very few, escaped but still no news and all of us hoping at least he was a prisoner. But there was no list he was in.

Now the next thing that happened came to me only through Ellen herself. Yes, she came alone on the MacBrayne boat to speak with me because she had been asking about quietly and cannily and in the end it came down to Neil and myself. But she had never liked Neil, the poor man, since he chased her off eating all the raspberries in the old garden and so it was myself she came to, and she spoke with great uncertainty until she found that I did not question the story. By that time we knew that John was back but also that the way he had escaped after the defeat at St Valery was something that could not be

B*

talked about and he had behaved so strangely and unaccountably that we did not know what to think.

So then came Ellen to make all clear. A few of them had found their way down a cliff path and had seized on a small boat the size of one of the old lobster boats maybe. They had got her afloat and were rowing out into the sea mist, for it was an unchancey cold fog that had stopped the kind of rescue that saved the Dunkirk lads. They were hoping if they rowed out that they might get picked up by one of our ships but before they were out of sight of shore they were fired on and two of them shot dead. But what was worse the boat itself was holed and though it was not coming in too fast at first it took one of them all his time with a tin to keep the water from rising on them. But by now they were into the fog belt and hoping, hoping that there might be some kind of craft to pick them up. They would shout and listen but the fog shut them in and the leak was gaining on them and they were dead tired with rowing and baling.

It seemed to me that young John had faltered telling this to his sister or it could have been that he was not able to remember right and who would blame him for that. But clearly the boat was foundering and they were loosening their boots to swim better, but there was no help and they were bound to die in the cold sea under the cold fog. John was a good enough swimmer and he had hold of an oar which kept him afloat; they called to one another and tried to keep together but the sea had hold of them and was pulling them this way and that. While she spoke of it to me I could see Ellen herself half living through it and her hands twisted tight together. 'There,' I said, 'there, my poor lassie,' but she did not hear.

So then John was aware that he was not in the water and not holding the cold wood of an oar and what he held was a bunch of white mane. And the sea horse was speaking to him, saying, saying— and here Ellen stood up and walked about the room and looked though the small window that faces west over the machair and the sea and I never ever opened that window because of the wind—and at last she turned to me and whispered: 'The sea horse told him it was because of me and the sugar lumps and the apples and kindness to a wet sandy foal stranded among the rocks.'

She stopped there and stared at me. I nodded and said: 'That would be it. Yes, that makes sense to me. And the horse landed him?'

She nodded. 'But he did not know where he was and I believe even he was not certain who he was. But they found out and he is beginning to come to himself. If it is himself he is coming to.' Then she stood stock still and asked: 'Can you believe any of this? Have you any reason to?'

'I can and do believe it,' I said. 'Though it is rare enough that any of that side of things should show any kindness or courtesy to ourselves on this side. But it is high time that you knew something which has been kept from you. Your father was not drowned. He was killed by the sea horse down there on the shore but only after he had cut its throat with his sword in a way which would have killed any horse of this world. And he died with a tangle of the beast's mane gripped in his hand so that we could scarcely loose it.'

'Who saw it?' she said, 'you?'

'Neil and his wife who is dead. They saw it when the sea horse was still lying there and bleeding. By the time I and the rest got down to the strand the beast was away, dead or alive, but your father was stone dead.'

'But why was I never told?'

'Your mother knew. It was for her to tell or not to tell. It was for us to keep quiet. So it has always been. You know now.'

'I cannot believe this!' she said with anger, yes, black anger against me.

'I know it is hard to believe,' I said, 'and it does not fit in right with the clever kind of world we have made. But this is how it was and your father was taking the doom on to himself. I think maybe he had hoped to get clear of it but that was not to be.'

'The doom,' she said, 'the doom. It is not a word that I care for. It has no meaning for me. It is something out of a story book.'

I said: 'This is no story and it is possible you may have broken it yourself when you were a young maid. But if it is broken there'll be some sign. On John.'

She stared at me for a long moment and then she said slowly: 'You know he was always left handed. But now he can only write—or—or strike matches or brush his teeth or use a knife with his right hand. Mother was wondering about this. And the doctor.'

'They need not wonder,' I said, 'nor need they be anxious. That is the sign on him.' Yes, truly, that was the sign.

NEIL McCALLUM

One Man Alone

The wind was driving a flurry of snow into the sentry's face. It was nearly midnight. The infantry training camp in the north of England was invisible through the curtain of blackness and falling snow. In the guard room the other sentries were stretched on their beds trying to sleep.

The room was hot. A cherry-red stove had turned the atmosphere into a dry unpleasant vapour that was thick in the throat. The black-out prevented ventilation. The room stank of old food and sweat and a conglomeration of ancient smells of human habitation.

In front of the stove three men were seated, two talking and making toast, the third absently squeezing the blackheads on his neck. One was the N.C.O. in charge of the sentries and the others were the bugler and the orderly.

Playing solitaire at a small table was the policeman on duty. His cards lay in bits of butter, jam, gravy, and breadcrumbs.

Except for the two who talked in low voices each man might have been alone. Each was alone with his own boredom waiting for the long night to pass.

The sentry outside banged his feet on the ground to knock off the snow that clogged his boots.

A bell rang and the policeman grunted. His eyes were sore from the bad light that fell on his cards. He spoke aloud but to himself:

'Let the bastard ring. That's the second time in half an hour.'

Above the electric bell on the wall a sign flickered showing that the occupant of cell number one was asking attention. The policeman continued with his game. He couldn't find the card he wanted. The bell rang again. The policeman swore, turned round on his seat and addressed the room: 'These bloody prisoners run this place. A police-man can't get five minutes to himself. Christ, I'm their wet nurse. When they want to wash or drink or go to the bloody lavatory I've got to go and hold their hands. Just in case they jump through the window. But this one's a deserter. Let the mucker ring.'

The N.C.O. at the fire saw a chance to enliven the heavy minutes with talk.

'How long has he been in?'

'Caught him today.' The policeman leaned forward, suddenly

anxious to talk. He wanted to unburden his grievance against the prisoner.

'We always catch these bastard deserters. You'd think they run away from the army just to get caught again. Always make for home, like bloody pigeons. When you hear they're missing you telephone the civvy police-station at their home town. Up go the police.' The speaker struck a pose and pretended to knock on a door.

' "Oh Mrs Brown, we've come about your poor wee man, God bless him, but his country needs him back." And every time the wee runt is hiding behind her skirts. These bastards should be shot. Where the hell would we be if every bastard started to desert? It's us would have to pay, you and me. What would happen to the army with all the soldiers running away to pop into bed with their wives, eh! Christ, I'd like to be at home myself, but if everyone goes where the hell would we be, eh?'

He glared at the N.C.O., indignant in his sense of righteousness. Then he spat into the fire and was going to start talking again when the bugler put down a mug of tea beside him. The bugler had listened in silence to the policeman. Now he spoke.

'Stop yer moanin',' he said.

'Who the hell's moanin'?'

'You are.'

'Who the hell made this tea?'

'I did.'

'It's bloody weak.'

'Then it's good tea. Strong tea's bad for your nerves.'

'Muck.'

The policeman took a long drink and banged the mug on the table. A spurt of liquid leaped over the side and mingled with the bread-crumbs and the butter smears.

*

In his cell the prisoner hesitated, his finger over a bell-push. He was a nervous little man. He did not want to ring the bell but his bladder was weak and he wanted to relieve himself.

He had deserted five days ago and he was still dressed in the shabby flannel trousers and blue pullover in which he had been arrested. He was confused and worried.

Perhaps if he had stuck it longer things would have turned out better. He had not intended to desert. He had run away on impulse, from something that had been overwhelming him. What it was he was not sure, except that it had surrounded him from the day he had been called up. The harshness, the indifference, the atmosphere of the barracks all choked him, unmanned him.

Sometimes he felt he wanted to apologise to the army for the nuisance he was being. It was not the army's fault, altogether. He was hopeless at everything, so paralysed by fear that his mind was incapable of translating the sharp commands of the N.C.O.s into action so that they had begun to believe he was shamming. With weapons he had been all thumbs, doing everything the wrong way.

Now he was tired and there was the policeman outside paying no attention to his ringing. His teeth fumbled with his lips as he went over mentally, again and again, the things that seemed to have been aimed at him personally—the sergeant who swore at him on the parade ground, the soldier who knocked over his plate of soup in the messroom and then laughed in his face.

When he had run away it had not been with any hope of deserting. He had never planned that. He just had to escape before he was crushed by what he saw was an inhuman organisation peopled by bullies. That was the army, he thought, inhuman. It did not understand him.

Now he wanted to relieve himself. He looked agonisingly at the bell-push. Then his mind went on again, relentlessly torturing himself. He would be tried and punished as a deserter. He could see that. They—the army—would never appreciate his feelings, never comprehend that he was really willing to do his bit.

Then a sense of his own futility brought tears in his eyes. God, why could he not assert himself? Perhaps after all he had only himself to blame. Why could he not deal with the army and yet remain himself, why was he overwhelmed by a sense of hopelessness?

His hand hovered over the bell-push. He wondered if he dare ring again.

*

The policeman finished the tea and turned to the game of cards. The first card he turned up was the one he wanted. He chuckled to himself.

The bell rang, very quickly and shortly. It stopped almost before the noise had reached the ears of the men in the room, as though the sudden silence would erase its demands.

The policeman paid no attention. He slapped the card on the table, still chuckling.

'It's coming out. It's coming out.'

GILES GORDON

Liberated People

—I suppose you expect me to . . .

The man, Joe McCrone, had moved his physical carcase along the
bar towards the woman, near enough that without shouting, without
causing a disturbance of the peace, he could address her. That was,
utter a few words which—amidst the hubbub of the pub—she could
hear and, if they spoke the same language, interpret and respond to.
Around them, not that they were a couple, not in any sense, not that
they were together, was laughter and voices and argument from groups
of people, mostly men but their women with some of them. The small
square pub was comfortably full around the seats and tables but few
people were close to the bar.

Had Maggie McGilvray looked in Joe McCrone's direction in the
first instance, before he moved and moved towards her? That was the
question. Or had he wanted her to look, yes, willed her to look,
dredged up from within him the power to persuade her to? I mean,
imagined that she had looked, turned her head like Rosie Redmond
(not that Maggie was that sort of woman, or Irish) and smiled at Joe,
beckoned? Sure enough her face wore a beckoning smile, a smile
to embrace even an indifferent Protestant, an indifferent member of
the opposite sex on a knife sharp January evening.

Jack MacBeth went on washing and polishing the glasses behind
the mahogany Victorian bar, dish towel inside glass as if he was a
conjurer performing an everyday trick. Which he was. He eyed the
pair of them, and the twenty or thirty others in the pub, but his eyes
were evidence of nothing, suggested nothing, proved nothing. What
he'd seen in the Cocker Spaniel, what he'd forgotten, was his business.
But he wasn't further educated, like so many these days. His job was
to serve drinks, not to join in debate, and he knew his job. And to
keep the pub tidy, whether or not the guv'nor was there. The oil
men, they were different from the locals, big and gutsy. Maybe
America was the country of the further educated. Either they were
all educated there or none of them were.

He looked into the warm soapy water in the chrome basin below
him, behind the bar. Little wisps of steam, like puffs of smoke from
a toy cannon, wafted up. He felt inclined to spit, to cool the water,

his complaisant response to the world in which perforce, and without particular qualifications, he had to make a living. But didn't. He was wearing a large white apron, wrapped around him like a linen napkin at the neck; though he wasn't the landlord, he stood proxy for him that night, and this was a responsibility.

Maggie McGilvray may have smiled at Joe McCrone. She wasn't especially a smiler but, it seemed to her, if you went to a public place, and where more public than a public house, you had to socialise, to smile if called upon to smile and not be a villain but to pretend and insist that a rough ravine of a throat and a twitching grinning head were prerequisites of the social life, to embracing your neighbour to your bosom (if you were that way inclined) or your mind (if you weren't). Metaphorically speaking, all—mind and bosom—metaphorically speaking.

She may have smiled at him. Which proved what, suggested what? She returned the smiles of most people who smiled at her. But he hadn't smiled at her. He'd have sworn that on a black book. Maybe she'd mistaken his everyday face for a smiling one? Impossible, he reasoned, shaking his head slowly, an oiled compass in a storm, unless she was a loonie, a daftie. In which case, who'd let her out, and were they watching her?

—Busy, Mr McCrone? asked Jack MacBeth, polishing still, continuing to wash and to polish.

McCrone looked round and up at him, as if the question was the most irrelevant the world could have devised, although he knew, if he thought about it, that it was one Jack used whenever he thought something untoward might be going to happen and he wanted to batten down the hatches before there was an incident, an accident. The barman had difficulty in thinking of questions, of making remarks that were opening gambits in conversations. Indeed, his 'Busy?' was one of a maximum of six questions, a minimum of six too, which he asked as opposed to someone else asking him questions. Rhetoric wasn't one of his major gifts.

The look in McCrone's eye was of such contempt that had the young barman been looking at him he would surely have dropped the glass he was fingering and it would surely have fragmented. Now had it been a mug. . . .

Maggie was drinking gin and tonic. The usual gin, an unusual American tonic, imported for the Yanks. Meaning that there was in front of her, crouching in a glass, two or three drops of gin, and a two-thirds empty bottle of effervescent water by her elbows, which leant on the polished bar.

She had bought herself the drink. No favours from anybody. No coat trailing as far as she was concerned. Woman's lib (she'd read about it, she read newspapers and magazines) was more honoured in her life in the observance than in the breach, and that was nothing to do with being married and having a family. If she was pining in melancholy she'd stay at home, not regale her woes to those, strangers or semi-strangers, who came together to forget their sorrows, whether mortgage or mate, whatever or whomsoever curtailed their freedom, stopped their imaginations from soaring. Naturally she accepted that she was a woman, that there were those who were older than her, and plainer but also that there were many who were younger and prettier. By the million, if you counted the world. And that was a lot.

His face lunged about in the air in front of her. The air in front of him too, for that matter. The space between them was filled with his head, his face. It seemed to expand but to show no sign of exploding. It occupied space that she'd chosen to keep empty, to give her a chance to breathe towards sanity and silence. There was smoke and alcohol, vaguely male smells around. Specifically male smells, to no degree neutralised by her presence, the presence of any woman.

He had spoken after shifting his body towards her. She had understood that his words were addressed to her. She tried to focus her drifting mind on what he'd said, words she had heard but hadn't concentrated upon. 'I suppose you expect me to. . . .' Then his mouth, the dry moving lips, reminding her obscurely of those folded paper fortune tellers she'd had at school, had ceased to move, to project the words beyond the face that spoke them, and the lips were clamped shut, like a decrepit ledger not needing to be referred to again.

What had he at home? A wife, three kids? In-laws to look after, or at least keep in victuals? A mother, or a father? Did he work in the Civil Service, in a clerking capacity, or on the rigs? He wasn't a fisherman, she was sure of that. The government somehow or other, she thought, a blue collar job, though his clothes were better than a disguise. A nationalised man. Perhaps he was a widower, not that he was *old*—he was between ages. He wasn't too old to change the world if that was his ambition, or his inclination. If he lived near the Cocker Spaniel it must either be in a block of flats or in a terrace house. Which again gave away nothing. He might have had a basement or a couple of rooms in an attic, or a room and a stove.

His face froze like a classical theatre mask, his features leered. It wasn't a comedy mask, certainly not. It was a face that had grown to petulance rather than through extreme suffering, not having earned the right to be considered tragic.

His words echoed in her mind, like a boulder crashed into her consciousness, and rippling out, rippling out, the intensity dissipating, thinning as awareness of it receded. What had she to do with him, or he with her? Couldn't she have a quiet drink in her local without being considered anti-social or snobbish? At least the barman wouldn't allow things to get out of hand. The days of knights in shining armour, Duraglit on brasses, blanco on webbing, and buttons, buttons, buttons had long since passed. Zips were everywhere. Chrome shone for itself. But some folk liked going on fighting the war. Humanity was the enemy, not the Germans. Or the Russians, or any other nationality.

Jack polished another glass, pulled another pint. Wind and piss, more wind and piss, but people had to spend their time and money somehow, between one Hogmanay and the next, though they did just the same then. Less likely to drive you to drink, your local was, than the muck at the end of the cathode tube. Andy Stewart in drag. Was that the best they could do? Jack had spent much of the last decade in England, and was still bitter that the oil had been discovered in his absence. Just like Livingstone in Africa, he thought. He wasn't alone in thinking that Stanley, although *he* hadn't had a drop of Scottish blood in him, had said: Dr Livingstone, *you* presume. The Scots had always liked to be left alone. In the Sudan, in the South Seas, at the football game and in their local. Livingstone died out there, in Africa, which hadn't done him much good. Jack had decided that he wouldn't leave Aberdeen again.

McCrone was, she sensed, suddenly focusing on the present, expecting her to respond. He'd clawed his way back from wherever he'd been. He'd addressed his words to her though she hadn't realised that that was what he was about. Common courtesy—no, rare courtesy —insisted that she reply. Why was he so aggressive? Why hadn't he spoken from the stool on which he had sat, raising his voice as necessary to reach her, rather than lurching towards her like a moulting bear in a third rate travelling circus?

She was certain she'd never met the man before. Maybe she'd passed him in a street somewhere but . . . there were millions of fish in the sea, and quite a few fishing boats around the coast, ten mile limit or no. She'd come here for a drink, her man being away and her not wanting to start drinking at home on her own, or with the children asleep, which came to the same thing. Yet she was deceiving herself: she'd drunk enough at home—not very much, but a couple of glasses of sherry—to persuade her out to the pub on her own for more.

—You expect to be bought a drink, don't you?

He was speaking to her again, his face at hers. This time her worn eyes held his, caught them like the beam of an inverted searchlight, caused them to drop, to look down. Two pools drunk dry by their own trout. And she was the social animal!

—And then another, and another.

He spoke on, the aggression less than before, softening, going. The voice still louder than necessary but no longer shouting. Had he been shouting? She thought of it that way.

—From one customer, or another. I'm sure it doesn't matter who. As long as you're bought as many drinks as you want.

Jack was covering him, marking his man with his eyes, in command by dint of his apron and position behind the mahogany.

—And then, the fivers like a soiled and greasy pack of cards.

That was it, even for Jack:

—Mr McCrone, he said sharply, a verbal pouncing. That wouldn't do, not to a lady customer, whatever her reasons for being there. He knew, Jack did, that more often than not people didn't have reasons for where they were, for what they did.

Maggie turned away from her assailant, knowing—as she supposed she had all along—that he was ultimately harmless, that he was trying merely to get to the bottom of something that worried him. She had been abused before in similar terms. If anything, she was mildly flattered that he thought it worthwhile. But she was his butt only because she was there. She spoke to the barman, and for McCrone to hear as well:

—I just want to finish up my drink, and be left alone. I don't want anyone to be in trouble because of me.

Jack said nothing, but eyed his male customer sternly, as if to say: Watch it.

Maggie looked again at McCrone, and was friendly, and dignified. She said:

—Not only can I afford to buy my own drink, I want to buy it. I'm not here to feel obligated to others.

McCrone looked bewildered, out of his world, not understanding her meaning though he knew the words, saw the sense they made as a sentence. She smiled at him, the smiler still, and as he didn't reply she went on:

—I won't even offer to buy you one.

He looked quite crushed, appealed with his eyes to the barman for reassurance that he wasn't going barmy, something he'd always been afraid of. But Jack MacBeth was not meeting his gaze. She spoke again:

—A woman in a pub on her own, whether waiting for a friend or not, shouldn't seem any odder than a man in a pub on his own.

He moved away from her. Enough was more than enough. He crawled back up on to his stool, perched on the slithery surface that was hardly large enough for his bulk. Jack polished another glass, and released much of the breath that had been pent up within him. He wasn't going to have to raise his voice, or go through the farce of trying to evict a harmless customer, or threaten Mr McCrone with a bobby.

She said it again, once more, her last intended remark in the conversation, the forced dialogue:

—I wanted a drink, that's all.

McCrone's face lost years. It was as if everything was revealed for the first time, that the scales hadn't so much fallen away as not been there, and he understood that he'd been anticipating the Second Coming:

—Me too.

A miracle, both decided, without considering that the other might have reached the same conclusion, by very different routes.

Around them, laughter and the noise of voices rose and fell, a cacophony of accents, and not all the sentences in English either. Drinks were requested and paid for and drunk. Nothing went on the slate. They heard none of this, nor noticed it.

*

Jack had been slipping his eyes at the clock for some minutes. In a moment he'd press the button that caused the bell for closing time to ring. Time gents, please; the last words, until tomorrow; and then the next day, and the next. Even on Sundays now.

McCrone said, from his high perch:

—I'll be having one for the road. Would you do me the honour of joining me?

He'd remembered that way of putting it from a film he'd seen years before. He recalled it was *The Massacre of Glencoe* but he couldn't think why it should have been, of what the connection could be.

She, from her equally high perch, said:

—A pleasure, Mr McCrone, if you'll allow me to buy the first round tomorrow.

And smiled. She'd had no intention, no intention at all of coming the next day. Neither, be it whispered in dusty corners and other secret places, had he. But his honour was satisfied, though it had taken over an hour. He nodded, then bowed, and spoke to Jack MacBeth, as if the barman was landlord, or that this order would buy the pub:

—Two of the same, Jack; for the lady and me.

Even then, he deliberately hadn't gone wild and ordered doubles. Restraint in everything.

Her honour was satisfied too, and certainly liberated ladies have a sense of honour. She wasn't to know because he hadn't told her that he'd be miles away the following day, in another part of the country where his work sometimes took him.

But tonight? They'd both, in utterly different ways, had a damned hard day, a God-given day of twenty-four hours, the nightmares and melancholia of the fastnesses between dark and dark not alleviating the waking hours, and the guilt and physical strain of adults growing no younger made it impossible, thank heaven, for either of them to behave as if he or she was sixteen or seventeen, or even twenty-one or thirty. Which assumes, in any case, that either or both of them had had the inclination, to allow the eagle to soar. They'd ties, responsibilities. There was no going back, no backsliding. Which was to say: people don't give up their lives that easily, that readily, however tough the going.

—Cheers, he said, his whisky glass touching her gin.

—Bottoms up, she said.

And they both laughed, and the smiles were there before the laughs as tends to be the case, and Jack MacBeth pressed the bell, and they said goodnight and pushed their way through the swing doors into the black swingeing night and went their separate ways back into their sober lives.

J. F. HENDRY

Peepshow

Once right in the middle of the theatre, his grandfather appeared. He could tell by the apparition of the long, phenomenal knees. To his delight, his grandfather sat down between the table and the bed and was the whole audience! His head was the gods. His knees were the Grand Circle, and his feet the Stalls.

The gods laughed when the marionettes moved in all their stilted gravity. Their actions did not matter. They could not do any harm. Set in the proper frame of the proscenium they were insulted in space.

The performance consisted chiefly of fighting and kissing. The figures bent over and embraced or jostled and pushed each other down. There was not much more they could do. The stage was rather small, and their reflexes therefore limited. Yet what they lacked in spontaneity and action, they made up in character and exotic interest. There were coloured scraps borrowed from his sister of Japanese ladies in nightgowns, combs and fans, winking penny-in-the-slot eyes, and pirates with their heads in turbans and a mouthful of fish-knives. There was a pale, newsprint Charlie Chaplin and a tomboy Pearl White in breeches. The trouble with the latter was that if you licked her too hard you saw instead of Pearl the printer's ink on the loss of the *Titanic*, which to David was as large as a broken mousetrap.

Between the acts there were no divisions as there was nowhere to go had there been an interval. The cardboard theatre which had formerly housed a gigantic pair of shoes, was not made to run to a curtain, did not perhaps believe in too great a severance from the auditorium. It was all rather a pleasant muddle than a play properly speaking, and it ended abruptly whenever dinner was ready. The characters could all be scrapped at once. There would be plenty more tomorrow.

His grandfather said it was a fine show, and David looked up his steep sides, giddy and amazed to find a grown-up so intelligent. Perhaps the beard had something to do with it. It must be a cult. Even the beard however did not explain the pat on the head he now received. For the first time David knew a comparative stranger who appeared to combine authority with validity. He was sorry when he went away into the night.

Later, he was to know him as the authority of integrity, when every Saturday, a tramcar took him with his mother out to Pollokshaws and his grandfather's hat.

There in the garden the boy walked up the path between the flowers, chrysanthemum the colour of burnt sugar, and tea-roses. Strange they should be called tea-roses. Some of them were white and beginning to wither. The rot was spattered on their petals like flakes of rust, or dried tea-stains.

He set down his glass-jar and waited for the butterflies. There were several cabbage whites fluttering high in the air, little dancing parachutes, at the foot of the garden where he never went. Once he had gone, through trees with cobweb claws, to look over the wall, against his grandfather's orders—straight into a horse's face.

He would wait for them to come up.

Now he idled about the grass, kicking the tops off dandelions. Suddenly there was a spark of flame. For a moment he could not think. Then, madly, he darted at it. A red-admiral! A red-admiral!

'Bobby! Bobby!' he shouted to his cousins in the house. Never had he seen one before. It was smaller than a white, with a web of black spots on the tip of each blood-red wing.

He careered after it, banging his net down on dandelions, cabbages, sometimes even on a clucking hen; but the red-admiral rose high over the bristling mossy wall by the blackberry-bush, in a ribbon of unfurling fire, and disappeared, dancing sparks.

Angrily he threw the net down.

'It's twopence wasted!' said Bobby later. 'I catch them with my hands.'

'You couldn't catch a red-admiral with your hands,' said David. 'It's too quick!'

'Yes I could!'

'Oh no you couldn't Bobby!' And Sandy, the smaller, a little blond with a face like the letter V, gave one of his jack-in-the-box giggles. He always sided with David, and that made Bobby fly into a tantrum, a veritable explosion of whimpering impotence. Coiling his lips with rage and snorting tears, he aimed a blow at Sandy.

'It's not a butterfly-net anyway! It's for catching baggie-minnows!' he screamed.

'This is a new kind!' shouted David, seizing his arm, 'And if you touch Sandy it'll be the last thing you'll do!'

Off Bobby stamped in a fury of mortification.

'He's going to cry to Bessie!' mocked Sandy merrily, a mischievous gnome.

Bessie was their foster-mother.

Together they built a tent of sacking round the rowan-tree, which, though they did not know it, warded off devils from the house of turrets. That calmed David's nerves, upset by Bobby's outburst. The tent beat out the heat of the sun, and smelt of straw and earth.

Then they made a sortie to catch the butterflies, still snowing on the soft undulating soil among the potato-blossom. When they had caught one, they returned to drink some soda from a halfpenny packet, through a tube of licorice.

'Shall we make some sugarolly water?' asked David.

'What's that?'

'You cut up the licorice and put it in a glass of water till it melts. It's great!'

'No time now,' said Sandy. 'The sun will soon be down and the butterflies will go home.'

'Home where?'

'I don't know. Sometimes they sleep on the wall alongside the blackberry-bushes.'

'These are moths!' exclaimed David, 'I've seen them. Big tiger-moths! Ugh, they look awful.'

'What's the difference?'

'Well, a moth has a thick body and small wings. A butterfly's wings are wide, and it has a thin waist and furry shoulders.'

Down they went again into the garden, but this time there was an interruption.

'Dauvit!' came a gruff voice. 'Come oot o' the totties! You too, Sandy!'

That was grandfather, revered figure in hat of tweed, with moustache and beard that seemed of the same material, only not woven, strandy straggling, with the same tobacco strands.

'If you want to help,' he went on, 'get the caterpillars oot o' the cabbages. Or dig up wireworms.'

'What are you going to do?' asked David boldly.

'Burn this rubbish.' Grandpa's gray eyes twinkled frost.

'Burn the rubbish!' the boys whooped. 'Can we help to gather it?'

'All right!' The old man nodded, still standing, bowed, a scarecrow in the field of destiny.

Soon all the magic of the garden mingled in the scent of the smoke from weed and bracken. In its purplish coils, so thick he could almost feel them, the dreaming boy saw ripe red rowan berries on a branch of fern. Sparks danced at their heart like red-admirals, and green sap burst from the rind of burning trees like the birth of apples.

He stood with Bobby and .Sandy round the fire as it mounted, but they saw nothing of his vision, except the westward sun aslant on the red and purple flames, that gradually dimmed its valour. His eyes streamed smarting tears of smoke in the lazing evening. He had some of that fire and some of that sun in his jar.

Looking down he saw the butterfly stalk up the wall of glass, clinging on hair-fine limbs, like spores of thistledown. Its green eyes, dabbled with black, stared huge as two revolving eggs; and the coiled trunk in between them seemed a fairy circus whip, through which it sucked a nectar from the flowers.

That was part of his fire and sun. A memory of his grandfather's library near the attic, where he ate 'cheugh jeans' and read *Tom Finch's Monkey*, or *Nansen's Farthest North*. So high and so quiet was it there, that he travelled for hours in another hemisphere. The books were huge and dusty, bound like ledgers and full of mysterious reckonings and figures dealing with the world of space about them. He could not always follow the argument, but sitting in the attic, near the sky, he wiped dust from their binding that somehow became the dust of stars to guide him, as the heavy tomes loomed, purposeful as the prows of ships, swinging into seas of silence and of wonder. Continents and years unfolded like a map, below.

Somehow the garden was one of these continents. His grandfather was Nansen in the Arctic, with frozen eyes and beard, the years' hero. And he, David, perhaps was the tropics, the fire and sun through the trees in the orchard, the butterfly, winging towards he knew not what. Seas of silence? Chill ice-caps? He was unafraid for Nansen had gone there before him, and now his grandfather too was there. What did it all mean?

Later, he walked alone among the cabbages, turning over the great ears of leaves to inspect the back, and picking fuzzy caterpillars from amongst the straggling veins. You had to bend close, for they looked like part of the hand of cabbage, green and struggling in an agony of light, like children severed from the wrist of stalk. These too, he dropped, numb and cringing little questions, into a jar as glassy as his eyes with wonder.

When it was quite dark, his mother appeared at the backdoor, thirty yards off. 'Come David!' she called, vague as a bird in a wood, 'Time to go home!'

He placed the net over the jar and walked towards her, plucking the heads off flowers on the way and dropping them nonchalantly in. Food for the butterfly in its transparent cell . . .

In the tram going home, he knelt on the seat, looking out of the window. It wasn't sore for his stockings were pulled over his knees. He wore his little glengarry. He should have had his rifle by his side too—the one that fired a bullet of cork—plonk!—on a piece of string! Instead, he clutched the long cane with the net at one end, like a forlorn sceptre.

'Look!' he suddenly shouted. It sounded like 'Luke'. 'There's a student, mother!'

He'd been watching for them. It was Charities' Day today, when University students all dressed up and collected for the hospitals, but to David, a weird day, full of irrupting, red-admiral magic. He looked down again at the butterfly in his jar. It was crouched on the bottom, antennae turning this way and that, as though listening for a possible way of escape, from this mirage.

Outside Red Indians were pushing policemen off point-duty. Negroes were chasing motor-cars with upraised axes. Their tram was filling up with strange creatures he would have liked to capture and keep in his jar. They flashed colour in all directions, deep-sea fish he had seen in an aquarium.

David held his breath. A huge man in a blue and yellow costume shook a tin before his mother and she dropped a penny in the slot.

At the back, where the conductor usually stood, was a resplendent being in blue blazer and velvet, tasselled skull-cap. Irrupting magic. That was being young. These people could do as they liked, and lived a life of laughter and sun like any red-admiral.

'What will you be when you grow up?' his mother whispered over his shoulder.

'A student!' he breathed, 'like that man over there, with the velvet tassel.' The thought was so daring he could scarcely bring himself to think it.

Now the trams swung over the river, blue sparks shooting from the pole on the wire. This was the part of the journey he liked least, when the centre of the town was left behind and they passed warehouses, factories, coal-depots, all looking like the animals he found when he turned over a stone.

His head swam. He felt he was going to be sick.

When they arrived home, the students were gone. In the chill lane of smoky sandstone tenements he covered the butterfly to keep it warm, but once in the small kitchen he took it out. It would be better here than in grandpa's garden, he thought.

'They live longer in houses, don't they mother?' he asked.

'Yes,' she said, taking off her hat, to light the fire.

'I can feed it on flowers and sugar and milk. It'll soon be tame and live a long time.'

He took it up in his hand. The powder-grains spread on his thumb metallic glitter, and the wings shone, glazed.

'Oh, look!' he cried. 'It can hardly fly! Have I hurt it?'

He stood the jar on the dresser and watched the butterfly agog on his thumb. 'It's beautiful!' he thought. Oh, he hoped it would live in the cold of the grimed tenements if he brought it flowers. The wind would not blow so hard. It was his youth. Every Saturday in the garden. Every butterfly he would pursue.

Gently he turned to the contortions of the anguished caterpillars. From their blunt, blind heads and from their diffident bodies too, would one day stream that irrupting magic. They would all be married to the sun. Carefully he placed them in the long bottom-drawer of the sewing-machine, and stuffed its compartments with leaves of fresh green lettuce. The butterfly itself he allowed to fly about the house. It was his friend, the magic he must tame and make his own, the good and true.

Darkness fell, and he closed the drawer, and sealed the jar, piercing holes in the cardboard lid to let in air.

Next morning, before breakfast, he opened the drawer, and at once little beads of corruption assailed his nostrils and eyes. Drawer, lettuce and caterpillars were one stench of green death. Never would they know the freedom now he had meant to give them. He had made them prisoner only in order to see the actual incursion of the magic, and now the magic itself had flown away.

In the chill jar he saw the butterfly, his inspiration, lying too, in death. Over its fallen, brittle petal the boy wept.

ERIC LINKLATER

Joy As It Flies

She has given beauty a new category, he thought, for she appears to be edible. She is the word made fruit, rather than flesh, and with sugar and cream she would be delicious. Her neck would taste like an English apple, a pippin or nonpareil, and her arms, still faintly sun-burnt from the mountain snow, of greengages.

'How old are you?' he asked.

'Nearly nineteen,' she answered, 'and I'm very mature for my age. We had lectures on all sorts of things at Lausanne. Really up-to-date lectures on genetics, and Cocteau, and the ballet, and—oh, everything!'

'And what's your opinion of Cocteau?'

'Well, I don't think the lecture on him was a very good one—what are you laughing at?'

'I'm sorry.'

'I never pretended to know *much* about him, did I? But I do know who he is, and what he is, and that's something.'

'It's a great deal.'

'Then you shouldn't have laughed at me.'

'You make me feel light-hearted: that's the trouble.'

'You mustn't be light-hearted about the match, or everybody will be furious. A Rugby International is very serious.'

They stood idly, in a moving throng of people, in the cold sunlight of March in Edinburgh. If they should step over the sharply drawn line between light and shadow, into the shadow of the tall stand, the darker air would be as cold as January. But the several thousands of people, hearty and red of cheek, who were streaming into the ground to see a match between England and Scotland, thought their northern climate could not be bettered. They brought their own warmth, a genial excitement, a general euphory that made men's voices ring louder and more kindly than usual and girls look vivid and pretty though they were not.

Latimer, when he woke that morning after a night in the train, had had no expectation of watching Rugby football. His mind had lately been occupied by a domestic issue of the greatest importance, and he had come unwillingly to Edinburgh on business that could not be postponed or delegated. For nearly two hours he had argued stub-bornly with an elderly and cantankerous Writer to the Signet who, having got his way with most of the disputed clauses, became suddenly jovial, insisted on taking Latimer home with him to a luncheon-party of ten people, and there persuaded him, easily enough, to go to the match. There were seats for all of them, but in different parts of the stand: two quarters and a pair.

'Latimer,' said the crusty old man, mellowed now by food and a second glass of port, 'you're an Englishman and England's going to be beaten. But you're my guest, so we'll need to provide you with pleasure of some kind. You'll take Corinna, and sit with her . . .'

'Oh, look!' she exclaimed, catching his arm and pointing to an ancient victoria, a shabby survival of carriage-days, that on creaking wheels rolled slowly towards them. It was drawn by a thin brown horse with enormous chestnuts depending from the inner faces of its large flat knees, and the cabman, in a greenish bowler and a short fawn-coloured coat, was small and old, pale of cheek but pink of nose, with a long unhappy upper lip. Three young men, who had done themselves too well at lunch-time and now regretted their extravagance, got hurriedly down, embarrassed by the attention they had attracted, and after quickly paying the cabman went off to their seats. The cabman, sour and dispirited, sat with the reins loose in his hands, and made no move to turn and go. The brown horse hung its head, and the pale sunlight showed the dust that lay thick upon the faded blue upholstery of the old carriage.

'Isn't it heavenly?' said Corinna. '*How* I wish we could go for a drive.'

'There's nothing to prevent us,' said Latimer.

'There's the match. Uncle Henry would be livid if we missed it. We can't miss the match, can we? But it would be fun!'

'You can look at footballers every winter for the rest of your life; but cabmen are dying out.'

'So a carriage-drive might be an historic occasion?'

'It might.'

'You don't want to see England beaten. You're trying to escape.'

'That may be the reason. Or it may be the lightheartedness I spoke of before.'

'We can't really go, can we?—Oh, he's driving away! Shout to him!'

'Cabby!' shouted Latimer.

'Where to?' asked the old man as the carriage tilted, the springs protested, they got in, and dust rose from the stained blue cushions to meet them.

'I don't think it matters.'

'Drive to the Castle,' said Corinna, 'and stop on the Esplanade. There'll be a view today.—Oh, isn't this the most wonderful thing that's ever happened?'

'I'm not quite sure how it did happen. I'm not sure if it should. Do you think, perhaps, that we ought to go back? Your uncle—'

'Must we?' she asked.

She had leaned heavily against him as the cabman wheeled abruptly on to a main road, and an antic fear had momentarily possessed him that he could not refrain from taking her into his arms and embracing her, regardless of the many latecomers to the match, now hurrying past on either side, who were already looking over their shoulders with amused or curious glances at the ancient carriage and its occupants so strangely going the wrong way. The impulse had seemed, for an instant, beyond control, and very properly it had frightened him. Only forty-eight hours before he had been sitting at his wife's bedside, his hands gripped fiercely by hers in her recurrent torment, and in his anxiety he had offered to the future all manner of extravagant bargains if she and her baby should survive their peril and their pain. For Latimer was in love with his wife, a lively black-haired girl, and the composure of his love was alarmed, as if a volcanic pulse had shaken it, by so urgent and unruly a desire to close with a young stranger. His conscience was perplexed, and over its surface ran the ruffle of fear lest he make an exhibition of himself. It was bad enough to be seen riding in a victoria, absurdly seated in an absurd vehicle trundling away from the football-ground that everybody else was moving towards; but to be caught embracing a girl, a lovely and seemingly edible girl of eighteen, under the bright intolerant sky of Edinburgh—oh, madness! Disaster shook its panic finger, goblin-eyed.

Out of his fear, then, he suggested going back, but when Corinna reproachfully asked, 'Must we?', he looked at her lips, become suddenly childish, and the blank disappointment of her gaze; and brusquely commanded his emotion. It was trivial enough, he found, he could rebuff it. As firmly as if fear had been a ball in a squash-court bouncing to his forehand, he drove it from him and said confidently, 'I was only thinking of your uncle—of my rudeness to him—but we shan't be missed, I'm sure. And you can see an International next year.'

'I've been taken to football matches ever since I can remember, and to go for a drive instead . . .' She turned and waved her hand to three small boys who whistled derisively from the pavement-edge. 'They're jealous,' she said. 'Everybody is jealous of us. Look at that deadly-dull woman leaning out of a window! Oh, what dull lives people lead! There ought to be more horses in a town, they smell so beautifully.'

On the causeway-stones the wheels rattled, the hooves of the thin brown horse beat in steady rhythm an old fashioned tune, and leather loosely slapped its hide. When the off-wheels were caught in a tram-line the carriage lurched and threw Latimer and Corinna close together, but in the same moment her attention was taken by a seagull, come inland from the Forth, that balanced solemnly on the rim of a large gilded mortar over the door of a chemist's shop; and he, having snubbed the panic impulse, now dreaded no mischance but felt stirring in his mind a high nonsensical pleasure.

'There are more dull people,' she said as they passed two women in respectable drab clothes, one of whom was old, and a narrow-shouldered man of depressed appearance. 'I couldn't bear to be middle-aged! I couldn't bear to be anyone else!'

'Some of us have our compensations,' he told her.

'Oh, but you're different.'

'Though it's true that many are unlucky. I once heard a man say, "I never got much fun myself, but some of my friends have had an amazingly good time."'

'How terribly sad!'

'So it seemed to me, but he didn't think so. He was a well-fed, apparently contented person.'

'But how could he be?'

'You don't know what secrets he had. You don't know anything about other people. You don't know what terrible strands of interest hold together those two dowdy women and the man with bottle shoulders.'

'Do you?'

'They may have a plot to strangle him after supper tomorrow, while he has a better plan to hit them on the head, with a stone in the toe of a stocking, after tea.'

'That's not typical of life in Edinburgh.'

'But you can't deny the possibility. You can't even tell me what the seagull saw that was sitting on the edge of a golden mortar outside a chemist's shop.'

'Do you think there was anything in it?'

'A rag and a bone and a little wooden box.'

'What was in the box?'

'The telephone-number of an old man who's forgotten what nobody else ever knew.'

'Goodness! You have got good eyes. Now tell me what he's looking at.' She pointed to a sailor who was staring into a fishmonger's full window.

'It can only be one thing, can't it?'

'Something horrible?'

'I'm afraid so. There's a flounder on the slab with his dead wife's ring in its mouth.'

'What a shock for the poor man! But perhaps she was a bad woman?'

'The worst woman in the world.'

They drove past houses set back from the road behind little gardens emptied by the winter, and looked at black or curtained windows, and the sky above them was as clear and cold as a great zircon. The old carriage groaned and rattled, and tall tramcars swaying on their shallow rails went shrilly past. Here and there, idly, Latimer read the name of a street: Roseburn, a shepherd's lyric deafened by stone, the remote Victorian echoes of Kew Terrace and Osborne Terrace, then a flour-mill and the vanished rural chaffering of the Haymarket, and so into shabbier thoroughfares till they saw mounting high and precipitous before them the darkly gleaming Castle rock. And all the way they spoke of nothing grave, of no material subject, and little even of themselves but for Corinna's recollection, now and then, of some ludicrous girl at school or a mistress's peculiar discipline and her outwitting. Latimer talked nonsense with an imagination as fluent as a hill-stream after rain—or a fortune-teller's patter in a booth—and Corinna's voice, like a swallow hunting evening flies, went to and fro in effortless arcs and charming cadences after topics so minute as almost to be invisible. But subsequently, when Latimer tried to remember what subjects had held them in conversation, he was inclined to believe that somehow they had touched—oh, lightly, it is true, but with conscious fingers—eternal themes and the poets' deeper chords.

He had made a joke about Byzantium—the architects of Edinburgh have sometimes had unlikely motives—but was it all a joke? He had described his sailing to the Fastnet in a leaking yacht improvidently manned, and made of dangerous misadventure a ludicrous tale; but surely in its burden had been the immemorial menace of the estranging sea? Corinna, talking of a concert solemnly attended by twenty schoolgirls, had described a plump and bespectacled friend's untimely woe, whom Gluck's *Orpheus* reminded that she had not prepared her necessary twenty lines of the Aeneid, Book IV, which they were reading—and then, oh surely then! they had fallen silent to think of Queen Dido in eternal grief upon the Africk shore. Such notes they had struck, he was sure of it in after years, though honesty could find no certain words to substantiate his faith. But a vibration of remembered light suffused his memory, as of goldfinches' wings above a thistle-field in the sun; and a sonorous echo of emotion, like a bell at sea, kept it alive.

They drove slowly up Castle Hill, and leaving the victoria on the Esplanade climbed to St Margaret's Chapel and looked northward over the Forth to the lands and the hills of Fife, dove-grey and glinting with gold. Corinna was confident of her geography and told him where the Bonny Earl of Moray had been slaughtered on the sea-wet rocks.

'Physical beauty was very rare in earlier times,' said Latimer.

'Beauty needs good food, and our ancestors fed poorly or foolishly. And because beauty was so rare it inspired a romantic devotion, while nowadays our appreciation is aesthetic—'

'Is it?' asked Corinna.

'Yes, I believe so. And aesthetic appreciation—'

'Is a little bit bogus, isn't it?'

'I don't think so.'

'Well, you're not really good-looking, but I like you.'

'I'm very glad. But are you being logical?'

'Oh, logic doesn't affect *people*!'

Slowly they walked down to the Esplanade again, and climbed into the waiting carriage. 'We'll be in Murrayfield before the match is over,' said Latimer. . . .

*

That was ten years ago, and he had not seen her since. War had invaded their uneasy climate, and Latimer, going to France in 1939, had retired hurriedly from Dunkirk a few months later, and served thereafter, sometimes dangerously on the field and sometimes in the mingled strain and camaraderie of a Divisional Headquarters, in North Africa and Italy. He had been more fortunate than many. He had recuperated pleasantly from a winter wound in Amalfi, and after demobilisation returned to his previous occupation without grave reluctance. His wife had suffered from the tedium and the huge accumulation of war's minor difficulties more deeply than he, and it was she who proposed, in the first autumn after the fighting stopped, that they should spend a few weeks in the relatively untroubled air, and among the splendid fleshpots, of non-combatant Ireland.

When the war was over, the victorious but thin-ribbed English discovered that Ireland, for so long a synonym of hunger and discontent, had become something like an Egyptian granary. The victims of old oppression had meat upon their tables and butter in their lordly dishes, while the heirs of the haughty Ascendancy, of the barons in their Pale and the squires in their parks, fed sadly on offal from the Argentine and the confected fats of chemical industry. So week after week, in their hungry thousands, the famished conquerors were humbly crossing the narrow sea to fill their bellies with neutral beef and mutton that had not—they now were thankful—been sacrificed to any common good.

After three weeks in Kerry, the Latimers were spending a few days in Dublin before returning home, when he, going into their hotel one evening, was halted outside by a girl who held in front of him a wooden collecting-box.

'What's it for?' he asked.

C

'For the language,' she said.

'What language?'

'The Irish language, of course.'

'I don't understand. Why should you collect money for a language?'

'So that we can teach it. It's to pay the teachers.'

'And who's going to be taught to speak it?'

'Every one of us. Or so they say.'

'Do you think that's a good thing?'

'I do not!' said the girl. 'I wouldn't speak it myself!'

'Here's half a crown for honesty,' said Latimer, and climbed the steps.

In the lounge he discovered his wife in a group of six or seven people seated round a table on which were twelve or fourteen cocktails, for which two warm and hearty men were disputing the privilege to pay. He was not much surprised. He knew that his wife had arranged to meet an old school-friend and her husband, and he was well aware of her faculty for gathering company, both old friends and new, with a celerity that he could never match. But he was astonished beyond measure when, in the midst of inaccurate but genial introduction, he perceived, with her back to the light, Corinna.

'You know her, don't you?' said his wife. 'She told me that you're old friends. Her husband is Nick's cousin, but he's not here and Nick hasn't come either. So like the Irish, isn't it? Darling, we've all been drinking far too much, you must hurry and catch us up.'

'This is a surprise,' he said.

'You haven't changed a bit,' she answered.

'But you have.'

'My hair,' she said. 'I used to hide behind it. But then I realised what a nuisance it was, and had it cut off.'

'It suits you,' he said, and looked at her with a sudden greed of attention while the great artery above his heart beat with a perceptible and disconcerting vigour. The soft roundness of her face had become an exquisite tension between cheek-bone and jaw, her eyes seemed the larger in consequence, and her short hair, finely curling, showed the delicate firmness of her head.

'It's incredible,' he said.

'That we should meet again?'

'That Time should be your beauty-parlour.'

'That's Italy!' she said. 'Your wife told me you were in Italy. You've been practising compliments in Rome.'

'On the contrary, I assure you. I was in Trieste with Tito's votaries.'

'Tony spent most of the war with the Northern Patrol and running convoys to Russia. His notion of being romantic is to build a roaring fire, close all the windows, and create a fug that brings the tears to your eyes.'

'Tony's your husband?'

'Yes. I'm an old married woman now. I've got two children.'

'We have three.'

'What a lot can happen in ten years! A war and two families!'

'I've had a very quiet ten years, except for a battle or two.'

'Well, so have I. There wasn't much hectic gaiety in being a wife and mother in the south of England during the war. It's only in the last few weeks that I've got my hands clean.'

'Do you remember driving to the Castle in Edinburgh?'

'Of course.'

'Do make the conversation general!' cried Mrs Latimer. 'We're all trying not to listen, but my own ears are vibrating furiously, and I'm not the worst. Where have you been, darling?'

'I went to see Michael again.'

'Is he any more cheerful?'

'Someone has asked him to write an article about a very brilliant young Irish dramatist, whose name I can't remember, and he's had to refuse because he isn't quarrelling with him at present. Apparently no Irishman can write about any other Irishman unless they're in a state of open hostility.'

'How very odd. So incense doesn't make the heart grow fonder?'

For half an hour they spoke of the meals they had lately eaten. Food, food and drink, was the English topic in the first years of their victory—the world had rarely seen a hungrier triumph—and in their laurelled heads were childish dreams of sugared cakes. They spoke of steaks with reverence, of cheese with sober joy. Ireland, said one of them, was in danger of acquiring a population of new Protestants, as hunger, that once had stripped her, now drew to her green acres her over-taxed and under-nourished neighbours. Ireland of the many famines, now glistening with fat, was England's dream of joy; and the conquerors talked of cream.

Then Corinna said she must go. She had to call for her husband, they were dining with a cousin of his.

'Let me take you,' said Latimer.

'Don't be late,' said his wife. 'We have a table at Jammet's.'

They went out, Corinna cool but he embarrassed.

With shuddering decision a taxi-cab was pulled abruptly to a halt, and the driver leaned towards them. He was an oldish man, burly of frame, with a friendly purple face and a watery eye. Latimer gave him the address, and got in. As violently as he had stopped, the driver started again, and a moment later nearly ran a cyclist down.

'He isn't very clever, is he?' said Corinna.

'Does it matter?'

'It may, if he meets someone as stupid as himself. I don't want to die with you.'

'Did your Uncle Henry ever discover that we didn't see the match?'

'No, I don't think so.'

'You didn't tell him?'

'I never told anyone.'

'Nor did I.'

'I've often tried to remember what we talked about. We talked all the time, and I've forgotten everything we said. What did we talk about?'

'Queen Dido and Byzantium.'

'It doesn't seem likely, but tell me more.'

'Dublin is ten years west of Edinburgh. We've less time than we had.'

The driver swerved widely to pass a halted tramcar, and in the lurching cab, filled momentarily with yellow light, Corinna fell into Latimer's arms, and made no move to escape again when his hands closed upon her shoulder and her side. The minutes passed—three, four, or five—before she moved away and said, 'We must be nearly there. Do I look as though you had been kissing me?'

'You look as if God had been kissing you,' he answered a trifle breathlessly.

'I don't think Tony would believe a story like that,' she said, and took out her powder-box. Then peering through the window, exclaimed, 'But where are we? We haven't come the proper way! I'm sure we haven't!'

She beat upon the sliding glass that divided them from the driver, and when he drew it open, asked him sharply, 'Do you know where we are?'

'I do not!' he said with wild vexation in his husky voice. 'I'm lost entirely.'

'Well!' she said. 'What do we do now?'

The driver, aware that he owed them some explanation, turned his purple face and shouted, 'It's drunk I am! As drunk as a pig!' And angrily closed the sliding glass.

'But this is dangerous,' she said, and let Latimer take her hand.

'He's going very slowly now. We shan't come to any harm,' he answered.

Again the driver opened the slide between them, and now in a more affable tone declared, 'But it's all right for you! I'm not charging you for this.' And pulled down his flag.

'Is that any comfort?' she asked.

'It's the handsomest thing I ever heard! *Bonosque soles effugere—*'

'Darling, you're not drunk too?'

'No, of course not. I'm misquoting Horace. Or is it Martial? I believe it's Martial.'

'But what does it mean?'

'You learnt Latin at school, didn't you?'

'What difference does that make?'

'None at all, none at all. But we haven't time to talk about education, have we? Listen to what I'm saying, it's most important. *Solesque*—no, that's wrong, you've put me off. *Bonosque soles effugere atque abire sentit, qui nobis pereunt et non imputantur.*—There now! Aren't we in luck?'

'How do I know, unless you tell me what it means?'

'Just what the driver said. No one's going to charge this to our account. Ireland, God bless it, is neutral still!'

The driver, deciding to try his luck in the opposite direction, turned right-about in the breadth of the street without slackening speed, and threw Corinna on to Latimer's breast before she could decide whether that was her intention or not. He, clasping her and advantage firmly together, began without loss of time to kiss her fondly, repeatedly, and with such enthusiasm as was bound to provoke a reciprocal warmth. The driver, looking this way and that but scorning to ask the help of any passer-by, turned east, west, north, and south to find a familiar landmark and the address that he had long since forgotten.

He looked for it in Ballsbridge and the neighbourhood of Glasnevin cemetery. He had a notion it might be in Ringsend, and not long after was out past Kilmainham Gaol and on the road to Mullingar. But open country frightened him, and he turned in a great hurry and drove at high speed past Guinness's Brewery, then loitered thoughtfully on College Green, and slowly, like a man in a trance, patrolled O'Connell Street and Grafton Street. He circumnavigated Merrion Square and went twice round St Stephen's Green to see if it was there. He remembered Rathmines and with fresh hope increased his speed again, but was perplexed by many streets that looked the same, and with a salmon's instinct in the spring turned north again to dawdle by the Liffey. Memory stirred more strongly in him, but a memory quite irrelevant, and for a long time he waited by the gate of the Rotunda Hospital, where he had been born. When at last he returned to Latimer's hotel and deposited Latimer, alone, he was nearly sober.

Latimer paid him off, and turning to go in encountered for the second time the girl with the collecting-box to whom he had spoken earlier in the evening.

She held the box in front of him, a little wearily. 'For the language,' she begged.

'Go home,' he told her, 'for you're wasting your time. There are no words for it in any language. Joy's inenarrable, as every cabman knows!'

MARGARET HAMILTON

Bung

In bright, blown-up raincoats they bobbed slowly along like bunches of balloons tied to a ragman's cart. Women and kids coming to watch the launching.

By the yard gate men stood waiting for them: workers in faded blue or brown overalls, fishing in pockets for a half-smoked cigarette. John Laurie, sulky-faced under the pushed-back welder's goggles, could see a bloated bit of green that was his wife, Katy, bending to jerk the child Ian's clothes to rights.

For a moment the two heads were together, insolently alike, with eyes like plumped-up raisins in the smooth warm faces. There was nothing of John in the boy, he sometimes half-wondered if . . . Ah, no good thinking like that two years after he'd married her because Ian was on the way. He glanced inside at the shed where Ginger Bain and the rest of the scrap-metal ring were standing in a corner, nervously flicking fag-ash behind them as they plotted their latest scheme for nicking brass from the yard in a big way. Ginger and Katy had once been pretty thick, but Ginger wasn't the marrying kind. The kid had ginger hair, but so had Katy—a crimpy auburn that sparked and crackled if a man ran his work-horned fingers through it.

As she crossed the street, a gust hurled grit and dirty paper in Katy's face. John could sense her muttering through the plastic shield of her dentures: *Shut up, Ian. What a climate, we can't be away too soon.*

Above him, as he stepped out to meet her, a Union Jack and a red-and-gold house flag snapped and snorted at each other. He dived to pick up Ian, grasping him by the thickly-clad waist to swing him high and clear of his mother. At once her attack began. 'You could have stayed at your work another quart'ran hour, you're only flingin' away dough!'

A lorry, backing into the yard, was silenced by the din inside—but not Katy. Men waiting to take children off the hands of their wind-ravaged mothers, could still respond to the rough comedienne's voice, which gave her words a blatant fearlessness and would make strangers grin indulgently at what she said.

He muttered: 'You needny worry. When did you ever get less than your pound o' flesh?'

What in heaven's name did she do with it, the unopened pay-packet handed to her every week? He never was away from work, except once when he'd had to go and see about that bit of skin trouble, brought on by her rotten cooking, beans and chips instead of the good grilled steak his mother always gave him. Tenderly exploring his chin with a blackened finger, he wished Katy would let him grow a beard. She was dead against it, remembering that at one time he had experimented with facial ornaments—handle-bars, beards, exaggerated sideburns—to attract certain girls who were said to be sporting.

Katy herself had been one of them . . . working at the time in a department store, conning women into buying clothes that made them look like frowsy tarts, and herself borrowing the clothes to wear with dazzling effect in the evenings. Till she was found out and sacked.

As he tried to settle the child more comfortably on his shoulders, she narked on as if he had not spoken: '*And* I'll bet you forgot to post the form about goin' to Australia. Nothin' gets done unless I do it myself . . . *Don't, Ian!*' She gave the kid's leg a stinging slap for trying to kick the wind-bellied front of her coat.

His automatic howl was cut short by the appearance of Thomson, the yard foreman. Wearing a grey, well-pressed suit for the occasion, he shot out on to the pavement, as if catapulted from the ways where the ship, *National Progress*, clung ready for launching. Before you could hear him, you knew he was muttering, *Where the hell have they got to?*

'Hear anything?' he roared to Paddy McGuire, the gateman. Slowly the old man cupped his hand to an ear whose drum had been mangled by years of boiler-shop din.

Thomson fiddled violently with his watch-strap, then turned to look inside the yard again—as if the minute his back was turned that ship would probably ramstam into the river on her own. Then he was out again—glaring along the street—pushing back the natty tweed hat as if it had been his usual squashed homburg. (It was not so many years since Thomson had discarded the black reinforced bowler, traditional foreman's protection against bolts and rivets dropped 'accidentally' from a height.)

Fathers of families, lingering by the gate, nipped out their cigarettes to become workmen again, hands forward, listening. Children were shushed. Against the yard noises, against the wind and the thunder of main road traffic fifty yards away, everybody listened. 'Is it too quiet for you, Mister, will I drop a pin?' said Katy, but softly, listening too.

Her husband moved back against the wall. 'They're comin'!' Then to Ian, squirming above his head: 'Here's the band, son.'

Thomson waited only long enough to make sure the small group of pipers and drummers was heading for the yard. Maybe he'd hoped for some hitch like the lack of a band to give him an excuse to approach the directors again about postponement. They must have insisted on the launching—Thomson would know it was daft to let her go today, a big empty hulk with no sense in her to tack and manoeuvre with a gale.

Ah, she had to go now, for the band was here. They were not a stylish turn-out, but a scratch bunch of local men who had learned piping or drumming in boys' organisations or the Orange Lodge, and now hired themselves out for football matches and launchings. The wind sported among their thin kilts and even tried to snatch the mace which the pipe-major tossed bravely as he entered the yard. There was a cheer from some of the men as he grabbed and caught it, less bravely.

'Well held, son!'

'That's a rare job, I wonder what bung they've to pay *him*.'

'None—he does it for love!'

'It's nothin' to what some folk'll do for love!' roared Paddy the gateman with a wink at John Laurie. Paddy was Katy's uncle, and she turned with a grin and a casual 'H'llo, auld yin!'

A grey-painted bow, with the name, *National Progress,* in gleaming white letters, dominated the yard. On either side the iron uprights, bare now of staging planks, swayed in the wind, while underneath her the shipwrights hammered away one by one the huge wooden supports, which they might almost have left for the wind to winkle out. Job No. 798 she had been, from the day the number was first pencilled on a blueprint by the foreman patternmaker till it was stamped on the last small prefabricated metal part imported into the yard. Two berths away lay No. 799, a few months off completion, with a prickle of staging planks on her stern. Between the two, No. 800, with only her keel laid, made a fine platform for watching 798 take the water.

Men glanced at the two unfinished shells, estimating how much work was in them for this or that trade. The speeches at the celebration luncheon were quoted in the afternoon papers, which had been given advance copies.

'D'ye see what the chairman's been sayin'?'

'Aye—"There may have to be sacrifices all round." All round about himsel', he means. Sacrifices in every home on Clydeside, but none for him and his pals!'

'Ach, they canny *make* work—'

'They canny make ships, you mean. We're the mugs that do that.'

Clouds hurtled over the sky, dropping a few fat samples of their load on waiting ship and people, then moving restlessly on. As restlessly as Katy, darting about with Ian by the hand, looking for a vantage point but choosing none.

'That's a nice boat you've got, son.' Paddy the gateman chatted kindly to his great-nephew, Ian. 'You should get the lady to launch it too.'

'Lady launch my boatie too!' the child cried excitedly, waving the toy sailboat he had insisted on bringing. 'Lady launch my boatie too!' he crowed, so that people standing near them laughed nearly as proudly as if he had been one of their own.

A man came up behind Katy, Ginger Bain putting his arm round her waist, his dirty hand crumpling the stiff P.V.C. coat with casual insolence. 'Hello, Katy, long time no' see. 'Ve you come to see the launchin'?'

(Did he think maybe she'd come to get down to it with a rivetting hammer?)

She answered with husky affability: 'Ach, Ian's daft about ships. Not that a tanker's much—just a big petrol can gettin' heaved into the water on its backside.'

'It makes a change for the kids.' Ginger was very civil now, treating her as a respectable matron only good for looking after another man's brats. Then deliberately he turned his back on her and sidled towards John, the ferret face full of imitation joviality.

'Is this your kid then, Johnny? Fine wee chap. Takes plenty dough to keep 'em goin' these days, eh, Johnny? . . . Now—me and the boys was just talkin'. We were hopin' you'd change your mind about comin' in wi' us. If it's only a matter o' steppin' up the bung, Johnny—just say what you want an' we'll see what we can do . . .'

John looked at him distastefully. The ring was dead keen to get him: a welder working for long spells near the keel of the ship where all the dirt and refuse gathered—he could hide stuff among the rubbish till they were ready to take it away. And his wife's uncle was a gateman who might be persuaded, for family reasons, to turn a blind eye on what was being carried out.

John had always steered clear of big theft, thinking you were bound to cop it sooner or later. It must be big stuff they were after this time—probably brass portholes by the dozen, since nothing smaller would pay off enough. They'd give him his whack for a week or two, but then his share would be cut, and if he tried to break with them the pressure would go on. Only last year Bill Carey, one of his mates, had got a prison sentence because he'd been made a scapegoat for the ring.

John shook his head. 'It wouldn't be worth while for all the time I'll be here—Katy wants to emigrate to Australia . . .'

c*

Suddenly they were everywhere, overalled men who knew they
had to stop work now if they were to see the launching. On the
ship herself riggers lined the deck-rails, and on the roofs of sheds
or underneath them other men stood close-packed as for a cup-tie
football match. Every now and then a single ironic cheer went up—
for the band, changing position, for someone in the official launching
party being photographed by a pressman. For Katy Laurie, diving
and swearing after Ian who, while John was talking to Ginger Bain,
had run dangerously near the prow of No. 800.

'Some folk's no' fit to be in charge o' a mongrel pup, let alone a
kid!' Lugging and shaking Ian, she strutted away on steel club heels
that John had not seen before. Another new pair—she must spend a
fortune in shoe-shops. Or . . . there was that place in Copland Road
where they had shoes on display on a rack outside. Katy was a com-
pulsive picker up of ashtrays and glasses in pubs, toilet rolls from
lavatories. *Ach, they owe us a bit o' bung for the prices they charge!*
she would grin with those ugly false teeth. All the beauty had gone out
of her smile when she had to have her own quartz-pebble teeth hauled
out because they went rotten after Ian was born.

Catching sight of Ginger Bain still hovering near, she stopped in
her tracks and began shamelessly to make up to him. 'Just like old
times, i'n't it, Ginger? D'you mind what the old bitch said when she
saw the van waitin' outside?'

As they went off together, John suddenly knew that her dismissal
from the shop had not been on account of borrowing clothes to wear
in the evenings. She and Ginger had been in cahoots, she slipping out
bundles of garments to a waiting van and telling her boss they had
been shoplifted . . .

'That one needs her backside warmed, and if her mother was livin'
she'd get it.' Paddy McGuire, Katy's uncle, was looking at her and
Ginger.

John shot him a look, but had an urge to confide in the old man.
'She wants to go to Australia,' he said.

'Ach!' Paddy spat, grinding the spittle with his boot. 'I remember
a green frock she once wanted when she was just a lassie—nylon
wi' a bunchy skirt. It was in a shop window in the Govan Road and
she thought if only she could get wearin' it at the school dance she'd
be queen o' the Clyde.'

'Likely she wasn't far wrong—'

'She never had half the looks o' her mother, nor the contented
nature . . . Her brother Mike bought her the frock, but she never
wore it because she discovered the other lassies were goin' to the
dance in sweaters and jeans . . . Now it's Australia. Her brother's in
Melbourne, doin' well for himsel'. He spoiled her rotten when she
was wee, so now she thinks everything would be hunky-dory if she was

there too. As if every thousand miles she travelled was a bit o' bung she was payin' for life to give her the best o' everything. . . .'

Bung, the shipyard term for bribery or graft. You slipped the craneman a bit of bung, a packet of fags for lifting a hunk of pre-fabricated shell into position so that you needn't stand idle waiting for him. Or you gave the foreman a bottle of whisky or a few quid (if he was known to be the kind who'd take it) so he'd put you on jobs where there was most money to be made on piecework, or when times were bad—as they were now on Clydeside—he wouldn't list your name among the men to be sacked.

Bung . . . some folk thought there was nothing it couldn't do if you offered enough of the right kind.

'Johnny!' Suddenly Ginger Bain was back beside him, grinning like a mangy cat that had just swallowed a bird of paradise. 'Johnny, I've got her talked out of it for you—she says she's no' carin' aboot goin' to Australia, providin' she gets a bit more dough to make ends meet. So gettin' back to that wee bit business we were discussin', Johnny—'

'*Aoh-aw!*' A low growl went round the yard as men realised the ship was 'coming alive'—trying to creep down the ways on her own. Thomson, the foreman, was hopping about, muttering, 'For Christ's sake, hold on to her!'—his talk profane because the shipwrights' fore-man would expect it, but subdued in deference to the platform party. They were now reshuffling for the launching, the official kicking of *National Progress* out of the yard with a broken bottle at her head.

A shout from Thomson was the signal for it to begin, for the bottle to be flung, the last stay to be knocked out, the *National Progress* to start moving. Eyes and cameras took her to themselves in a series of nose-to-tail impressions chasing each other with growing rapidity. Everything moved to receive the ship, turbulent water, hovering tugs, draggled sky . . . and wind.

Now she was cleaving the water . . . and a scream cleaved the air. The familiar outraged protest of Ian Laurie being prevented from doing what he thought was right and just to himself.

Unnoticed by either parent, he had snaked to the very front of the people on No. 800. He laid down his toy boat, the better to clap and jump to the music of the band as the ship went down the ways. As Paddy had prophesied, there was a second launching, for the wash from the ship flooded the new keel and swept away his boat.

Ian tried to snatch it back, and was himself snatched back by his great-uncle Paddy who, unlike the child's parents, had seen what he was up to. Struggling in mid-air, Ian screamed against the in-justice of a world where boats were launched and taken from you.

It was different with the *National Progress*. Before tugs could control her the wind rushed in, forcing her sideways, slowly, back to the land. With a splintering crack of staging-planks, her stern rammed the stern of the partly-finished No. 799.

And John Laurie rammed his wife.

Triumphantly, even as the tugs got busy charging and leaping and putting out smoke, he roared at her: 'Of all the bloody rotten mothers —he could easy have been drowned—I suppose that would suit you fine—save you the bother o' lookin' after him—'

'You were nearer. If you hadny been standin' dreamin'—'

'You might as well know it now, you're goin' to Australia, whether you like it or not. I've made up my mind.'

'*You*'ve made up *your* mind, I like that.'

'And you're goin' nowhere near Melbourne, you're goin' to the outback where there's nothin' but sheep and you'll have to pay attention to the kid . . .' She'd have to be nice to her man too, there'd be no competition but kangaroos and Aborigines.

She laughed in his face and strutted away, still yapping at Ian. 'Shut up, you'll get another boat the very same. Oh, all right, you'll get one o' the big clockwork ones that go round and round the pond'— as if she were already confident of having extra money between her fingers. A few yards away Ginger and the rest of the ring stood grinning, confident too.

Other men, moving slowly back to work, looked at the damaged ship, already on her way down-river for fitting out. 'That'll be a bit o' overtime for somebody, goin' to Greenock to sort her plates.'

Paddy McGuire, staring at the wind-scoured empty berth, said: 'You miss a ship when she's awa'. She kept the draught oot o' the yard.'

'There's others comin' on.' John waved towards the growing No. 799 and the embryo No. 800.

'And after that?' Paddy as a young man had lived through the hungry thirties, when this and other yards had been a forest of rotting cranes and empty uprights.

There were hard times coming again. You couldn't lift a paper or switch on the telly without getting more bad news. Maybe he'd better take a chance with Ginger and the rest, John thought, for the sake of having a few quid behind him when the crash came.

As if he had read the thought, Ginger moved in close to John. 'Look at Thomson messin' his pants for what he'll say to the directors about the bad launchin'.'

'What's he worryin' aboot?' Paddy McGuire, time-pitted hook by which the ring must hang or fall, looked John in the eye. Then he roared above the growing sounds of work re-starting: '*Even the directors ken the wind's like a guid gateman—it'll no' tak' bung frae anybody!*'

ANGUS WOLFE MURRAY

I Want To Go Now

Shona waited in the forest overlooking the road, watching through trees for her brother to return. He had been gone three years. His name was Calum. He was a revolutionary.

She did not understand the workings of wisdom nor the manifestations of political power. Her brother, Douglas, called her 'simple', even to her face. Calum called her 'ma wee daffy'.

He wrote letters.

'Freedom is the ability of all people to learn the truth. There will be war. I love you.'

She read the letters to her wolfhound, Skornag.

In the islands to the west she was known as the wild child of Glen Rahsig. Her beauty, they said, affected her mind. She was twenty-two years old.

Douglas was the eldest. He managed the estate.

One night, when Shona was fourteen, he grew as tall as Ben Rogaht. He walked like a mountain. He waded the loch. Floods swept the village. Mrs Kennedy at the Post Office floated out to sea.

'Skornag saw you in the river,' Shona said.

Mrs Kennedy popped a butter drop into her purse.

'Then it was so.'

Smiling.

They were together, as they had always been, Shona and Skornag, on the hill overlooking the road. It was the second week of the atrocities.

'I wonder if he'll bring us something,' Shona said. Meaning Calum.

Skornag lay in the bracken, his eyes reflecting sun like the steel tips of lances.

'He'll bring us silver drums,' she said.

They listened for music above the hiss of insects dying.

*

The house lay back from the road, protected by pine trees and rock, a solid stone building in the tradition of northern architectural practicality. Lawns, sculpted from bare hill, created an illusion of calm. Rhododendrons tangled in ruins beside the drive.

'When are they coming?'

Douglas's father paced the boards of what was once the ballroom. 'Frankly, I'm at a loss.'

He was a serious man who had worked conscientiously and with aptitude for the benefit, or so he believed, of others. He did not expect treachery, nor defeat. He expected reasonable compensation. Events (implausible, illogical) had taken a hold on rationality, leapt fully clothed into the arena, and the Emergency Government, created as a direct result of the oil riots four years ago, had been overthrown, literally, at the Assembly Buildings by an army of skilfully trained commandos led by an associate of his boy, Calum. Their fate was not yet known. Nothing was. Communications had been cut, irrevocably, it seemed. These men, Ministers of the Government, were his friends, his colleagues. He had worked with them, legislated, helped write laws for the new Constitution, mould a country from a union with the dedication of a native son. (Who said that? Was it one of *his* speeches? Why not? He'd use it.) Now all was fraught, *ruptured,* as if time and energy, effort, love and care was for nothing, wasted. He accepted (no, no, he wouldn't deny it) that the Emergency Government had been forced to take authoritative action to contain violence in the streets. Camps had been set up as temporary holding zones for prisoners awaiting trial. There was no evidence of brutality. Regular checks had been carried out. (He had read reports.) And yet because of the extremity of power, essential to law and order at the time, and of his involvement in the Government as a loyal and dedicated servant of the people, he was in danger of forfeiting his land, his home, even his life. It was a cruel, bitter, ultimately fruitless gesture.

'How do we know they're coming?'

'We don't,' Douglas said.

'And what are they going to do when they get here?'

'Kill the cows for starters.'

'Rubbish!'

Debate, argument, invective! It seemed absurd, here, in an empty room in the autumn of the last year of sanity.

Douglas, his heir, stood 6ft 10ins in stockinged feet, an added reminder that honour, decency and duty was seldom repaid with a fair distribution of good fortune. He had three children, a white giraffe, a stunted red-headed maniac and a beautiful girl with the brains of a bird. It didn't appear proportionately representative.

*

Calum on the road, alone, darkness bubbling up the backs of the mountains, filling the glen like jaundiced piss. No more wondrous place in all the world. His own. Where he grew, or (in his case) didn't. Riding a bike up the last hill with the loch on his left, bare rising rocks to his right. The house hidden in trees.

His father was mad. Of this he was certain. Only madness could save him. He constructed a case for the defence as he pumped the pedals.

'Brothers,' he said, speaking to the Committee For National Security later in the long dialogue of post-revolutionary analysis. 'My father was the victim of isolation, privilege, bourgeois romanticism and loveliness. He was made mad by beauty, having the money to indulge it and the time to enjoy it.'

Sky falling across the water. He sped down hill, a dwarf shielded in the shadow of the forest, second son who became a soldier for the forces of change and destruction.

*

Skornag, in the trees, heard sounds on the road. Shona watched his face.

'Who is it?'

Skornag stiffened, standing in dead bracken, shook his rough, grey hair.

*

Shona's mother walked from the garden, an angular lady, across the lawn, wearing brogues, bog brown tweeds and a coat like a bulldozed groundsheet.

It was still cold.

She had lived thirty years in this house. Thoughts of leaving it had never, until now, disturbed the peace of her mind. Happiness was the recognition of her children's devotion and her husband's acceptance and success. Love and duty fused in a simple ritual of containment with care. Her heart, not her arms, embraced them.

Voices on the drive. Cries. Like laughter. Skornag bounded over the gravel, a body on his back, a rider.

She hurried up the bank.

Shona came running, pushing a bicycle.

'Mama, oh Mama!'

Breathless.

*

Douglas took stock. He was aware of certain facts. One of which was fear.

No one knew whether the forces that had taken the capital controlled the country or whether groups in the north had rallied. Already in the village there were rumours of marauding gangs, killing hostages, burning farms to the south. His father had escaped the coup and returned. And now Calum also.

Nothing would be the same again. The solidarity of a stable, essentially feudal society had been replaced by terror, uncertainty and almost inevitable deprivation. The pattern of revolution was repetitive and predictable.

Douglas worried about the animals.

*

Calum entered the ballroom. There was no furniture except a sofa and a low table before the fire. Carpets had been taken up. Curtains remained but had not been drawn. Calum's father was standing in front of the window with his back to the door.

'What are you doing?' Calum asked.

His father did not answer.

'We never *use* this room.'

*

The night lingered. Time hung on the wires.

Calum's father ate from a tray, alone. The others gathered in the kitchen. Calum spoke of the war. They had experienced nothing.

Shona touched him.

'Don't be afraid,' he said.

She sensed changes like heather burning between them.

'You're a bloody traitor!' Douglas shouted from the kitchen corridor.

Calum returned to the ballroom.

'You've brought this upon yourself,' he said. 'You've condemned your family.'

'We deserve no credit for the things we achieve in the failure of our duties,' his father said. 'The one inexcusable folly in political life is to awaken the susceptibility of the common man, unless you *are* the common man, in which case you become elated, for a moment, until, quite easily and quickly and with the minimum of fuss, you are defeated, pushed aside and thrown into the bin.'

*

Shona felt the foundations of her dreams dusty in a wind blowing from spaces beyond her knowledge and understanding. She could not hold them together. Not any more.

Calum had returned for another purpose. To make them fear him.

He talked of why they must leave, what would happen, plans for their future, for the country's future. She did not listen. Trees and mountains beckoned, holding back their tears.

She slept with Skornag. She whispered to him.

'Ah my love, my love.'

*

It rained during the night and in the morning a group of men arrived. Calum met them outside. The leader of the group was Calum's age. They spoke together.

Calum's father recognised some of the men and walked across to where they were standing to shake them by the hand.

'These are difficult times,' he said. 'For all of us.'

The men appeared uncomfortable, even nervous.

Douglas stayed with his mother on the lawn. She squeezed his arm.

The men in the group had .22 rifles and 12 bore shotguns. Most of them were from the district although four or five were strangers, smartly dressed in green corduroy, carrying modern weapons.

'I expect they will burn the house,' Douglas's mother said, as if discussing a cure for greenfly.

*

Upstairs Shona fought Skornag, holding him under the water of a deep enamel bath, screaming to avoid the sounds. He thrashed like a horse, his great head locked in her fists. She pressed him to the base, her body arched over the edge, hair falling in curls across his face. A thousand years passed. His legs splintered against the sides. A thousand nights and days. She felt the weight of his life sink. Suddenly still. And so burst with a passion beyond that of desire for flesh to be warmed by the sun or for happiness requited in dreams made real. A god flowed out of her mouth, howling and spitting. She was fierce with the spirit, hearing bells ring at the gates of heaven.

She left the bathroom and came downstairs. She wore a dress of summer flowers. Her eyes, they said, were shining. She stood at the door of the house. Calum turned, startled at her appearance. The men with guns waited. No one moved.

It seemed that she would fly. It seemed that she would open her wings and fly over the trees.

'I want to go now,' she said, and walked towards the cars.

EONA MACNICOL

The Man in the Lochan

My mother's girlhood home was a croft above Clachanree proper, over its skyline, in the middle of the moor. A solitary place; I doubt if there were any other houses within view. Only the smoke from the houses of Tallurach and perhaps the school-house behind the Planting gave hint of neighbours at all. We looked on to a sheer hill face called the Leitir which overshadowed Loch Laide, famous for its trout and for the waterfowl that lived secretly among its reeds.

A solitary place. When once I spent a whole summer there I found it too solitary. When I grew tired of watching women's ploys about the house I had to go about with my grandfather, tending his fields or rounding up his sheep. It must have been on an expedition with him that I discovered behind the Leitir a habitation I had never known about before.

It was a tiny croft, an islet of cultivation in the middle of the heather. There were only three fields, one of hay, one of turnips, one of potatoes, with a little grassland heavily encroached upon by tufts of bulrushes, even starred here and there by bog-cotton flowers. But in my eyes the smallness was its charm. On the greensward round the little house some half-dozen hens daintily strutted. A cow and her calf munched near by, and a pony lay taking his ease in shelter of the single tutelary rowan tree. An old woman could be seen busy on one of the fields, singling turnips.

I do not think it was the custom in Clachanree for women to work much in the fields. True, they would help out at harvest or lambing time. Here was a woman who every time I passed that way with my grandfather was at man's work. I admired her greatly. She was only of average height, but stalwart and strong. How nonchalantly would she swing a hammer down upon a post in her fence; how confidently catch and harness her pony; with what careless ease cut rushes for his bed. Her clothes were the dark long-sleeved blouse and the full skirt that all elderly women wore, but she had man's boots, stout hob-nailed affairs; and I thought her worthy of them.

I persuaded my grandfather one day to pass near enough the

house to hail her. 'Well, well then, Oonagh, and how are you the day?' She dropped her hoe and came silent though smiling to meet us. She wore her hair, of a silvery gold colour, in a pile on the top of her head, as the fashion then was or had been. Her face was brown with the sun, the corners of her eyes wrinkled from squinting against it.

I got into the habit of giving my grandfather the slip and spending with Oonagh the time I was out under his care. I made advances to her, and she accepted my presence in her silent way. I had the privilege of assisting her out of doors; gathering her cut hay, or making a mixture of milk and meal for her calf. Soon I was permitted entry into her house. Its thatch was adorned by a plume of heather sprouting all joco from it. Inside it consisted of only one room—well, one and a half, for the boxbed was virtually a room in itself. Everything was as spic-and-span as if Oonagh expected company. The coverlet of patchwork though frayed was immaculately clean; the table was covered in a shiny, bright-coloured stuff called, I think, baize; the bowls and jugs upon the dresser made as brave a display, proportionately to the size of the dwelling, as did ours in the croft house of Druim. Even the rag rug before the hearth was clean—clean, I began to realise, because few feet trod on it. There was no plant on the window sill; instead there was a brown jam-jar of pink-spotted flowers with a heavy clinging scent which vied with the usual smell of damp and peatreek. I had not at that time seen orchids. Oonagh in few words explained to me that she found them away out on the moor, among the peat bogs. I resolved I would go myself and find some.

Only one thing seemed to me to spoil the charm of the little dwelling; for joined on to the one room, like an envious poor neighbour, was the other half of the original house, now in a ruinous state. When I asked Oonagh why she did not have the old walls carried away she laughed, colour rose in her face, and she said, in a rare burst of talk, 'Who knows, *m'eudail*, but some day there will be need of them?'

She was not only silent, but strange. Yet I found it pleasanter to be with her than in jollier homes where there was always the likelihood of tedious talk, likening one's face to this and that past member of the family. Oonagh did not tease me with talk at all. In friendly silence we worked together, or rested; for sometimes she would fetch me out a glass of milk and a hunk of oatcake, and would herself sit down, her legs in the dark skirt spread comfortably upon the grass. She might hum to herself, or sing, more often in Gaelic but sometimes in English learnt at school. One song was a ballad of great length the chorus of which I picked up:

'I wish I were,
But I wish in vain,
I wish I were
A young lass again.
But such a thing
Can never be
Till an Aipple grows
On an Oarange tree.'

Other times she might bring out of her pocket a clay pipe, and light
up and puff away as good as any man.

One day as I was making my way to Oonagh's I heard a creaking
sound, as of wheels on a rough rocky road. It was Oonagh going up on
the high moor to turn her peats. And the sound was like a fairy pipe
to me. I longed to be up on the heights, in the sea of heather. Maybe
too I should find those exotic pink-spotted flowers. The cart had got
a start on me, yet it was going slowly, the pony straining with the
effort of pulling, Oonagh walking beside.

I took short cuts and made up on them. I called a greeting to
Oonagh, who said nothing in reply but looked as if she were not
averse to my presence. She was smoking her clay pipe, curls of grey
smoke floating backward in the wind. We plodded uphill behind the
pony, who kept on nodding his head, poor thing, as if endorsing our
unspoken complaints about the steepness of our way. At last we gained
the peat moor, and Oonagh got busy turning, puffing the while at her
pipe, saying nothing.

I for my part was content; there was so much to see. Among the
heather grew blaeberry bushes with their vivid green, and staghorn
moss paved that hidden world which is inhabited by lizards and
beetles. But I found no flowers. And after a while I came back to
Oonagh where she was turning the wet sides to the wind. The wind
had teased out strands of her grey-gold hair, and she squinted against
sun and smoke. An old woman, with little power to amuse. I began
to think it was time we were getting home.

But Oonagh took her pipe out of her mouth and said, 'Sheep.' I
gathered she was uneasy about their whereabouts and wanted to scan
the hill grazing ground. We left the pony patiently switching from
his flanks the flies that settled whenever the wind dropped. We went
round a hillock. I gasped with delight.

There lay a lochan, sleek, still, its dark surface sprinkled round
the rim with water lilies of purest white. As fast as I could through
the deep heather I made my way to it, and threw myself down on
my stomach, stretching out a greedy hand for the nearest of the
exquisite flowers. I secured one, but it had a long rubbery stem
which seemed endless as it came up out of the water. I broke off the

flower head. But so far from feeling satisfied, I felt greedier than ever and reached out farther for another flower. It was beyond my reach. I called to Oonagh, who had come back but made no effort to assist me, begging her to see if her longer arm could secure it.

I remember she came slowly, as if weighted down by her long heavy skirt and heavy boots, then got down awkwardly beside me. The wind had dropped for the moment. It was so still that reflections appeared in the water as if in a glass; the dark shape of the hillock; the clouds patterning the blue of the sky; a wild duck flying up to meet its counterpart flying down. Close to the brink our two reflections appeared. Then a small breeze came, and wrinkled the surface. The images were gone. Oonagh put out her arm. Her brown fingers closed below a flower and she pulled at it, dragging the stem like a discovered thing up and out. Another and another she procured, some six or seven, cheerful and humming, her pipe laid down by her side.

I was about to say I had enough and restrain Oonagh from further effort, when I found there was no need. The wind had dropped once more. The surface of the lochan was smooth, with images appearing on it again. Now Oonagh was bending so low her face almost met the water, shading her eyes with a hand spread on either side.

'What is it, Oonagh?' I asked. 'What are you looking at? Are there fish?'

'Aye are there fish!' She turned her head over her shoulder to address me. Her wrinkled sunburnt face wore a radiant smile. 'Put you your head down low and keep looking, *m'eudail,* and you will be seeing them. Grey like silver they are, leaping this way and that. Then suddenly they will leave the water and fly through the air.'

'How can fish leave the water? They would die.'

She said 'Tst!' impatiently, and turned from me to gaze into the water again. I felt I was missing something and followed her example, bending down so low I smelt the heavy smell of water thick with weeds.

She was staring in, rapt, like a clairvoyant.

'What are you seeing now?' I pestered her.

She pointed. 'See, see! See the palm trees moving.' I could see the stems of the water lilies swaying to some little depth, the currents moving them.

'That's not—' Something stopped the words on my tongue, the realisation of the absurdity of it: how could palm trees grow in this cold windy place? I looked closely at Oonagh to see if she were joking at my expense. I took it upon myself to say, 'See will you fall in!'

She cried sharply, *'Bith sochd!'*—Be quiet! Her pointing finger moved like a magician's over the still water. 'Look now, what bonnie! A lily pool, it is lined with white stone, and a fountain in the middle of it, and the fishes are golden—look at them jinking this way and that way between the flowers. White the flowers are, as sheets laid—' If I had a question I could not ask it, for something froze the words upon my lips. 'See yon! There it is, the house itself. It's coming. Look at that now!' She turned her face towards me, smiling but with eyes unfocused, then turned to the water again. Her voice was so low it was all I could do to catch what she said.

What house? What house? I had heard—who has not?—of houses, villages, overwhelmed by water, but away up here on the moor who had at any time built houses? And how could a little lochan cover them?

She put a hand on my back and pressed me down. 'Here, look down here. Can you not see the house? It's down there, deep, deep in. The white pillars and the steps and the roof with a shine on it. That's the stars, *m'eudail*, bonnie stars they have there.'

I would have liked to ask her to let us leave the lochan and be going home. Indeed I rose up on my knees, but she was talking still, chuckling to herself. 'Aye there's them! There's the dark men, it's coming this time, the dark men with the bright clothes on them.'

I felt a longing for home keener than my past longing for water-lilies. The game, if game it was, was over for me. I should never be able to see more in the lochan than lily stems and the reflections of hill and cloud and our own faces. There clear in the water I saw Oonagh's face, and was startled out of my senses; for the face in the water was young, the curve of cheek and chin like a girl's. I looked in astonishment from the reflected to the real face and found it was indeed bright, youthful, transfigured with joy.

She was chanting to herself in an ecstasy. 'When it is quiet he will come, himself will come. Out from between the pillars of his house, into my arms.' Her ecstasy melted into tears, and she cried with both smiles and tears, '*Tha m'ulaidh ort! Tha m'ulaidh!*'—I love you! I love you!

I cried out to her in fear, 'Oonagh!' And just as I spoke, a stiff breeze came. It ruffled the water from middle to brink. The still mirror was gone.

She jumped up and looked round at me in intense anger. Her face, old and brown, menaced me. Then, as if passing through a double enchantment, she was quiet and serene again, familiar, friendly, my companion of the summer.

She said, sighing, 'Aye aye, just so. It is always the way. He willna stay for long. There's aye a something. But when it is his time, he will come and stay.' She looked down at her knees where the damp peaty earth had stained her dark skirt, and stooped and picked up her clay pipe and stuck it between her lips. She took it out once to ask me, 'What were we doing at the lochan?' But I was now the silent one. I left my lilies behind, and walked with dragging steps after the cart and pony.

*

I was late home that evening. My mother was helping my grandmother at her churning. She called to me. Where had I been? My grandfather had come home without me.

I said I had been talking to Oonagh. Then, in a sudden longing to be reassured, I told the whole of it; about the lochan and how she had stared down into its depths and spoken of things she could see. My mother cried out, then stopped short with a hand at her mouth. It was left to my grandmother to speak. 'You must not go far from the place with Oonagh. It is not safe. Your grandfather should have warned you.'

'Why?' I cried, angry at the hint of blame.

My mother had regained control over herself. 'There is nothing against her, Ellen. Nothing at all. She is a good woman. For all they do not like her in their houses at such times as churning, she is respected. She has never done harm to a living. She is even mindful of the means of grace'—by which she meant she was a churchgoer— 'All the same, you will do well to keep away from her when she goes near water.' She made a signal to my grandmother.

But my grandmother did not see it or did not heed. 'She fell in love with the lochan itself, they say.' She paused maddeningly, took off the wooden lid and pulled the plunger up, a weird mass of horsehair and cream, and tested for butter forming. 'Some say the *eachd uisge* [waterhorse] has put a spell upon her.'

My mother cried out along with me in remonstrance. My grandmother at last saw what was required of her and said nothing more, but began to churn mightily, singing a Psalm to swallow up any inauspicious influence and make the butter come firm and sweet.

My mother came to me when I was in bed. 'About the *eachd uisge;* you must not be afraid. There is no such thing. Your father, at any rate, would not approve of it. And about her being in love with the lochan; that is all nonsense, for she had a human lover. That is to say, there was a man she loved.' Her blue eyes grew thoughtful. The story hid within them. I lay still in my bed, listening with an eagerness near to apprehension. Yet it was like a story told already, I needed only the details.

It was some childish disappointment—my mother thought that Oonagh's new dress, such a rare possession, had been usurped by a sister—which made her run away over the moors to the lochan to hide her tears there. By its brink she should have been alone, but she began to hear the small clatter of oars in rowlocks. Curiosity drew her. It was not Jock from Corrie, nor Lachlan from Reneudin: it was a stranger. He was as startled as she was—and no wonder!—to see as if growing out of the moor this fair young girl. When he saw that she was weeping, however, he pulled in to the shore. 'Why are you weeping?' He asked it in Gaelic, that tender language; and in the same tongue she answered him, 'For nothing at all.' For suddenly it seemed as nothing. When he put a kindly hand to her head, straightening the snood ribbon, a feeling she had never known swept all through her, swept over him too.

Often after that, so ran my mother's whispered tale in the darkening room, they met at the lochan. He had come for a holiday to Glen Urquhart, for the fishing. He would take his boat out and sit with dipped oars, while she knelt at the boat's rim trying to see his image in the water, too shy still to look directly at him. Later they would lie by the brink. What passed between them my mother did not say, nor would I have known.

Summer was almost over when he told her what surely she must have known all the time. He was going away, not to the town, not even to Aberdeen or to Glasgow; over the unimaginable seas to a foreign land. Seeing her face, he avowed, 'I will not forget you. One day when I have got rich I will come back and we will be always together.' She saw his image there in the water as he said it; saw it plainly in the still water, for all time, for ever. Then a breeze came and it was gone.

I could picture Oonagh as winter set in, snow on the far mountains, a bitter wind searing the nearer hills. In the cold of the morning she would crouch at the hearth, relighting the fire, clinging to her dreams, unwilling to leave them for the long vacuous day. But she was not forgotten, my mother said. Letters, a great novelty, came from foreign parts. Many people would have liked to examine them, but she would snatch them and run away with them over the moor to the lochan. It was in her light step and her singing that the contents of the letters could be guessed at. But sometimes she talked of the marvels of life abroad. So fantastic it seemed that people laughed as if at a jest.

Then after a while—did I not know?—the letters stopped coming. Months went by, seasons went by, and years. I pictured them in the mutations of the rowan tree: its young leaves; its pale blossom; its berries going from green to orange to red; then the tree bare again. But the reality was toil, long toil, hard toil, many reverses, little to eat. Years went by; father and mother dying; sisters marrying and settling in other homes; Oonagh left where she was. Even if she had had the inclination to look into the small dim mirror in the house she had little time. Only in the coming of young men about the place might she have known she was comely to look at. They had brought gifts, as wooers; but never could she give answering love, and by and by they had grown discouraged—who could blame them?—and had found other girls as beautiful and not so strange. For she had strange ways. She would leave tasks in the midst and run off over the moors to the lochan. She began to say she had a lover, a husband, a home in its depths.

At last only one brother remained, and a hard life he had of it trying to keep the croft with her fitful aid. He took a dislike to the place. He had a sweetheart whose family moved to the east where farming was more rewarding. He could go there, and take his sister with him.

But when he told her of the plan, Oonagh would not hear of leaving. How could she leave her home, the trysting place, where alone she had hope of being with her lover? And perhaps in his heart her brother was not sorry to escape.

'She has lived ever since, as you see, alone.' My mother rose to go, but I held her back.

'He never came again then, her lover?'

She paused, as if reluctant to continue the story, but at last she said, 'Yes, he did come. That was the funny thing, he did come back to her.' One day a carriage and pair was observed coming up the Brae, along the main road past Druim, to Loch Laide. It stopped where some men were working at the side of the road. A gentleman got out, dressed I suppose in old-world style, twin gold chains reposing on his stomach, one for his watch, one for his sovereign case. To the surprise of the men he put his question in Gaelic. 'Was there a family living yet in the moorland croft behind the Leitir? And a girl called Oonagh, was she married yet?' The older among them knew then who he was, and I have no doubt they left the ditch un-cleared to go and spread the news. The time was come at last. That poor solitary woman, whom some shunned as unlucky because love-lorn, would get her due reward at last. There was no mistaking the eagerness on the stranger's face.

I cried out, 'Then why—?'

My mother seemed to shiver. He returned in less than an hour. This time he did not speak, but went as fast as he could away. The account of their meeting came from a child who, curious, ran over the heather and got near enough to witness the manner of it. Oonagh came to the door to receive her caller, then stopped short at seeing a stranger. He held his hands out. 'Do you not remember me? I have come back as I said I would.' She stared at him bewildered, making no move towards him, no sign of recognition. 'I have never loved anyone as I could have loved you. I am home now. I will make up to you for all the years I have left you forsaken.'

'Then why? Did he not live long after coming?'

'He lived all right. He is still alive, alive and prospering. He is in business in the town. It was Oonagh who would not. . . . It was as if she had never seen him before. She would not let him touch her. She said the only man she loved was in the lochan. I tell you only what you know.

'From that the story has grown that she is in love with the spirit of the lochan, or even that the *eachd uisge,* about which your father will tell you there is no such thing, has put his spell upon her. Now she is past the time of women it is easier for her. It is only now and again the idea takes hold of her. She is quiet and has done no one any harm. All the same, Ellen, if you go to her place you must not go out on the moors with her.'

I needed no forbidding. I was a timid child. I doubt if I went to the tiny croft ever again. And she never asked me. Whenever we met, at school-house service or on the Druim road, she would smile from her wrinkled sunburnt face, if she were not contentedly puffing at her clay pipe. That was all.

But sometimes, when I heard the creaking sound of a cart upon a rocky road, I would be visited by a perverse longing to go with her again to her lochan and see that ecstasy I might not share.

EDWARD GAITENS

Growing Up

The boy lay awake all night in the light of dreams about the adventure of his first job. He was fourteen years old. It was only a month since he had reluctantly left school, but he forgot now how bitterly he wept when his mother told him he must go to work and contribute to the family income. Because only last night his father had asked him: 'Would ye like tae come wi' me to the shipyards tomorrow, son?' and his mother chimed in: 'Aye, take him wi' ye. Mebbe ye'll get him a start wi' big money.' And the boy nodded eagerly: 'Oh, yes, da!'

His father, who had been a long time unemployed, had suddenly addressed his wife with unusual optimism. 'Ye know, Mary, I've a feelin' I'll get a start tomorrow for sure! They're layin' a big ship down at Clydebank. They say it'll mean a year's work for hundreds o' men.' The wife looked sceptical, but the boy believed his father would find work and that he, himself, would get his first job in the shipyards, away out where the Clyde neared the sea!

His father had washed and shaved to avoid a rush in the morning, for they had to be up at half-past four, take a hurried snack and cup of tea and catch the five o'clock tramcar. The boy washed also, exulting as he laved arms, neck and face, and went through the lobby to the concealed bed in the front room, his glow of anticipation burning away desire for sleep.

A job in the shipyards! He had often listened intensely to his father and brothers talk of those worlds of fabulous energy and mighty achievements where thousands of men and boys toiled night and day and the clang of hammers never ceased. He would see battleships launched and immense ocean liners. He would help to build one and earn big money! He was dazzled with pride.

Night and the wonder of quiet was ending; he heard the homeward footsteps of nightshift workers and day workers going forth, then the hum of the first workmen's tram afar, as dawn stared at the window, innocently entering, filling the drab room with beauty of light. Slow-fading silence, the slow growth of clarity and rising tempo of sounds, thrilled and awed him. Soon he would hear, through the wall, from the set-in bed in the kitchen, where his parents slept, his mother saying: 'Eddy, will ye get up, now! It's half-past four!'

and his father exclaiming: 'Eh! Wha-a-at? My God! Eh! What's up?' and jumping agitatedly to the floor, as he frequently did. Then, the boy was aware, it would be hardly after four.

'She won't have to wake me!' he boasted to the silence, smiling at the cracked, blistered whitewash of the bed-ceiling. He would be up and dressed before his da! He regarded his two elder brothers who were sleeping with him with condescension. They would be abed for three more hours, then James, the eldest son, would return from nightshift at seven, have breakfast, read a newspaper and retire to the yet warm bed at eight o'clock. But he did not envy them!

Quivering with eagerness he rose, pulled on his flimsy tweed trousers and slung minute braces over his boyish shoulders, disappointed that he hadn't moleskin trousers, a thick, leather, heavy-buckled belt and big hobnailed boots, like his da. He was still enjoying the novelty of his first pair of long trousers. Aye, he was a man in these! And they were more comfortable, too. They didn't chafe him above the knees like the short breeks he had thrown off a week ago! He heard the kitchen window-blind whirr up and the clang of a tin kettle planked on the stove. That was his mother up. Wouldn't she be surprised when she called him and he was all ready! Perhaps he had better say a prayer to the Blessed Virgin? She would get him a job! Quickly he put on stockings and cheap boots with papery uppers, and kneeling at the bed held forward clasped hands to a coloured china effigy of the Madonna, gracing the centre wall. Unaffected by the raucous snoring of John, he muttered two very quick, devout 'Hail Marys', then, half-ashamed, added the improvisation: 'Hail, Queen of Heaven, the Ocean Star, pray for me and get me a job this day!' He rose pleased, happier, firmly believing the 'Holy Mother' would intercede with the powers that dole out work to men, and went into the kitchen.

His father was leaning against the bed pulling on his trousers, his mother, at the gas-stove, was frying thick slices of bread in dripping for their snack, and the kettle whistled a plume of steam into the room. While he stood by to let his father wash first, in the iron sink at the end of the dresser, his mother turned, pouring boiling water in a large enamelled teapot, and said, half-sullenly: 'Ye'd better put yer collar on. Go an' clean it. An' don't spit on it! Wash it properly wi' soap an' flannel. Ye must be respectable!'

He turned to the parlour, his eagerness dimmed by her sullenness, and lifted a celluloid collar and stringy brown cotton tie from a glass dish on the sideboard where he always placed them when undressing. He had wanted to go like other apprentices, like his da, with a knotted muffler or nothing at all round his neck, and he regarded the collar indignantly. That wasn't like a working man! Did she take him for a jessie or a message-boy?

While his father dried himself he washed the collar at the sink, rubbing it vindictively with a piece of red flannel, then washed himself, anxiously hoping his parents wouldn't quarrel. They were often sulky and short with each other, and sometimes he had been wakened at this hour by a brutal altercation, when his father had struck her and rushed out, crashing the door, and she had yelled after him she hoped he'd be killed at his work. He could not understand the real cause of the strain between his parents—their thin love blasted by the worry of recurring unemployment; his mother's suspicion that her husband didn't try hard enough to get work and his offence at her distrust.

Their tea was ready and he ate the hot, fat-soused bread and drank the bitter brew deliciously, his appetite big with excitement and pleasure. They stood to eat, his father glancing continually up at the clock. His mother said: 'Yer pieces and tea and sugar are ready, there!' At the corner of the table lay two lunches wrapped in newspaper, a huge one for the man, a smaller one for the boy, and on top of each a penny Colman's Mustard tin filled with dry tea and sugar. The boy felt manly as he regarded it; he had begged it from his mother, who had made up his tea and sugar the night before in a screw of paper, and, in good mood, she had emptied the newly bought tin into an egg-cup, gratifying his wish to be as possible like his father. They were ready to leave and stuffed their pieces into their jacket pockets, the boy imitating his father's movements.

His father begged the loan of a sixpence and the wife answered complainingly: 'Och, shure I lent ye sixpence yesterday! Could ye no' walk some o' the way?' but she took her purse from under her pillow, where she kept it to prevent him filching coppers while she slept, and gave him the coin unwillingly. Suddenly he exclaimed: 'Isn't that Saint Peter's bell just striking the half-hour? Och, ye've got us up too soon. We could have slept longer!' Unperturbed, she answered: 'Well, ye're better to be early. Ye'll have time tae say an' Our Father an' three Hail Marys for a job!' He slung his cap irritably on a chair and knelt in unprayerlike mood at the bed, making the sign of the cross. The boy, palpitating to be off, was almost in tears. 'You say a wee prayer, too,' advised his mother. 'Och, maw, I said two Hail Marys before I came ben!' he grumbled. 'Say another two an' make sure!' she answered obdurately. He knelt beside his father and while their mumbled 'Aves' ascended to holy images on the bed walls, the woman sat to drink a cup of tea. The man cocked an eye frequently at the clock and suddenly crossing himself, rose, donned his cap and said: 'We'd better be gettin' away now!' The boy rose simultaneously and as they went out his mother warned her man to do his best and not be too late home!

The boy was aware of an outreaching sense of freedom when they

emerged from the narrow entry. At last they were away! As they
boarded a tram he ran before his father to capture a front seat and
leant forward gallant and unenclosed as charioteer, while the packed
tram passed all stops. He saw smoke jut from hundreds of chimneys,
blinds shoot up, curtains parted and here and there a woman leaning
akimbo on a sill four stories high, contemplating the street. He
tried to see into rooms, but speed blurred his vision and he laughed
at the phenomenon. Ah, this was better than rising at eight and
crawling to school at a quarter to nine. This was rare! And perhaps
tomorrow or next day he would be dashing along like this while his
former schoolmates were asleep. And when the trap stopped at a crossing where services went all ways, the names CLYDEBANK, YOKER,
SCOTSTOUN, ANNIESLAND, DALMUIR, DUMBARTON, glowed with
romance, magic as the names of foreign lands to him who only knew
back-streets. And here they were in Dockland! The funnels of liners
and masts of sailing ships above the warehouse roofs, the flags of
many nations afloat in the warm breeze.

Shortly the shipyards' region surrounded him with new wonder.
His father decided to call at a firm ten miles out, and as it was still
very early they sauntered about the vicinity till starting-time. The
boy glued his eyes on great cranes rearing over housetops like figures
in a monstrous ballet, and his spirit followed their rhythm while he
fired shrill questions at his father, who answered in his detailed,
laborious manner. Then at a minute to six they followed the last
worker going through the wicket door of the immense gates, and his
father craved an attendant commissionaire's permission to enter and
interview various foremen. The personage let them pass and immediately the boy was stunned in an ocean of sound, then as soon, struck
by a tragic stillness. A procession of begrimed, bareheaded workers,
bearing two stretchers, wended towards the ambulance-house at the
gate. The boy's father stopped; other men paused a moment, removing their caps, then hurried to their work. The procession passed,
the man on the first stretcher gallantly smoking a cigarette, smiled
at the boy, but the face of the body on the following stretcher was
covered.

The father removed his cap, bowing his head; the boy copied
him. 'My, there's been a man killed already! It's terrible. Terrible!'
The boy looked up, asking: 'Do they not stop the works when a
man's killed, da?' His father answered, 'No, the work goes on, son.
The work goes on!' The shipyard ambulance appeared, the bodies
were placed within, a nurse closed the door and the vehicle sped
through the gates.

The boy forgot the dead man as they went on through the yard
amid mammoth sights and sounds. He saw a warship near completion, the mere ribs of ships just begun, liners in repair dock and the

pathetic end of a worn vessel in the hands of the breakers. All men seemed midgets here, the riveters' catchboys everywhere in the skeleton ships, like imps, handing red-hot rivets from portable fires to the holder-on, and his small self had never felt so insignificant. Then in pride at being here, he strutted along cloaked in rare distinction. 'Ye can smell the sea here!' said his father, but he only smelled rust, iron and steel, machine-oil and the smoke and heat of furnaces.

All the while seagulls decorated the air, but their cries were unheard in the symphony of Labour. The boy crouched within himself as cranes swung overhead steel plates vast as two floors of his tenement home, and his father showed him a steam-hammer pounding gargantuan objects of molten steel. 'I've seen a hammerman place an egg there and bring the hammer down to rest on it and not break it! They get so skilful!' The boy marvelled, breathless with questioning, while his father hurried to interview foremen in various shops and the holes and corners of ships—great, strapping men who shook their heads distantly or spoke amiably, and canny little gaffers with frowsy moustaches, glasses and peaked caps, who sized up his father shrewdly.

None had jobs to offer, and when the breakfast-time buzzer blew, his father took him to the smiddy's shop, unhitched a tin can from his belt, filled it with water and boiled it on a smiddy fire. Never had he seen so many smiddy fires gathered in one place, nor water boil so swiftly as he worked the bellows handle and his father held the can on a rod. They washed down their food with milkless tea, sitting on a great anvil, while his father discussed with the blacksmith the chances of work in another shipyard.

Crossing by ferry to the opposite shore was the next brilliant event. Now the river was mad with sunshine and against passing and anchored ships the water splintered like golden glass. Amidstream, his father pointed out famous shipyards. 'Yon's Fairfield's away back, and there's Harland & Wolff's. That's John Brown's where we're going next, and yonder's Beardmore's! Yon's the highest crane on the Clyde!' And the boy looked far through smiling space at the goliath moving with relentless deliberation at its task.

And once again they were at shipyard gates, hanging about till the dinner-hour, when his father rushed forward to intercept a little man in a dungaree suit, spectacles and a sailor's cap among the hundreds of men streaming out. While the interview proceeded the boy could not take his eyes from the man's ardent red nose, abnormally small, above his grey moustache. 'Weel, I'm no sure!' said the foreman, 'I'm no sure! I'm pretty full up the now. But see me here tomorrow at six! And is this yer wee laddie? Will ye be wantin' a job for him, too? Weel, bring 'im wi' ye! One o' my platers wants a boy. Ye'll be puttin' him to a trade later on?' and walking in a queer, staccato style, he left them without waiting reply.

'God be praised!' the boy's father exclaimed jubilantly. 'That means a start for me tomorrow! He wouldn't tell me to come if he hadn't a job for me! An' you'll get a job, too, son, wi' fifteen shillin's a week!' The boy couldn't believe it. Fifteen shillings a week! Fifteen shillings a week! Immediately he was rich and in imagination scattering money right and left, buying long-desired things for himself, presents for his mother, father and brothers, making fabulous plans. They walked along with more inspirited step. 'Ye'll have a pay-poke on Saturday the same as me!' said his father, and the boy set his cap a little rakishly, plunged his hands into his pockets manfully and looked at life with tremendous satisfaction!

They could not afford to buy tea in a coffee-shop, and his father took him to a lodging-house where he could boil his can on the hot-plate. They turned down a side street into a narrow lane. From a distance the boy read the black letters on a white-glassed, antique lamp over the narrow door: GOOD BEDS FOR MEN, 4D. AND 8D. PER NIGHT, and when they reached the place, THE THISTLE HOTEL above the entrance.

They passed into a hot, low-roofed room, with settles and a long, narrow table at which two shirt-sleeved youths played cards with a dog's-eared pack. The place stank vitally of foul life; on a form against the wall a powerful, barefooted negro lay asleep. The boy was amazed at his cavernous mouth, slackly open, exaggerated by full, negroid lips, then his frightened glance fixed on an elderly tramp with one raw, blear eye, the other large and glowing, huddling against a brickwork stove which occupied an entire end of the room, shivering scratching himself and unwrapping dirty toe-rags from his feet. He stared hypnotized at the brilliant orb as the old man ogled him with a toothless grin.

'You sit there, sonny,' said his father, placing the tin of tea and sugar on the table and going to fill his can at a hot-water tap on the stove. The boy waited timidly, afraid to look about the villainous surroundings, and he started, alarmed, as a thick-set, apish man who leant against the stove reading a newspaper padded across on rope-soled slippers and stood over him. The boy's glance travelled slowly up his loose, greasy trousers and recoiled at the black hair, thick as a dog's, on his enormous arms and breast, showing through his open shirt. The man's little red eyes regarded him with savage contempt, and as the young face turned away he calmly lifted the mustard-tin, turning its oval in his fingers. That moment the boy's father turned and shouted: 'Hi, you! Put that down! That's mine! Put it down!' The brute swung round, deliberately removed the lid, poured the contents on the table and threw the tin at his feet.

The boy was transfixed by that black-and-white spill, a lurid insult, like a spit in his father's face. He jumped back as his father leapt, his left hand seizing the bully's shirt, his right followed by all his weight smashing into his face. He heard a crack and a ripping sound and waited, petrified, certain the big man would beat the life out of his da, that all here would set on him! The two youths started up, the negro shouted, swaying, staring like a sleepwalker, the tramp cackled like a crone: 'Heh, that was a rare smack ye gied 'im! My, that was a guid yin! Right on the chin! Right on the point!' But no one interfered and the big man sprawled back on the table, breathing heavily, then sat up dazed, rubbing his jaw, his torn shirt slopping between his thighs, hair showing down to his paunch. The boy's father pranced, shaping up to him. 'Come on, ye bastard! I'll beat the jelly out o' ye, big as ye are!'

They all turned as the dosshouse proprietor, a stout, carroty-haired man, rushed in tucking a soiled white apron at his waist, shouting furiously: 'What's goin' on here? What the bloody hell! Here, you! Get to hell out of here! Come on, out you go! You don't pay for a bed here! What's yer bloody game, comin' here to use my hot-plate without payin'?' The boy's father faced him defiantly, inclined to fight him also, but he only said: 'All right! Keep yer shirt on, man! We're goin'! Come on, sonny!'

In the lane his father hitched up his belt arrogantly, pleased at besting the dosshouse bully. 'Did ye see that, sonny? One good right, straight from the shoulder, an' down he goes, the get! I bested the cur!' He went through the fight again, shooting out his fists, then swaggered along at tremendous pace, thumbs in his waistcoat arm-holes. He put an arm round his son's shoulder. 'Eh, we're a couple o' rare fighters! They can't best us!' he chuckled and walked faster, looking slyly down. The boy strove to pace him till his heart pounded and he fell behind. His father slackened with a great laugh. 'My, ye're a rare wee walker, sonny!' and the boy smiled, breathing hard. How proud he was of his da! He was the best da in the world! 'Come on!' cried his father. 'We'll eat our dinners down by the water. Damn the tea!'

They walked by the river along the grassy banks. The boy clutched at his father, crying excitedly: 'I can smell the sea now, da! I can smell it!' He lifted his head and inspired and the adventurous tang filled his little breast. They ate their pieces and his father smoked a clay pipe, then lay down with a big, white-spotted red handkerchief over his head. And the boy sat beside him watching river-life—barges, yachts, pleasure-boats, tramps and great liners from all corners of the world, going along the sun's path of gold, always to the accompaniment of riveters' hammers, clanging on bulkhead and deck. 'Oh, da, look at yon bonny boat! It's like a swan, isn't it, da?' and he

D

pointed at a suave steam yacht, white as snow, anchored midstream, its brasswork and gold paint flashing as it bowed to the smooth flow. His father said: 'Eh! What's that? A swan? Ay, a swan!' and fell asleep, snoring outrageously, and the red handkerchief burbled on his face.

And the boy's happiness rose with the waning day. This warm, light-hearted May day seemed eternal, and he could have sat here for ever, watching life, listening to the echo from shipyards across the water, sending his heart to follow the wild gulls. He was not lonely because his father slept. In this hour all life was his. He was content. He thought how the river widened to the ocean, and only then felt lonely for a bit as a sense of the world's immensity over-awed his tiny comprehension. Then a liner from India in tow of pilot tugs crawled past, shutting the white yacht from view for several minutes. A crowd of half-naked lascar sailors leant on the ship's rail, chattering, laughing, singing an Eastern song. One waved a bright scarf to him and he waved back with his cap. He had often watched lascars shopping in the slum markets. Why were they always happy and laughing? The liner passed. At once the world was friendly, all his happiness was restored and he smiled again at the white yacht.

His father started awake when the sun was some way down, and exclaimed; 'My God! It's late! Yer maw'll be mad wi' us. We'd better get home!' The boy was in a state of sheer bliss with all he had seen that day. No boy had seen the wonders he had witnessed, and all the long ride home he fought sleep, wishful to miss nothing. When he had gulped down his tea he rushed into the back-court to tell his tenement friends. They were rooting for any objects of interest housewives might have thrown into the communal midden, which was beginning to exude its summer stink. They rallied, a charmed, envious circle, while he narrated, a little Homer of the back-streets. He had seen a dead man and the highest crane on the Clyde! His da had knocked a man 'right oot' over a table!—by now his father's adversary had attained prodigious proportions—and he had got a job in the 'Yards' with 'big money'. Suddenly he broke off importantly with: 'Well, I'll have to be gettin' home now. I've got to be up gey early for my job, ye know!' and swaggered away.

There was unusual tranquillity in his home that evening. His mother was pleased because all her menfolk would be in jobs, and she and her man were almost friendly. The boy tried to read a book, but the print danced and he could think of nothing but his fine job with big money. He would give his mother every penny. Keep nothing for himself. He would be a good son to her. She would see! He stumbled to her where she sat smiling, knitting a sock. 'Ye won't let me sleep in tomorrow, will ye, maw?' he said. She tousled his hair. 'No, son. I'll call ye fine an' early.' His father shook his shoulder ruggedly.

'Ye're a fine standing-up man, sonny! Ye'll soon be as big as yer da!' He staggered through to the parlour bed, drunk with the sweet opiate of healthy fatigue, hearing his mother say: 'Puir wee soul! He's gey tire't!' and his father: 'Ay, he's had a long day for a wee laddie.' Immediately he fell asleep, thinking vividly of the morrow's job, smiling, with the cries of seagulls in his ears.

All night he dreamt of exalted shipmasts and tall cranes bowing, proudly lifting, swinging their loads, while wild birds circled around them in brilliant sunshine. And the gallant Clyde, pursuing its historic journey to the mountains and the sea, flowed through his dreams.

Five Green Waves

I

Time was lines and circles and squares.

'You will go home at once to your father,' said Miss Ingsetter, rapping her desk with a ruler, 'and tell him I sent you, because you have not prepared the mathematics lesson I told you to prepare. Now go!'

A rustle went through the class-room. The pupils looked round at me, wide-eyed. A few made little sorrowing noises with their lips. For it was a terrible punishment. My father was a magnate, a pillar of authority in the island—Justice of the Peace, Kirk Elder, Registrar, Poor Inspector, a member of the Education Committee itself. He was, in addition, the only merchant in the place and kept the shop down by the pier; even before I was born he had decided that his boy would be a credit to him—he would go to the university and become a minister, or a lawyer, or a doctor.

Now, this summer afternoon, while blue-bottles like vibrant powered ink-blobs gloried in the windows and the sun came four-square through the burning panes, my stomach turned to water inside me.

'Please, Miss Ingsetter,' I said, 'I'm sorry I didn't learn the theorem. I promise it won't happen again. I would be glad if you punished me yourself.'

The bust of Shelley gazed at me with wild blank eyes.

Her spectacles glinted. Down came the ruler with a snap. 'You will go to your father, now, at once, and tell him of your conduct.'

The bright day fell in ruins about me. I crossed the floor on fluttering bare feet, and was soon outside.

'You, Willie Sinclair,' I heard her shouting through the closed door, 'stand up and give us the theorem of Pythagoras.'

A red butterfly lighted on my hand, clung there for a moment, and went loitering airily across the school garden, now here among the lupins, now there over the flowering potatoes, as if it was drunk with happiness and didn't know on what bright lip to hang next. I watched it till it collapsed over the high wall, a free wind-tipsy flower.

Inside the class-room, the formal wave gathered and broke.

'. . . is equal to the sum of the squares on the other two sides,' concluded Willie Sinclair in a sibilant rush.

'Very good, Willie,' said Miss Ingsetter.

Despised and rejected, I turned for home.

II

The croft of Myers stands beside the road looking over the Sound, and the hill rises behind it like a swelling green wave. Sophie, a little bent woman, her grey shawl about her head, was throwing seed to the twelve hens.

She smelt me on the wind. 'Hello, there,' she cried. I muttered a greeting.

She peered at me. 'And who might you be?' she said.

I told her my name.

'Mercy,' she said, 'but you've grown.'

Our voices had roused the old man inside. He was suddenly at the door, smiling. Peter's face was very red and round. He had been a sailor in his youth. The backs of his hands, and his wrists, smouldered with blue anchors, blue mermaids, blue whales. 'Come in,' he cried.

It was like entering a ship's hold, but for the smells of peat and kirn and girdle. I breathed darkness and fragrance.

They ushered me to the straw chair beside the fire. I had hardly got settled in it when Sophie put a bowl of ale between my hands. The sweet heavy fumes drifted across my nostrils.

Peter sat filling his pipe in the other straw chair. The old woman never rested for an instant. She moved between the fire and the window and the bed, putting things in order. She flicked her duster along the mantelpiece, which was full of tea-caddies and ships in bottles. The collie dog lolled and panted on the flag-stones.

'And tell me,' said Peter, 'what way you aren't at school?'

'I got sent home,' I said, 'for not learning the lesson.'

'You must learn your lessons,' said Sophie, setting the fern straight in the tiny window. 'Think what way you'll be in thirty years' time if you don't, a poor ignorant fellow breaking stones in the quarry.'

I took a deep gulp of ale, till my teeth and tongue and palate were awash in a dark seething wave.

'And tell me,' said Peter, 'what will you be when you're big?'

'A sailor,' I said.

'If that wasn't a splendid answer!' cried Peter. 'A sailor. Think of that.'

'My grandfather was a gunner on the *Victory*,' said Sophie. 'He was at Trafalgar. He came home with a wooden leg.'

'That was great days at sea,' said Peter. 'Do you know the ballad of Andrew Ross?'

'No,' I said.

A hen, shaped like a galleon, entered from the road outside. She dipped and swayed round the sleeping dog, and went out again into the sunlight.

'Woman,' said Peter, 'get the squeeze-box.'

Sophie brought a black dumpy cylinder from under the bed, and blew a spurt of dust from it. Peter opened the box and took out a melodeon.

'Listen,' he said. A few preliminary notes as sharp as spray scattered out of the instrument. Then he cleared his throat and began to sing:

> *Andrew Ross an Orkney sailor*
> *Whose sufferings now I will explain*
> *While on a voyage to Barbados,*
> *On board the good ship* Martha Jane.

'That was the name of the ship,' said Sophie, 'the *Martha Jane.*'

'Shut up,' said Peter.

> *The mates and captain daily flogged him*
> *With whips and ropes, I tell you true,*
> *Then on his mangled bleeding body*
> *Water mixed with salt they threw.*

'That's what they used to do in the old days, the blackguards,' said Sophie. 'They would beat the naked backs of the sailors till they were as red as seaweed.'

'Damn it,' said Peter, 'is it you that's reciting this ballad, or is it me?'

> *The captain ordered him to swallow*
> *A thing whereof I shall not name.*
> *The sailors all grew sick with horror.*
> *On board the good ship* Martha Jane.

'What was it Andrew Ross had to swallow?' I asked.

'It was too terrible to put in the song,' said Sophie.

'I'll tell you what it was,' said Peter, glaring at me. 'It was *his own dung.*'

The sickness began to work like a yeast in the region of my throat. I took a big swallow of ale to drown it.

Peter sang:

When nearly dead they did release him,
And on the deck they did him fling.
In the midst of his pain and suffering
'Let us be joyful,' Ross did sing.

'He was religious,' said Sophie, 'and the captain was an atheist.
That's the way they bad-used him.'

The captain swore he'd make him sorry,
And jagged him with an iron bar.
Was not that a cruel treatment
For an honoured British tar!

The house took a long dizzy lurch to starboard, then slowly righted
itself. My knuckle grew white on the edge of the chair. The good
ship Myers burrowed again into the fluid hill.

'Mercy,' said Sophie, 'I doubt the boy's too young for a coarse
ballad like that.'

Justice soon did overtake them
When into Liverpool they came.
They were found guilty of the murder
Committed on the briny main.

'High time too,' said Sophie. 'The vagabonds!'

Soon the fateful hour arrived
That Captain Rogers had to die,
To satisfy offended justice
And hang on yonder gallows high.

I stood erect on the heaving flagstones. 'Going be sick,' I said.

'The pail!' cried Sophie, 'where's the pail?'

But she was too late. Three strong convulsions went through me,
and I spouted thrice. The flagstones were awash. The dog barked.
Then the cottage slowly settled on an even keel, and I was sitting in
the straw chair, my eyes wet with shame and distress. Not even
Andrew Ross's sorrow was like unto my sorrow.

Old Sophie was on her knees with a wet clout and a bucket.

Peter patted me on the shoulder. 'Don't you worry,' he said. 'You're
not the first sailor that's been sick on his maiden voyage.'

III

Below the kirkyard the waves stretched long blue necks shoreward.
Their manes hissed in the wind, the broken thunder of their hooves
volleyed along the beach and echoed far inland among corn-fields
and peat bogs and trout lochs, and even as far as the quiet group of
standing stones at the centre of the island.

I made my way shoreward, walking painfully along a floor of
round pebbles. One had to be careful; Isaac of Garth, going home
drunk and singing on Saturday nights, was in the habit of smashing
his empty bottles on these rocks. He had done it for so many years
that the amphitheatre of pebbles above the sand was dense with
broken glass—the older fragments worn by the sea to blunt opaque
pebbles, the newer ones winking dangerously in the sun. If one
of the sharp pieces scored your foot, you might easily bleed to
death.

There was no one in sight along the wide curve of the beach, or on
the road above. In the kirkyard the grave-digger was up to the hips
in a grave he was making for Moll Anderson, who had died at the
week-end.

Quickly and cautiously, under a red rock, I took off my clothes—
first the grey jersey with the glass button at the neck, next the trousers
made out of an old pair of my father's and finally the blue shirt.
Then I ran down to the sea and fell through an incoming wave. Its
slow cold hammer drove the air out of my lungs. I thrashed through
the water to a rock thirty yards out and clung to it, gasping and
shivering. 'Lord,' I thought, 'suppose Miss Ingsetter or my father
saw me now!' A shred of cloud raced across the sun, and the world
plunged in and out of gloom in a second. And then, for an hour,
I was lost in the cry and tumult of the waves. Shags, dark arrows,
soared past my plunging face. Gulls cut gleaming arcs and circles
against the sky, and traversed long corridors of intense sound. Seals
bobbed up and down like bottles in the Sound, and grew still every
now and then when I whistled. For a brief eternity I was lost in the
cry, the tumult, the salt cleansing ritual of the sea.

The grave-digger paused in his work and, shading his eyes beach-
ward, saw me stumbling out of the waves. He shook his fist at my
nakedness. The sand was as hot as new pancakes under my feet. I ran
wild and shouting up the beach and fell gasping on my heap of
clothes. I lay there for a long time. From very far away, on the other
side of the hill, a dog barked. The rockpool shimmered in the heat.
The music of the grave-digger's spade rang bright and fragile across
the field. Suddenly three words drifted from the rock above me: 'You
naked boy.' I looked up into the face of Sarah, Abraham the tinker's
daughter. She rarely came to school, but whenever she did she sat

like a wild creature under the map of Canada. She was sprawling now on the rock with her legs dangling over. Her bare arms and her thighs, through the red torn dress she wore, were as brown as an Indian's.

Sarah said, 'I come here every day to watch the boats passing. When the sun goes down tonight we're moving to the other end of the island. There's nothing there but the hill and the hawk over it. Abraham has the lust for rabbits on him.'

The tinkers have curious voices—angular outcast flashing accents like the cries of seagulls.

She jumped down from the rock and crouched in front of me. I had never seen her face so close. Her hair lay about it in two blue-black whorls, like mussel shells. Her eyes were as restless as tadpoles, and her small nose shone as if it had been oiled.

'Sarah,' I said, 'you haven't been to school all week.'

'May God keep me from that place for ever,' she said.

With quick curious fingers she began to pick bits of seaweed out of my hair.

'What will you do,' she said, 'when you're a tall man? You won't live long, I can tell that. You'll never wear a gold chain across your belly. You're white like a mushroom.' She laid two dirty fingers against my shoulder.

'I'm going to be a sailor,' I said, 'or maybe an explorer.'

She shook her head slowly. 'You couldn't sleep with ice in your hair,' she said.

'I'll take to the roads with a pack then,' I said, 'for I swear to God I don't want to be a minister or a doctor. I'll be a tinker like you.'

She shook her head again. 'Your feet would get broken, tramping the roads we go,' she said.

Her red dress fell open at the shoulder where the button had come out of it. Her shoulder shone in the wind as if it had been rubbed with sweet oils.

She stretched herself like an animal and lay down on the sand with her eyes closed.

I turned away from her and traced slow triangles and circles in the sand. I turned a grey stone over; a hundred forky-tails seethed from under it like thoughts out of an evil mind. From across the field came the last chink of the grave-digger's spade—the grave was dug now; the spade leaned, miry and glittering, against the kirkyard wall. Two butterflies, red and white over the rockpool, circled each other in silent ecstasy, borne on the stream of air. They touched for a second, then fell apart, flickering in the wind, and the tall grass hid them. I turned quickly and whispered in Sarah's ear.

Her first blow took me full in the mouth. She struck me again

D*

on the throat as I tried to get to my feet. Then her long nails were in my shoulder and her wild hair fell across my face. She thrust me back until my shoulder-blades were in the burning sand and my eyes wincing in the full glare of the sun. She dug sharp knees into my ribs until I screamed. Then she ravelled her fingers through my hair and beat my head thrice on the hard sand. Through my shut lids the sun was a big shaking gout of blood.

At last she let me go. 'Next time I come to the school,' she said, looking down at me with dark smiling eyes, 'I'll sit at your desk, under the yellow head of the poet.' She bent over quickly and held her mouth against my throat for as long as it takes a wave to gather and break. Her hair smelt of ditch-water and grass fires. Then she was gone.

I put on the rest of my clothes, muttering through stiff lips, 'You bitch! O you bloody bully, I'll have the attendance officer after you in ten minutes, just see if I don't!'

As I left the beach, walking slowly, I could see her swimming far out in the Sound.

She waved and shouted, but I turned my face obstinately towards the white road that wound between the kirkyard and the cornfield. The salt taste of blood was in my mouth.

IV

The grave-digger had finished making Moll Anderson's grave. He was sitting on the shaft of his barrow, smoking a clay pipe. As I turned in at the gate he wagged his beard at me, for he did not associate this shy decently-clad boy with the naked insolence he had seen running out of the sea half an hour before. I wandered away from him among the branching avenues of tomb-stones—the tall urns and frozen angels of modern times; the fiery pillars with the names of grandfathers on them; the scythe-and-hourglass slates of the eighteenth century; and the lichened leprous tombs of a still earlier age. This small field was honeycombed with the dead of generations— farmers with stony faces; young girls rose-cheeked with consumption; infants who had sighed once or twice and turned back to the darkness; stern Greek-loving ministers; spinsters with nipped breasts and pursed mouths. I stood on the path, terrified for a moment at the starkness and universality of shrouds; at the infinite dead of the island, their heads pointing westward in a dense shoal, adrift on the slow tide that sets towards eternity.

My dreaming feet brought me to a low tombstone set in the east wall:

HERE LIES BURIED
A FOREIGN SEAMAN,
OF UNKNOWN NAME AND NATIONALITY
WHOM THE SEA CAST UP ON THIS ISLAND,
JUNE THE SIXTH, 1856

*'Though I take the wings of
the morning, and flee to the
uttermost places of the sea.'*

I closed my eyes and saw a little Basque town between the bay and the mountains.

The feast of Our Lady of the Sea was over. The nets and the oars had been blessed. The candles were still burning in their niches among the rocks.

Now the young people are dancing in a square that lies white and black under the moon.

The musician slouches, as if he were drunk or half asleep, against the fountain. Only his hand is alive, hovering over the strings like a vibrant bird.

The young people are dancing now in long straight lines. The partners clap their hands and bow to each other. They shout; the dark faces are lit up with a flash of teeth. They move round each other with momentarily linked arms. They incline towards each other, their hands on their knees, and stamp their feet. It is all precision, disciplined fluency, a stylised masque of coupling.

Older men and women sit gossiping on the doorsteps. Occasionally they sip from tall glasses. One, a fat man with a yellow beard, looks often through a gap in the houses, at a ship anchored in the harbour.

An old shawled woman stands alone, in the shadow of the church. No one speaks to her; the seal of separation is on her. She is the guardian of the gates of birth and death. In this village she comes to deliver every wailing child, she goes to shroud every quiet corpse. Her eyes are in the dust, from which all this vanity has come, and to which it must return.

The hand over the guitar moves into a new swirling rhythm. Now the square is all one coloured wheel, a great wavering orange blossom.

Suddenly there is an interruption. A tall bearded sailor appears at an alley-opening and walks slowly across the square. The guitar falters. The dance is frozen. The old dark woman raises her head. The officer points to one of the dancers and crooks his finger: he must come, immediately, the ship is sailing tonight.

The seaman—he is only a boy—turns once and looks back. A girl has raised her apron to her face. The yellow-bearded man rises from his doorstep and makes a gesture of blessing: 'Lady of Waters, guard him this day and all days till the sail returns to the headland.'

Above the village a cross stands among the stars. Through a long silence comes the sound of the sea. The last votive candle gutters and goes out among the rocks.

The little town of moonlight and music will never see that sail again. Her voyage has ended on a northern rock. All her sailors have vanished down the path of gull and lobster, scattered in a wild Atlantic storm. One broken shape only was lifted out of the seaweed. Curious hands have carried the nameless thing in procession across the fields. They have clipped the rags from it and combed its hair, and covered the crab-eaten face. And though there was no priest to sing Latin over it, a Calvinist minister said, 'All flesh is grass, and the glory of flesh is as the flower thereof'—the orange-blossom of Spain and the little blue Orkney primula, whose circles of beauty are full and radiant for a short time only; and then, drifting winterward, or broken with June tempest, lay separate shining arcs in the dust. . . .

My slow circuitous walk had brought me to the new gaping hole in the earth. The grave-digger was still sitting on his barrow. He bored a sidelong glance into me and said: 'There's only one way of coming into the world, but ah, God, there's two or three ways of going out.'

'That's a fact,' I said.

'Would you like,' he said, 'to see what a man *truly* is?'

Not understanding, I gave a quick nod. He groped with his hand into the small hill of clay beside the open grave, and brought out a skull. Carefully he wiped it on his moleskin trousers. 'That's you,' he said, 'and me, and the laird, and Frank the idiot. Just that.'

He laughed. 'There's nothing here to make your face so white. It's as harmless as can be, this bone. It's at peace, and not before time. When it lived it had little rest, with its randy eyes and clattering tongue. This skull belonged to Billy Anderson, Moll's grandfather. He was twice in jail and fathered three illegitimate bairns. O, he was a thieving, drunken, fighting character, and it was a good day for him when we threw him in here. Wasn't it, Billy?' he said to the skull, blowing smoke into its eye-hollows. 'Wasn't it, boy?' . . . The skull grinned back at him.

From the other side of the loch the school bell rang the dismissal.

Over the hill from the village, like a procession of beetles, came the mourners.

V

After I had finished my lessons that evening, I was summoned into the shop.

My father was sitting at the counter between a barrel of paraffin oil and a great dark coil of tobacco. There was a jar of sweets at his elbow. Over his head hung jerseys and scarves and stockings, with price tickets on them. The lamp swung from the hook in the ceiling, smoking a little. There was always a good smell in the shop.

'It's thee, John,' he said, raising his head from the ledger for a moment. 'Sit down, boy.' He counted the sticks of toffee in a glass jar and then said, 'How did thu get on at the school today?'

'Fine,' I said.

'I've been thinking about thee,' he said, 'what to make o' thee, once thee school-days are over.'

He gathered up a handful of coins, and rang them one by one back into the till. Then he marked the ledger on his desk with a pencil.

'There's no future in this shop, I can tell thee that,' he said. 'The profits are getting smaller every year. The reason is, the folk are leaving the island. They're going to the cities and the colonies. Not a month passes but another family leaves.

'And then they send to the mail-order places in the south for their clothes and their ironmongery. A great lot of them do that. They forget that we depend on each other for our livelihood in a small island like this.

'And there's debts too,' he said. 'For instance, Mistress Anderson who was buried this afternoon died owing more than six pounds. So it'll be a poor inheritance for thee, this shop,' he said.

He licked his pencil and wrote more figures in the ledger. His hair glittered frailly in the lamplight.

'I had a word with Miss Ingsetter this afternoon about thee,' he went on. 'She called at the shop after school for some fly-papers. She seemed surprised thu weren't home yet . . . I made a point of asking her about thee. She says thu're an able boy, good beyond the general run at reading and writing and history. Not so bright at the mathematics. Sometimes thu're inclined to be inattentive and dreamy, she says. At times, only at times. But there's no harm in the boy, she said, and he's by no means stupid. And it's my opinion, she said, he ought to go to the grammar school in Kirkwall for a secondary education, once he turns twelve.'

'I want to be a sailor,' I said.

'The dreaminess,' he said, 'you take from your mother . . . After the school comes the university. That'll cost money, a power of money. Still, I'm not barehanded, I haven't neglected to provide for things like that. With a degree in thee pocket, thu could enter *the professions*. Think of that.'

'It's the sea I have a hankering for,' I said. 'Uncle Ben said he could get me into the Saint Line, any time I wanted.'

'The ministry is an honourable profession,' he said. 'There isn't

a lot of money in it, but you get a free manse, and I can tell you old
MacFarland doesn't spend a fortune on food. He gets a hen here and
a pound of butter there and a sack of tatties from the other place.
On his rounds, you understand, his visitations. Cheese at the Bu, and
fish from Quoys, and a fleece for spinning from Westburn, all for
nothing. And nobody can say the work is strenuous.'

'Supper is ready,' my mother sang out from the kitchen.

'Now doctoring is strenuous, there's no doubt about that. They
haven't a moment to call their own. They can't even be sure of a
night's sleep. There's always somebody thundering at Doctor Leslie's
door after midnight with the toothache, or a pain in the guts, or a
hook's got stuck in their hand. It's no wonder he's taken to the drink
lately. But, putting all that aside, medicine is a fine calling. Plenty
of money in it too, if you can get them to pay their bills.'

'I spoke to Mother,' I said. 'She would like fine for me to be a
deep-sea captain. She's going to write to Ben.'

'The law,' he said, 'is a different thing. Not that there's anything
wrong with it, if you understand, but there's a shady side to it, there's
a certain amount of trickery about it that makes the ordinary honest
man wonder sometimes. You can hardly open a newspaper without
seeing some lawyer or other in trouble for embezzling his client's
money, and carrying on. You'll hear a couple of them arguing a case
like mad in the courts, and then, half an hour later, there they'll be
walking down the street together cheek by jowl . . . John,' he said,
'never go to law if you can possibly help it. Not but what there
aren't honest lawyers too.'

He unscrewed the lid from a bottle of black-striped balls. He took
out a couple between his fingers and handed them across the counter.

'If there's one place I have a longing to see,' I said, 'it's Japan.'

He suddenly withdrew his hand and dropped the black-striped balls
back into the jar.

'Not before your food,' he said, licking his fingers. 'I forgot . . .
Then there's teaching—'

'Are you coming for your supper,' chanted my mother impatiently,
'or are you not?'

Outside the dog began to bark. There was a clattering of hooves
and wheels over the cobbles. The poultry squawked like mad in the
yard. 'Mercy,' said my father, running to the door, 'it's the tinkers.
The hens!'

I followed him out, into the moonlight. The tinker's cart was
opposite the door now. Abraham sat on the shaft. He cracked his
whip and cried to the grey pony. In the cart sat Mary his wife with
an infant slung behind her in a tartan shawl. Sarah walked alongside
with her arms full of wild lupins.

They were going to the other end of the island where the rabbits were thick, to camp there.

'Giddap!' cried Abraham and cracked his whip. 'That's a fine dog you have there, Mister Sigurdson,' he shouted to my father. 'I'll take a half-pound of bogey roll, and I'll pay you when I come back along next week.'

'No,' said my father sternly, 'you'll pay now, for you owe me sixteen and six already.'

'Hello, Sarah,' I said. She stood on the road and looked at me through the dark blue congregated spires of lupins.

'Are you seeking a tin pail, mistress?' yelled Abraham to my mother who had come out and was standing at the corner of the house guarding the hens.

'Yes,' she said, 'I'll need one when you come back by next week.'

Suddenly my father was furious. 'We need no tin pails!' he shouted. 'There's plenty of tin pails in the shop!'

'Next week-end, mistress,' cried Abraham. He stood between the shafts and cracked his whip. 'Giddap!' he yelled. The wheels rolled in crazy circles over the cobbles and stars streamed from the pony's hooves. There was a sudden wild *cluck-cluck-clucking* from inside the cart as it moved off. Sarah stood looking at us, smiling through her screen of lupins.

My father went back into the shop, muttering. My mother stood at the corner of the house and watched them out of sight. 'One of the hens is missing,' she said. 'I darena tell thee father. He would have the police at them for sure.'

A wave of purple blossom rose in front of the moon and showered over me.

Soon the racket died away at the far end of the village. Sarah's mockery sounded from a distance of three fields. I turned back into the house. My face was wet with dew and petals, and the moon raged above the mission hall wilder than ever.

'The very idea!' cried my father from inside the shop. 'A sailor! A tin pail! *The thieves!*'

Time was skulls and butterflies and guitars.

JANET CAIRD

Destiny Obscure

Like all good local papers, the *Invermurchan Chronicle* devotes a good deal of space to obituaries: and nowadays I tend to look at these first, assessing my survival rate against that of erstwhile contemporaries. Not that Hector McGillivary was a contemporary: he was a lot older than myself, more of an age with my father; in fact I was quite surprised to learn he was still alive when I read his obituary—if you see what I mean. The *Chronicle* did him proud. 'Mr Hector McGillivary of Vorlich who passed away suddenly yesterday morning was a well-known member of the community and will be long remembered' etc., etc. I read cursorily but my attention was gripped by the penultimate sentence: 'He yielded to none in his affection for Vorlich and chose to spend his life within its confines though his talents undoubtedly fitted him to shine in a larger sphere.'

Ha! That showed insight, and I wondered how many people apart from my father and myself knew just how Hector achieved his position in Vorlich, deploying a skill in intrigue and manoeuvring which would have taken him far in any career, though in his case neither power-seeking, nor money, nor even malice provided the motive. It was simply that he could not live anywhere but in Vorlich.

Hector was not a native of the place. He arrived there at the age of seven to live with his aunt Mary Macleod, the postmistress, having been left an orphan when his mother died in Glasgow. How she died and who his father was no one ever knew, for Mary Macleod, like all good gossips, could be as close as a clam about her own affairs. The child was an unhappy, sullen, frightened small boy, with shabby ill-patched clothes. For months he would shrink back if approached too suddenly. He seemed to have had no schooling to speak of and was aggressive in the playground, always ready with a blow, and when he did speak it was to shout obscenities. He did not 'play fair' and would kick, punch, bite. Soon he was left alone to moon in a corner by the wall that fenced the school from the road and the shore. At night he would waken screaming. But gradually, under the love and kind care of his aunt, who was endlessly patient, he became a normal small boy, growing up in surroundings which might have been designed to give small boys all the scope they want for engrossing ploys.

There had been a crisis when he went to secondary school and had to live in a hostel from Monday to Friday in Invermurchan. Twice he had run away, headed back to Vorlich and taken refuge in a cave on the shore. But this had been straightened out too.

All this my father learnt from his predecessor as minister in Vorlich. By the time I knew Hector he was firmly and deeply rooted in the community, and most people had forgotten he wasn't a native. He succeeded his aunt in the post office, which at Vorlich was a 'proper' post office, not a mere sub—for although Vorlich had a population of only six hundred or so, the post office served a wide area. Hector ran it very well, and it became a model of spruce efficiency. Once Hector had got it organised and had trained Billy the Post to take (unofficial) counter-duty, he had plenty of time left for fishing (legal), shooting (illegal), Gaelic choir, dramatic club, eldership in the kirk—in fact the whole fabric of life in Vorlich.

But disaster struck. Hector was promoted. He was to go to Dundee as assistant postmaster in a post office in a near-slum area at almost double his salary. To Hector it was like a death sentence.

He brought his trouble to the manse. From the study came the rise and fall of voices; not in anger, but like the sad pull and surge of the waves on a bleak day. A subdued Hector shook my father's hand dejectedly as he left and walked slowly down the garden path.

Over the dinner-table that day my mother said:

'I can't understand why Hector's so upset about going. He's an intelligent man, and could do much better for himself than being postmaster in Vorlich. Did he say anything to you?'

My father hesitated, and she said:

'Don't tell me if you think you shouldn't.'

'Oh, he didn't give away any secrets. I tried to tell him that perhaps it was his duty to take on greater responsibilities, given that he has the capacity to carry them out. I got the impression that he wanted to tell me something . . . that he was almost afraid to leave the place . . . He even talked of giving up the job altogether.'

But Hector's wife, Elspeth, hitherto a meek and amenable woman, announced firmly that she would leave him if he put himself deliberately out of work. So the sad day came when a crowd gathered to watch Hector, Elspeth and their gear, all in the same removal van, take the road over the hill on the way to Dundee and a new life. As the roof of the van disappeared over the crest, there was a little silence and Murdo McCann said portentously:

'The end of a chapter. The place will not be the same without Hector.'

'He'll be back,' said Ronald McFadyen the butcher. 'Hector is not the man to be pushed around. He'll be back.'

'I doubt it,' said Murdo. 'Not even Hector could take on the Civil

Service of Britain and win. You perhaps do not appreciate the workings of the Civil Service, but I do seeing. . . .'

'Seeing your son is a civil servant in London. We know,' said Ronald, 'but Hector will be back.'

Hector's successor at the post office turned out to be a mild and amiable man from Lincolnshire, with a wife and two children. Possibly Murdo's son in London might have been able to explain the workings of a system that could tear George Pigott from the fat flat lands round the Wash and set him down on a narrow littoral between great heaving mountains and the Atlantic surge. He and his wife tried hard to adapt but it was not easy for them. They were very anxious to please; George behind the counter even addressed his clients as 'sir', or, in my case, 'young sir.' But in time, Vorlich's initial hostility was replaced by condescending acceptance, helped by the fact that George ran the office just as well as Hector.

News of Hector filtered back mainly through Ronald McFadyen who was married to Elspeth's sister. At first Hector was reported to be so miserable that he had decided never to return to Vorlich because once back he'd not be able to bring himself to leave. As time went on the tone changed. We heard that Hector was 'settling down' and attending various courses with a view to promotion. Murdo McCann was even heard to prophesy, at Angus Macdonald's wake, that Hector would 'end up as Postmaster General yet, and we'll not be seeing him again.' Ronald McFadyen said nothing, but gave a wee smile into his glass.

Autumn turned to winter, winter to spring, to summer. People had adjusted to the change. Mrs Pigott became friendly with Isabel McFadyen, Elspeth's sister, and 'was never out of Isabel's house,' as Mary McCann remarked with a sniff. 'I hope she keeps a discreet tongue in her head for it wouldn't do for her to be telling who all is getting the Assistance.'

But as far as business went, Ethel Pigott was discreet enough, though perhaps not so wise about her personal affairs.

It was Ronald who broke the news that Hector was going to spend his three weeks' holiday with him and Isabel, and this was taken to mean that Hector was now quite settled in Dundee and able to return to Vorlich with equanimity. He and Elspeth stepped off the bus looking prosperous, if not as ruddy-cheeked as of yore, and after a day or two it was hard to remember Hector was only on holiday. He resumed all his old ways and was even back behind the post office counter. Going in for a stamp one day I found Jean MacDougall there, her black eyes bright with speculation.

'Well, well,' she was saying, 'just fancy seeing you here! Anyone would think you were wishing you were back.'

Hector beamed with disarming beneficence.

'Not at all. George and I were just having what in government circles they call a "useful exchange of views".'

A day or two later, when my father and I were coming home after an evening's fishing on the loch, about eleven o'clock, we were surprised to see a light in the post office. Just as we were passing, the door opened and Hector appeared with George behind him. My father stopped and said:

'Good evening Hector, and you too George. You're working late.'

'It's you, minister,' said Hector. 'I'll just walk up the road with you.'

As we walked away, Hector said:

'I have been passing on to George some of the useful tips I have been getting on the course I was sent to. He says he's very grateful, but och! it was no bother to me—just a matter of showing him one or two ways of doing things and not doing things.'

'That's very kind of you,' said my father, but I could hear the note of reserve in his voice.

'Well, I am in a way sorry for him,' said Hector. 'He is wanting to get back to his own place in Lincolnshire—the way I used to want to get back here. So I can feel a sympathy with him. Yes, indeed.'

'But you are quite settled in Dundee now?'

'Oh yes, indeed. And with all these courses I have been sent on, I think the future is quite bright. But here we are at Ronald's door, so I will bid you goodnight.'

My father walked home in thoughtful silence.

Hector's time passed quickly. It happened to be one of those spells of idyllic weather that sometimes hit the West Coast. Tranquil sunny day followed tranquil sunny day. Murdo McCann's son Hamish arrived, to the immense pride of his father. Hamish was a pleasant and relaxed young man, who slipped back at once into the ways of the community, and if it had not been for his father's proud comments, no one would ever have taken him for the brilliant young administrator he actually was. He and Hector had more than one day up on the moor with their guns; more than one brace of grouse appeared mysteriously at the manse back door. . . .

On the morning that Hector and Elspeth left, I happened to come on him as he was waiting for the bus. He was looking over the sea to the tumble of mountains on the other side, and his face was so full of the sadness of farewell that it even impressed me, careless boy though I was, so that at tea I remarked to my father:

'I think Hector wished he could stay in Vorlich.'

My father looked at me meditatively.

'Do you now?'

Summer went. Autumn and the storms came. Vorlich drew in on itself and resumed its own closely-knit life. But even I was aware as autumn darkened into winter of a change in the feeling of the place.

Mrs Pigott's friendship with Mrs McFadyen dwindled; the poor woman seemed to withdraw into herself and didn't even appear at the whist-drives where she had shown herself to be a skilful player. George began to look anxious and drawn; and more than once the light from the post office beside the harbour burned long after working hours were over. One evening my father and mother and I were driving up-country to visit friends, when, passing the harbour, we saw a solitary figure at the end of the jetty looking out to sea. It was George. My father stopped the car, jumped out and strode down to him. They spoke for a few minutes and then my father came back.

'He says everything's all right,' he said, 'but I wonder . . .'

Some time into the New Year two strangers came off the bus one morning; discreet men, with black hats and brief-cases. They went to the post office. By evening everyone knew that George was suspended from his job for fiddling the post office money and that a stranger was acting in his place. By the end of the week, George had been driven away in a sleek black car and Mrs Pigott and the children had also left in a small furniture van with what suddenly seemed a pathetically meagre assortment of household goods.

And in a month a large van came over the hill, and sitting up in front smiling a smile of—yes, it *was* triumph—was Hector.

It was a sensation. For once, no one had suspected what was going on, though Murdo McCann was heard to remark he ought to have known something was up seeing the McFadyens were going round looking 'as pleased and smug as if they had been left money.'

Attempts to find out what was behind it all were baulked by Hector's smooth reticence. He had acquired a truly professional capacity for rotund statements that meant nothing.

'My predecessor' (he never referred to George by name), 'my predecessor found the book-keeping side of the work somewhat beyond his capacity,' was the most he would say, and after two or three attempts had produced the same reply, people gave up trying; except my father. He felt he had failed George Pigott, that he should have been able to help him and prevent the débâcle. My mother disagreed and said so:

'If Hector was determined to come back, I don't think you could have stopped him.'

'You sound like Ronald McFadyen,' said my father irritably, 'but I'll get to the bottom of it somehow.'

A week or two later we met Hector face to face, and after the usual exchanges about the weather, my father said:

'What about an evening on the loch?'

'That would be very nice, minister. We must fix it up some time.

'What about today? The weather is right for it.'

'That's so, minister, but I am very much occupied in the office just now.'

'Oh come, Hector, we don't expect *you* to have to work late. I promised the boy some good fishing and you did once say you would take us . . .'

I think Hector realised he was caught. So he put a good face on it.

'As you say, it is good weather. I could postpone the business.'

So it was arranged. My father walked home, whistling under his breath, and I had a shrewd idea it was more than trout we were going after.

We had good fishing and my father said never a word about the post office until I was oaring us back to the landing-stage. Then he looked round at the hills reflected deep in the clear evening water and said:

'You'll be glad to be back, Hector.'

Hector, puffing at his pipe, stiffened, nor could he keep a wariness out of his voice.

'I am indeed, minister.'

'Tell me, Hector, seeing we're alone except for Peter, and he knows never to repeat what comes to the manse, just what happened?'

My father was a mild man but at times he could put into his voice a chilling note of authority, and it was there now.

'Well now, minister, I was thinking I should maybe be mentioning the circumstances to you, for to tell you the truth, my conscience is a little troubled.'

He paused hopefully, but my father said nothing. Unawares, I stopped rowing and the boat bobbed gently on the water.

'You see when I was telling my predecessor all about the course I had been on, I was telling him, among other things, what we were told to be on the look out for if ever we were in charge of an office, in the way of jockery-pockery and fiddles among our subordinates. There are some very clever tricks people could get up to and you have to be able to recognise them . . .'

'You showed George Pigott how to embezzle?'

My father's voice was as cold as the fish in the creel.

'No, no. I was showing what we were taught in our promotion course. I wasn't to know what he would do with the knowledge, was I?'

'You knew he was anxious to get back south. You knew he was poor—you hoped—you were almost sure he would do what he did do. Hector McGillivray, how could you? You have been the means of sending a man to prison, ruining his life . . . and his family . . .'

'He's not in prison, minister, and he won't be. They said if he paid the money back they'd drop the case. The Service doesn't like scandals.'

There was another silence. Then he added:

'The money that was needed was sent to him anonymously.' But my father was not to be deflected.

'You can't buy your way out of wrong-doing. If you think that, you've been living a lie.'

I could see Hector's face from where I sat, and now it changed like the loch when a sudden gust of wind whips it.

'I know very well what I've done. I didn't do it for spite at poor George. I did it for this.' He swept an arm round at the hills, the loch, the quiet water. 'You don't think that's any reason at all. For you Vorlich's a place. For me? Look at this minister.' He drew up a leg of his trousers. There were three white scars across the bone of his leg. 'That was done with a red-hot poker. I came here as a child out of hell, minister. Before I could speak right I knew how to lie and twist and cheat. Some scars heal; others don't. What would you say if I told you some of my scars began to bleed when I was away? A man will do anything for wholeness. It was George or me.'

His pipe shook as he filled it. The water of the loch was still, the reflections deep and black. My father said sharply:

'You've stopped rowing, Peter. It's time we were home.'

*

I went to Hector's funeral, driving up through the golden autumn to Vorlich, and, as always, wondering why we had ever left it. There was a 'grand turn-out' at the burial, and I took my turn at carrying the coffin on the track to the graveyard.

Walking back from the grave-side, I was joined by a tall grey haired man whom I had noticed earlier and felt I should recognise.

'Peter Scott?' he said. 'Perhaps you don't remember me—Hamish McCann.'

Of course. Sir Hamish McCann, K.B.E., one of the great civil servants, now retired.

'Of course. How are you?'

'Very well. I was on holiday with friends at Invermurchan and thought I'd come over to Hector's funeral.'

'He'll leave a gap.'

'Yes indeed. A remarkable man. It's a pity he opted out. He could have gone far in the Service. He had the right gifts.'

'Had he?'

'Definitely.' Hamish McCann stopped and leaned on the stone wall that bordered the road, looking out over the sea. 'Did no one ever wonder how it was that when George Pigott had to go, Hector got his old job back?'

'I was only a boy. I can't remember.'

'I'm sure your father, your very shrewd father, must have thought about it. You remember I spent my holidays here the summer before? And went fishing and shooting with Hector?'

'I do seem to remember . . .'

'After I was back at work, I got a letter from Hector, saying that if ever George Pigott had to leave Vorlich, he'd like his old job back. And in the blandest possible way, he pointed out that we had been poaching that summer. It was in fact, polite and gentlemanly blackmail. I don't know if there was much risk, but at that stage I couldn't afford the slightest breath of scandal. So, when George went—and I'd like to know how that was engineered—I was able to—well—put in a word—you know how it's done.'

Yes, I knew how it was done.

'All the same,' he went on, as we resumed our way to the village, 'I do think it's a pity he didn't find wider scope for his talents.'

I looked across the water to the tangle of mountains with their corries, cliffs and pits of darkness and said nothing.

ALAN JACKSON

The Conspiracy for Arthur

Once upon a time there was a conspiracy. It was a conspiracy for Arthur. Began this way.

About half past nine on a Friday night, in the Spotted Dick, Colin saw this willowy and billowing, thrilling and dare-devilling, dark-haired whitefleshed longdressed whish of a chick.

She was really a person called Moira. But Colin was young, drunk, a man, with friends—he saw a chick.

She saw a chin, a moustache, nice lips, fond hot honest humorous eyes watching and letching.

She stayed watching his eyes and he stood witching hers, so she, not to move too quick and give the game, raised her little drinking glass and smiled behind it, knowing the smile would not look definite, would leave him doubtful, but that, if there *was* anything in this, 'twould be enough.

He waited, she waited. He cracked jokes with mates, she said to girl-friend: 'No, not yet. Might as well wait a minute or two.'

Bogwards bound Colin casually to both of them (only slightly lingering on Moira):

'Fancy coming to a party?'

Friend looked at Moira—oh just a light glimmer. Moira nodded back—oh just a tot.

'Yeah, all right. Why not?' says friend.

*

Is there any hope for us? Any hope for Arthur? Why not straight to Moira did the cleanbrowed Colin go saying:

> Say no and you will slay me.
> You are so fantastic I
> 've just got to ask you out.
> Please believe.

'S rarely done so well.

'S mostly done in a glancy, dead cool, modern, unromancy, self-protect, frightened to be wrecked, we'd only have necked, vile style.

But for wee Arthur, wondrous wee wet Arthur's sake, it worked.

*

Oh who was closer in a taxi that night than Colin and Moira as they began to chat, and, amongst others, gather the whereabouts of each other's flat?

She was a saucy typist but not daft. He was a thinking man, hence unemployed.

'Thought we were going to a party. Where drink?'

'What? Not smoked pot? Just as thought. You wait, remember the date, off by rote. For tonight, sweetpie, you fly, you float.'

He rymbled on. She, won by words' delicious flow, sat glowing warm, not melted quite, almo.

At the party (i.e. the pad arty—always enough people about to pretend there was something happening each week-end) Colin's prob. was to separate Moira off; find somewhere genial and venient where they could, if she would, was in the mood, start to doff.

His urgent though relaxed manoeuvrings met with success. In ten minutes they were out of the press:

'Let's go somewhere where's it's less . . .'

and they were in his little room,

'scuse mess.'

Sitting on the one clear space, the bed, they knew it. They sat and said nothing while he rolled a joint and she looked round it and they still knew. They caught each catching other looking and they knew it again. Were so suspended they could hardly smile but they did smile and when they both really knew both knew, she lay back on his arm as he put it round her and both were down. And as she looked his looking face came near.

Kissed. A long time. A long time to find and to lose a long time. Sometimes he opened his eyes and hers were shut and sometimes one knew other's were open and stayed shut until all were open and nothing was shut. And they laughed at each other.

Almost a cry, although merry, inside such a laugh, and a shy, and a stir of fear, for whatever was happening was happening in time and by chance.

*

The conspiracy of Arthur has begun.

His eyes were blue and hers were brown and I feel no need to go on describing further down.

The eyes for the wise are the prize and nothing else that may open or rise should surprise.

Arthur's eyes are blue, his hair quite fair, considering the darkness of the pair. He's eighteen months, runs about, piddles and chatters.

Two have become one and that's what matters.

IAN HAMILTON FINLAY

The Old Man and The Trout

He was tenant of a red-roofed cottage where we spent a summer holiday once. I suppose I must have been about eleven or twelve years old at the time. It was late on in the summer evenings the old man used to spin me his sleepy yarns. While he yarned we sat together on his wooden garden-bench, in view of his green and yellow honey-suckle bushes full of late-shift bees. Behind us was a big field of ripening corn, with a lot of poppies like blood-spatters in it, bright crimson in the rusty gold. The old man sat well forward, his vein-knotted arms laid flat along his trousers which were pulled up tight, showing his carefully polished boots.

I can't remember much of what the old man said. Mostly he talked about his mole-trapping days, or about his own boyhood, when he'd lived down South. He still had a trace of the Southern way of talking and it was perhaps that that gave his voice such a tickly, sleepy sound. But somehow the mole-trapping was not true to the old man's char-acter as I saw it. A lot of things I said or did would bring a mo-mentary clot of sadness into his hazel eyes.

Once I talked the old man into taking me out fishing. I made him give a solemn promise to catch me a trout. I couldn't catch a trout myself, hard as I tried, every day. Still, the fish there were lovely to look at—fat and sleek, though a bit on the fly side, I thought.

When the old man had said he would take me fishing, we went round to the back of the cottage to gather worms from the hen-coop. The coop was round in the long, narrow garden the old man looked after, with the help of his sister, who was tying string round the currant bushes just then, as we began to dig the worms. The old man suffered from rheumatism, so he held the worm-tin while I dug at the dunged soil with a fork.

It must have been a very hot day, for I remember the old man had first unbuttoned his waistcoat, then taken it off and hung it on a bush. His woolly vest showed white through the slits in his thick, grey shirt. Once I broke a worm in half as I was pulling it from its escape-hole, and he stepped forward and ground the bits to nothing with his polished boot. 'They have feelings the same as we do,' he said, looking at me gently. As he spoke, the apple in his throat wobbled up and down, and I was suddenly saddened to see the brown crinkles in his neck, where his shirt-collar was missing. Then his sister called over to him from among the currant-bushes, and while he was gone to help her knot the string, I gathered up the worms and we were ready to start.

I took my rod from the shed where I always left it, never taking the pieces down, or untying the hook. It was an old shed. In the dusty corners of it stood cobwebbed washing-mangles, and the kind of big, brass basins in which black-currant jam is made in season. There was a steady drip of sunlight through the tiles down to the floor of brown earth. I liked just to stand in there, sniffing the dusty-damp smell which reminded me of something—something I could almost, but never quite remember.

The blue tar on the road had melted in the heat, and I left the marks of my rubber-heeled shoes on it as I walked along. At first, the old man carried the fishing rod while I was left to carry the tin of worms. It was an old treacle tin with a tight-fitting lid in which I had made a few holes with a hammer and nail. 'They have to breathe the same as we do,' I thought of the old man saying. I carried the tin inside my shirt to keep the worms cool and wet. I was scared they might close up like accordions and become no good for the trout.

It was almost no distance from the cottage down to the stream. On the way, though, we had to go by the Big House. Just as we drew level with the lawn, with its neat rhododendron bushes, the old man put the fishing rod into my free hand, and looked away into the fields on the other side of the road, as if he had caught sight of something. I could not see anything there myself. He took back the rod as soon as we were by the Big House and in sight of the stream.

Now that I could see the water running out from the bridge, I thought it might be better after all if it was me who fished. But I waited behind the old man while he slowly climbed the fence. Then we began to make our way down the bank of the stream which was grown all over with a strange kind of weed, like garden rhubarb that had jumped a wall and gone wild. This weed, said the old man, would hide us from the trout.

Instead of starting to fish right away, as I knew we ought to, we walked on down to the deep corner pool. There, the old man stopped, and soon we sat down among the false rhubarb. Flies buzzed round us noisily. A motor-bicycle whizzed up the road, leaving its sound spread out behind it like a long, black snake.

The pool was dappled on the far side with the shadows of trees. The clear water, as it swirled among their roots, was soiled by a drain that poured out rusty stuff, the colour of spate. It certainly was a fine place to fish the worm. I knew that several big trout lived under the trees, for I had often seen them feeding there, from the other bank. They always ignored the worms I threw down to them, except when I threw just the worms without the hook.

At length, the old man screwed himself up to spear on a worm. He told me to sit still where I was, and not to stand up, or shout, or I would scare the fish. Then he began to crawl towards the pool carrying the rod in one hand, and, with the other, clearing away the stems of the weed. The big green leaves kept closing back like the sea. I had to stand up just a little to see him cast. He threw the worm out in a way I thought terribly clumsy. It fell just by luck, though, in the mouth of the drain and began to float down slowly into the shadow of the trees.

To my surprise, the old man laid down the rod with its tip balanced on the edge of a rhubarb leaf. He crawled back towards me, and I could feel him creak. Seeing that I had half-stood up, he waved his hand at me, and I dropped down so as not to spoil his crazy fishing. At the same time I kept my eye on the tip of the rod. Almost at once, it was jerked down from the leaf. A trout had taken the worm. I shouted, and the old man stood up and made a grab for the butt.

Except once in a fishmonger's shop, I had never been so near to a big trout. While the old man wound hurriedly at the handle of the reel, the trout followed upstream in a slow, aloof sort of way. At first, I thought he was going to snag the gut on the barbed-wire cattle-fence which ran across the shallow water at the top of the pool. But he suddenly turned and swam back down towards the roots of the trees. He could not quite reach them because of the dragging line. He leaped out from the water with a big splash then surprised us both by swimming almost to our feet. I could see the red spots on his sides, and his baleful eyes. Then he swam away again, taking the slack of the line.

While the trout splashed in the water, in the shadow of the trees, the old man looked around for a place to land him but there was simply nowhere. The banks were steep, and we had no landing-net. It was a rotten situation.

At length the fish began to turn sideways on the top of the water, and the old man reeled him across the pool till he lay right below us. He lay almost on his back, with his mouth opening slowly and regularly as a clock ticks at night. All at once I felt sorry for him and I wished we had him on the bank.

The old man handed me the rod, and began to push up his jacket sleeve to above his elbow. Then he kneeled down over the trout, and closed his fingers on it, below the gills. He was raising it from the water when suddenly it slipped, and he was left holding only the gut, broken off a good way above the hook. I dropped the rod and looked after the fish as it swam away, with my hook in it.

The old man stood quite still for several minutes, looking after the trout. Then I picked up the rod and the worm-tin, and we walked up the road to the house, saying not a word to each other. I was worried about losing the hook but, as it happened, I had another one hidden away among the hankies in my drawer. I stopped worrying. I went in for my tea, and while I was eating I saw the old man's stooped figure cross the window, and I heard his chair scrape back as—it must have been—he took off his boots.

When I had finished my tea. I went out and sat on the bench sort of waiting for the old man. He didn't come, so in the end I went along and knocked on his door. It was his sister who answered my knock. She was wiping her red hands on a white dish-cloth, while behind her I could see the wallpaper with its pattern of faded roses, and a wooden coat-stand with a pair of the old man's galoshes down below. She took me through to the kitchen where the old man was sitting in a chair drawn in by the fire.

When he saw me come in he sat up. A grey shawl was thrown about his shoulders. He had taken his stocking-soles to ease his feet, and his boots were laid by in the hearth, the firelight dancing in the polished leather. His sister told me he got the rheumatism from being down at the stream fishing, but the old man said it was a sure sign of rain. That cheered me up.

I did not wait long in the old man's private kitchen. He was going to bathe his feet in a papier-mâché basin which his sister carried through from the scullery, and put down for him on the woolly rug. I waited only till she had filled the basin. I heard him groan as he bent forward to drag off his socks; and afterwards, when I was in the garden, I heard the water gurgling away mysteriously down the hidden drain.

Sure enough, there was rain as the old man's rheumatism prophesied. The big drops splashed on the honeysuckle bushes, outside the window, all night. I woke up early. After breakfast, though, it was still raining and I wasn't allowed to go out. Then in the afternoon it faired up, and I was let take my rod from the shed, with its new, puddled floor. The smell in there was a whole lot different that day— sad and exciting somehow. I didn't have to waste time digging for worms. They had come up to the top of the ground, and one or two of the pink ones had wriggled across the road and were squashed thinly on the blue tar. All I had to do was to lift them up.

The sunlit water looked like lentil soup. Twigs and other things were bobbing round in black-ripples, and I let my worm drop in beside them and I caught a good trout. I ran back across the fields and gave it in to the old man. His sister was pleased. She put the fish on a white platter, with little bits of green grass still sticking to its red-spotted sides. I went in to stare at it several times before it was gutted and fried.

The next day the water was almost clear again and I couldn't get any bites. I went down, after a while, to the corner pool, to see if I could spot the big trout. I saw one big fish, but I didn't think it was him, so I went on down to the next pool, and the next one again. This pool was like a big deep hole, with a lot of rotten branches half-buried in the mud down at the bottom of it. It was a pool where you could easily lose all your hooks.

I was just going to walk right by the pool, as I usually did, when my eye caught on something that was glinting down on the mud. I clambered down the bank and picked up a dead branch which snapped. I threw it away. When I had found a branch strong enough, I thrust it down through the water, and poked at the big fish to get him where I could lift him out. Little pieces of mud flaked off the bottom and whirled round him like smoke. He sank up and down like a balloon each time I thrust. When at last I was able to get hold of him, I dropped him on the bank and he was quite stiff. A blue-bottle came and crawled on his eye but I shooed it away.

After I had looked at him for a long time, I took out my pen-knife and got back my hook. It was a little rusted, of course, but there was enough of the bloodied gut left to tie back on my line. I wondered what I ought to do with the trout and, eventually, I pushed him into a hole in the bank and pulled the long grass down on top.

When I had done fishing and got back to the house, the old man was sitting out on the garden bench waiting for me. His rheumatism was a bit better, and he yarned for a while about moles, and said it was an awful pity we'd lost the big trout. It was on the tip of my tongue to tell him what had happened, but I never did for I guessed that if I had it would have broken his heart.

JAMES ALLAN FORD

The Mourners from 19D

After the funeral we went for a drink. Davie's widow told us that we would be welcome at the house, but Alec said that we would have to be getting back to work, and the rest of us just shook hands with her. Although we had all known Davie well enough, none of us except Alec had ever visited him at home, and I suppose that even Alec would have felt like a stranger if we had accepted her invitation and gone back to the house with the folk who had gathered together, like relations, close to the grave. He had stood with the rest of us during the ceremony, on the gravel path, where I could hardly hear the minister and could not see the coffin being lowered. We stood in a row, the five of us, as if we were drawn up for roll-call at Camp 19D.

The day was blustery, with a north-east wind blowing up from the Firth of Forth and scattering thin showers of snow over Edinburgh. My stomach was grumbling with the cold, and I was glad when we were on the move again, following the other mourners out of the cemetery. Just as we had formed up in line for the ceremony without Alec or anybody else suggesting it, so we brought up the rear of the procession out of the cemetery without anybody deciding out loud when we should leave, and I am not sure whether we were showing respect to Davie's kin or just thinking of Fergus, who lost a leg at 19D and has never since been able to walk far or fast.

For longer than was comfortable we were gripped by a silence which, I suppose, came from memories of Davie and the thought of death and the stiffness that slows down even fitter men than Fergus after they have been standing for a time in the cold. At 19D, which was in the north of Japan, you could become so stiff standing outside the hut for morning and evening roll-call in the winter that you had to clench your fists, to bunch up your will-power, before you could move away after Alec shouted out the order to dismiss. There was a kind of reluctance in you as well as a stiffness, and I believe that freezing may be one of the easiest ways to death. One winter night at 19D an American called Chuck Stormer was tied to a stake as punishment for stealing a pack of Japanese tobacco from the camp office, and in the morning he was as stiff as the stake and as dead, and his face was peaceful.

We started talking before we reached the cemetery gates but, although we had not seen each other for a long time, we did not at first say much about ourselves. Our minds were still on Davie.

'How old a man was he?' asked MacAndrew, ex-sergeant and work-party leader at 19D. We had called him Big Mac until we were moved to 19D, where we nicknamed him 'Hancho', which seemed to mean 'ganger'. He was one of the few big men who had survived. The bigger you were, the less chance you had of keeping yourself alive on a daily diet of two bowls of millet and rat shit and two cups of salted water with a few shreds of vegetable floating in it. He was still a big man, tall and straight, but there was not enough of him to fill his skin, which hung from his jaws and was rucked around his neck.

'About fifty-six,' said Alec. 'About the same age as myself.'

'Only fifty-six?' Fergus stopped for a rest. 'And what sort of disability pension was he getting?'

I could have answered that, for Davie and I sometimes met at the Ministry office when our pensions were being reviewed. But I let Alec answer.

And I had a fair idea of what Fergus would say next, for he had always been a grumbler. Even in a place like 19D where everybody had grumbled, his bitching and binding had stood out enough to make him a byword. If you ever had a stroke of luck, like getting a cigarette from one of the Japanese civilians who laboured alongside us in the foundry, someone was sure to take you down a peg by saying: 'Only one? That's not enough for Fergus.' And 'Enough for Fergus' came to mean twenty-three meals a day (allowing time for sleeping) or a whole hutful of Betty Grables (each with four breasts and four thighs) or, as Alec put it, something else within the dreams of avarice.

'Only twenty per cent?' Fergus said. 'A man in his condition?'

Alec caught my eye but did not share my smile. 'Davie was reasonably fit for most of his life,' he told Fergus.

'But it wasn't what you'd call a very long life,' said Fergus sarcastically. 'And I don't see how anybody could deny that it was 19D that wore him out early.'

Even if Fergus lives long enough to get a telegram from the Palace, he will still be inclined to think that his time has been cut short by 19D. But you cannot turn him aside now with a laugh and 'Not enough for Fergus.' We have not ridden him about his grumbling since his leg started to blacken in 19D.

'Well, it's all over,' said Hancho MacAndrew. 'The world's a different place. Most of the Japanese we knew will be dead themselves. It's maybe time we forgot some things.'

'Forgot?' Fergus seemed more astonished than angry. 'How can

E

we forget things like that? How can we ever forget what those bastards did to us?'

Batty Dodds, who had a smell of whisky on his breath, spoke up. 'Slant-eyed yellow bastards,' he said, spitting the words out. Then he looked around us, grinning.

Another shower of snow came swirling up, and Alec opened his umbrella. 'Come on and have a drink,' he said in his officer's voice.

*

As we walked to the pub, I began to feel that I was not myself. It may just have been the break in my usual daily routine that made me slip out of my ordinary way of thinking and start seeing myself in much the same way as I saw the four other men from 19D. But I have broken my routine at other times without feeling this momentary freedom from my own skin. And I believe not only that I was experiencing something different from the distraction which often comes when you are left outside your habits but also that I was sharing the experience with the others. I believe that Batty's words had taken us all outside ourselves, that he had made us all feel our nearness to each other. We walked up the road in a silence that was no longer uncomfortable, the kind of silence that does not separate. We had suddenly fallen back into an old awareness of each other and did not have to keep talking like strangers.

I have never been a man to live in the past, to tell old soldier's stories in the regimental club, to attend reunions of prisoners-of-war. Alec himself once said in 19D, 'If we ever get out of this, I hope we'll find better things to do than remember it.' And I have always tried to find better things to do. After we came home, I did not even help Alec in his welfare work for other survivors who were in poorer health than we were, or out of work or still nearly out of their minds. When I left 19D, I left it all and kept walking away from it and tried never to stop walking away. Davie's funeral was the first thing that made me stop. There have been other funerals, plenty of them, but Davie's was the first I have attended. I went to it, I suppose, partly because of the kind of man he had been and partly because of the kind of man I had become, old enough and closely enough wrapped in my own affairs to look back without losing myself. But my memories had started running as soon as I met the four others at the cemetery gates and began to mark how little they had changed over the years. Then Batty, speaking up for the first time, speaking straight from 19D, made us feel for a few moments that nothing had changed.

The different camps I was in had different ways of life, different ways of reaching for survival. And, if anything could sum up 19D's ways, it was Batty's words, 'Slant-eyed yellow bastards.' There, the last camp I was in, it was hatred that kept us going, nothing but hatred for the Japanese. 19D was the worst of all the camps any of us had been in, not just because we were near the end of our tether but also because the Japanese were near the end of theirs. And the harder they tried to beat us into the ground, the harder we had to make our hatred. 'S E Y B,' we would say to their faces, and even the interpreter was foxed. 'Slant-eyed yellow bastards,' we would say among ourselves, until I could feel the hissing hatred of the words hurting me inside. Hating does hurt, and that was why, after we left 19D, I tried to stop hating, to stop hurting myself.

The pub was crowded with lunchtime drinkers, and we could not find a corner for ourselves, a place where we could talk in private. We had to squeeze into an alcove that had already been taken over by a group of young men, youths really, who were none too keen to make room for us. A bunch of the kind who are all hair and prickles. It was a poor start to the occasion for men of our age, but the drink helped to loosen our tongues and we started asking about each other.

Fergus had a part-time job in an office on a building site. Hancho MacAndrew was no longer a commissionaire but had hopes of being taken on by a Government department as a temporary clerk; he is quite an educated man, Hancho. Alec, we all knew, was still a lawyer, and from the look of his clothes he was a good bit more prosperous than he had been as a lieutenant.

'And what about you, Batty?' asked Hancho.

Batty Dodds grinned and nodded. He has never minded being called 'Batty'. He has never much minded anything, except the Japanese. 'The Corporation,' he said.

Alec explained, 'Batty's working at one of the cleansing depots.'

'Heavy work?' asked Fergus.

'Heaviest in the whole place,' Batty boasted. 'I'm not one o' them long-haired boyos that can't get off their arses.'

He looked as strong as ever, although he was carrying a lot more fat. He had always, even in 19D, had the kind of strength that frightened me, that made him seem as if he would burst out of his skin one day. And he still knew the power that his strength gave him, for he grinned straight at the long-haired lads beside us when he spoke. He had taken more punishment from the Japanese than any other man in camp, and he had asked for a lot of it. He had lived his hatred in a way that was beyond the rest of us, and we had relieved some of the hurt of our hatred through him, watching how he provoked the guards, how he stood up to them when they screamed at him and slapped him and kicked him, when they beat him with sticks and rifle butts.

Then Alec, with an eye on the bully boys scowling at Batty, asked me what I was doing. He knew well enough the work I had come back to, and he knew that I was never one for chopping and changing. He was trying to ease Batty into the background rather than to find out anything about me, and I did not give him much of an answer.

'You had other ideas once,' he said, smiling.

'We all had great ideas then.'

There had been a time, before 19D, when we had helped to keep ourselves going by making plans, great plans, for what we were going to do after the war. But nothing came of my plans or, so far as I know, anybody else's.

'I was going to raise chickens,' Hancho recalled.

We used to be puzzled and tickled by that. None of us could see any connection between Big Mac and chickens.

Fergus butted in. 'If I'd kept both my legs—'

'See if you can get a chair for Fergus,' said Alec.

He was speaking to me, for I was nearest the tables and chairs at the other end of the pub. But Batty moved first, elbowing me and one of the lads aside as he went.

'Watch it, dad,' the lad warned him.

'Get stuffed,' said Batty cheerfully.

He brought a chair back for Fergus, who was still talking. 'I might have surprised you all. I knew where I was going.'

He was always going in circles. He would never be left out of the planning but could never settle on a plan of his own. He kept changing his mind about the future, as he kept foreseeing the snags of every way of life he could imagine.

'You think we haven't made enough of ourselves?' Hancho asked him.

'Well, have we?'

Hancho took no offence. 'I've sometimes wondered myself.' He emptied his glass. 'Maybe the wrong ones survived, eh? Think of young Williamson, the wee fellow from Gorebridge who could count three columns of figures at the same time. He'd have made something of himself if he'd lived.'

'We've done well enough ourselves,' said Alec. 'We've kept going.' He too drained his glass. 'And it's time I did just that—kept going. I'll have to get back to my work.'

But nobody else was quite ready to leave. We had come a long way—thirty years—to this meeting. And our minds were now quick with memory.

'We'll have a pint of beer,' Hancho suggested.

'Ach,' grumbled Fergus, 'you can't get the good old Edinburgh beer I used to dream about in 19D.'

*

While Alec and Hancho fetched the drinks, Fergus and Batty spoke of 19D. I was still thinking of Alec's words: 'We've done well enough. We've kept going.' With a whisky in my stomach and the sound of old familiar voices in my ears, I stood there comfortably aware of myself, a free man, thirty years and half a world away from 19D. I could feel the space I took up, the warmth I contained. The feeling of survival. And it took my mind back to the times in 19D when I would lie down on my mat and shut my eyes and put my hands over my ears and listen to the pulsing of my blood, the sound of my living.

'Aye, aye,' said Fergus, at the end of some story, 'how can we ever forget?'

Batty's face was bright with good humour and sweat. He had always sweated after drinking more than a mouthful of anything, and it was plain that he had been at the bottle before the funeral. I could understand that. I could remember how he had avoided looking at corpses. Only death itself had ever really frightened him.

'I don't forget,' he said. 'If I could lay my hands on some of them bastards—'

It struck me that, although they had survived, Fergus and Batty had never freed themselves. Nothing else in their experience had been bigger than the wooden fence with the barbed wire on top, and they still lived inside it, angry about what had happened to them but ready to boast about it, as survivors often do if they have nothing much else to boast about.

'I'll never forget the day,' said Fergus, 'when Takahashi and the guard with the celluloid teeth tried to batter you cold.'

'I showed them.'

'They had you down four or five times—'

'Six times.'

'And you kept coming back for more.'

I could remember that day and the lump of shared suffering and pride in my throat as Batty kept staggering to his feet and facing up to Takahashi and the guard. Anybody else would have had the sense to lie still the first time he was clubbed to the ground, but nobody else would have given us the kind of legend that helped to keep us going. I did not grudge Batty his moment of remembered glory. 'It was a great day,' I told him.

'I showed them.' Batty bulged inside his skin. 'And I'm still ready to show anybody else.' He was boasting now to the lads beside us.

They were a hard-faced bunch, although they were all rounder in the shoulders and shallower in the chest than Batty, the old soldier. It was understandable that they were angered by him. When we looked at him we could still see the young Batty whose slow mind and dour courage had helped to save us from the kind of humiliation that kills.

But when they looked at him they would see nothing but a red-faced man in his fifties who was taking up too much room with his beef and his boasting.

'Look, dad,' said the one who had spoken to him before, 'why don't you go back to the old folks' home and sleep it off, like?'

Batty was still surprisingly quick on his feet. Before I could even think of diverting him, he had side-stepped me and whipped his arm around the lad's head and was squeezing it against his chest. 'Piss and wind,' he said savagely, 'there's nothing but piss and wind in your kind.'

The lad wriggled like a parcel of eels, lashing out blindly with arms and legs, trying to knock holes in Batty with fists and feet. His mates started to twitch, shuffling and hunching and jerking glances at each other, none of them ready to move in until all were ready. And I was trying to find something to say or do myself, when Alec was suddenly among us, snapping at Batty in a way that broke off the action. 'Give over,' was all that he said, but he said it as if he had a squad of regimental police at his back.

'Outside!' shouted the younger of the two men behind the bar. 'Outside, the lot of you!'

But it was Alec that Batty was listening to. He let the lad go. 'No harm done,' he mumbled, his anger used up. 'Just a bit of fun.'

'Outside!' shouted the barman again.

Alec stood there, facing Batty and the furious lad, his mouth tight, the reflection on his spectacles hiding his eyes from me. At his back there was only Hancho, holding a tray of beers and muttering, 'We've paid for them and we'll drink them.'

The young barman pushed in among us. 'Did you hear me? Or do I have to get the police to you?'

'We'll drink up and go,' answered Alec very coldly.

'Right. Just do that, as quick as you like.' The barman was nervous, and all the bossier for it. He turned on the gang of lads. 'I want you outside in two minutes flat. You get me?'

'Look, mac, we didn't start nothing.'

'Am I asking you who started something?' He was sweating, the young barman. He must have felt terribly tired afterwards. 'I'm telling you to get the hell out of here or I'll have the law on you.'

Then the other barman, the older one, called across in an easier tone of voice: 'Drink up and go, lads. I've my licence to think of.'

'And leave your glasses,' added the young one, to show that he could handle a thing like this without help.

They had less left to drink than we had, and they were moved out first, with the young barman at their heels like a terrier. But they took their time in walking to the door, swaggering a bit and lifting their heads in a way that I could understand, that anyone who had suffered humiliation could understand.

After the door had closed behind the lads, the barmen left us—the five short-haired, well-dressed, middle-aged customers—in peace.

'Some pub, this,' muttered Batty, with his head down.

'No harm done,' Hancho assured him. 'It was about time for us to be making tracks anyway.'

Nobody else was ready to say anything. We gulped our beer, and I took another look at them all. It struck me that I would never know anyone better than I had once known them and Davie and a few others in 19D. I had never had closer friends and was never likely to have. And yet we had seen very little of each other since the war. We had gone our own ways as soon as we had found ourselves free to choose our ways, and this was the first time in thirty years that the five of us had come together. It seemed to me that we should have more to say to each other, that we should not be standing apart.

Then Alec turned to me and, as he had often done in 19D, gave me the uneasy feeling that he could hear me thinking. 'You haven't had much to say for yourself.'

Before I could say anything for myself Hancho chipped in. 'He was always the quiet one, always a bit of a loner.'

Alec was watching me, and it began to irk me that he was still playing the officer, still trying to keep an eye on everybody. He used to worry about my silences, because in a prison camp you can never be sure whether the quiet ones are holding their own. There is a kind of silence in which courage fails. 'Not really a loner, were you?' he said. 'You couldn't have done solitary any more than I could.'

I agreed. In 19D you needed somebody to pity besides yourself.

Batty lifted his head again. 'I done more time in that doghouse than anybody else,' he boasted.

When you were punished with solitary confinement you had to go down on your hands and knees in the yard and crawl through a hatch in one side of the wooden guardhouse and twist yourself into a space just big enough to hold you crouching with your legs bent tight against your trunk, and your head bowed over your knees.

But Alec was not ready to forgive Batty. 'Drink up,' he replied abruptly, and Batty raised his glass in submission.

Fergus grumbled that he needed more time to enjoy a pint.

'You're not the only one,' said Alec. 'Drink up and I'll see you all outside. I'd better make our apologies to the landlord before I go.'

Still playing the officer, still trying to take our responsibilities away from us. I think we were all beginning to feel the weight of his manner. We took our time about moving. We needed the time, not to empty our glasses, but to show him where we stood.

Batty, his face shining like a lamp, said, 'It was just a bit of fun.'

Hancho nodded to Alec. 'Best forgotten.'

Batty's eyes looked pitifully naked. 'I'll tell the man at the bar myself, if you like.'

But Alec, although he has always made much of Batty, has never really understood him. It's only the mind of a man that Alec seems to understand, and Batty's mind explains very little, even to himself. He clapped Batty's arm and said to him, in a kinder voice. 'I'll see you outside.'

As he turned towards the bar, Batty and Fergus made for the door, but Hancho and I went to the toilet. It is easier to say some things in a toilet than in other places, but Hancho and I did not find much to say. I was wishing that I had not attended the funeral and muddled myself with memories, and he must have been thinking the same.

'It was all a long time ago,' he said.

I agreed.

'That's all that's worth remembering,' he muttered. 'That and the funny bits.'

I found a smile. 'There were a lot of funny bits.'

My mind was suddenly loud with remembered laughter. Through all the years of our imprisonment, even in 19D, we never forgot how to laugh. Sometimes we may have laughed at things that were more pitiful than funny, but prisons are places outside the ordinary world and you cannot expect prisoners to behave in ordinary ways.

'We should just have laughed at Batty today,' I suggested.

Hancho grinned. 'I can remember laughing once at the sight of his backside twisting and turning when he squeezed himself into that doghouse. That big backside of his looked more worried than his face did.'

We turned to each other, ready to laugh again. There were plenty of things to talk about now, true things, things that were worth remembering and would not hurt us.

'Come on,' said Hancho, 'we'll away out and raise a smile on their solemn faces.'

Alec was already on his way to the door, and he was outside before we caught up with him, standing by himself in a blinding swirl of snow that brought us up short and took the breath from me. Then we heard Fergus calling excitedly on Alec and, turning, we saw him hirpling towards us from the corner of the street.

'They got Batty!' he shouted.

We ran, all three of us. Round the corner we found Batty lying face down on the pavement.

'It was that bunch of young hooligans!' Fergus was greyskinned and trembling. 'They were waiting for him, they all went for him.'

'The police,' said Alec, 'we'll have to get the police.'

Hancho knelt down on the pavement. 'Anything broken?'

'I'm all right,' muttered Batty, but his voice was thick with pain.
'We'll need an ambulance,' Hancho decided.

'We can phone from the pub,' said Alec. He was looking at me,
but I was not looking at him. He swayed uncertainly on his feet,
then hurried back to the pub himself.

'I'm all right,' Batty insisted. 'I could show them yet.' He tried
to raise himself, and I saw that his face had gone as grey as Fergus's
and that blood was dribbling from his nose and mouth.

'Lie still, man,' said Hancho. 'They've run away.'

'I could show them,' boasted Batty. He made another effort to rise,
and Hancho and Fergus must have been remembering, as I was, how
he had struggled to his feet time after time to face up to Takahashi
and the guard. But that was a long time ago, and Batty could not
raise himself from the pavement. He sank down, his broken breathing
sounding like sobbing. And he too must have been thinking not of the
young lads who had knocked him down but of Takahashi and the
guard with the celluloid teeth, for he gasped out, with all the hatred
left in him, 'Bastards—slant-eyed yellow bastards!'

We waited with him, and Hancho brushed the snow from his head.

E*

FRED URQUHART

Maggie Logie and the National Health

Maggie Logie was a poor, simple, but well thought of widow body in the village of Cairncolm. She was liked because she was aye pleasant and not a one to talk behind her neighbours' backs. After her man was killed in the sawmill in 1928, she cleaned the school, did odd bits of washing and cleaning for the minister's wife, and what with that and her widow's pension she managed to get by.

Tam Dodds, the beadle, who had been a mate of Andra Logie's visited her every Saturday afternoon and split a bit of kindling for her fire. He brought a bundle of wood from the mill with him, and after he'd split it, Maggie would give him his tea and they'd have a wee crack in front of the fire.

Usually there was only a bit handful of coal in the grate, but Maggie's big range was aye so highly polished that it gave the impression that the fire was bigger and brighter than it was. The steel fender shone like silver, and Maggie spent a lot of time and elbow-grease on the designs she squiggled with white and red pipeclay on the hearth. A couple of red china dogs with bold black eyes—Pomeranians they were, and they'd belonged to Maggie's Granny—sat on either corner of the mantelpiece; and there was a blue china clock with panels of Greek goddesses with very little on standing in the middle. It had been a wedding present, but it had never gone right since Andra was killed. Occasionally Tam tinkered with it and it went for a few hours, but it aye stopped again. Tam didn't seem to have the knack.

It wasn't long, of course, before the village jaloused that there was something between Tam and Maggie, and gossip was rife. But whenever folk asked about Tam, saying: 'Is it no' high time he was puttin' up the banns for ye baith,' Maggie would simper and say: 'There's nothin' definite, but he's aye comin' aboot.'

Things went on like this for a long time. Tam was thirty-four when Andra died—a couple of years older than Maggie—but he lived with his mother, a cantankerous old body who demanded a lot of attention, and so he was never able to pop the question. By the time the war started he still hadn't popped it, and the auld wife seemed to renew her youth like the eagles when evacuees were billeted in the village. Mrs Dodds made sure she wouldn't get any evacuees herself, for she was bad with phlebitis in the legs and the doctor gave her a certificate to say she mustn't be trauchled with extra work. But this didn't stop her from having wee tea-parties and even taking the bus to Stranraer to go to the pictures with some of the wifies from Glasgow. Maggie got evacuees, of course, and a bairn broke one of the china dogs. Tam patched it together again with secotine, but it never looked the same.

By the end of the war the whole village was changed. The RAF and the Yanks had left their mark, and what with bigger money coming into nearly every house, folk were on a wave of prosperity, the likes of which they'd never dreamed of. Women that used to have just one good frock for Sundays and Women's Rural meetings and that had never even had enough clouts to use as dusters, began to talk about getting washing-machines. And nearly everybody had Hoovers or Electroluxes to keep their new carpets clean. Maggie Logie was now the only one who still hung her bit rugs over the fence in the back garden and walloped them with a stick. Although she'd had a wheen RAF boys and Yanks billeted on her, like most of the village folk, Maggie's house looked much the same as it was that day Andra Logie was brought home feet first.

Whiles Tam asked if she didn't think a wee modern fire would be more economical and easier to work, but Maggie aye said she couldn't be fashed with anything new-fangled. 'And if it's saving the kindlin' you're thinkin' about, Tam Dodds,' she said, 'a modern grate'll take as long to light and need as much wood as that yin.'

And so Tibby the cat, the great-great-great-granddaughter of the first Tibby that Maggie had had when Tam first came about the house, still sat in front of the old-fashioned range. She aye sat there, with her eyes half-shut, on the rag-rug that Maggie had made before she got married. Throughout the years it had got worn with the scuffle of army boots and the claws of Tibby's forebears, and every now and then Maggie would repair it with rags she got from the folks she worked for. The original pattern had disappeared long syne.

Mrs Dodds died the year after the war finished, but it made no difference to Maggie. Tam stayed on in the cottage behind the old smiddy and still came regularly every Saturday afternoon to break Maggie's kindling. Folk said: 'When's he goin' to hang up his hat wi' ye?' but Maggie would just give a bit skirl and say: 'There's nothin' definite yet. He's aye comin' aboot.'

The only thing different that happened was that Tam branched out and bought a motor-bike on the proceeds of his old mother's insurance money. And now every Saturday, after he'd split the kindling, Tam would reive away for a bit hurl with Maggie on the pillion. Whiles they went to Stranraer to the pictures, and whiles they'd go farther afield as far as Glenluce or Port Logan. When folk saw the bike whizzing past with Maggie in her Sunday coat and brown felt hat sitting bolt upright behind Tam, they'd give a bit grin and say things like: 'Love's young dream had better get their skates on before they baith land up in a ditch!' For Maggie was busy with the change, and Tam was a douce, settled man without a black hair left in his head.

At first Tam wore a cap and goggles when cycling, but after a while he got one of these berets that had been so popular with sodgers in the war. It suited him gey well, and when some of the younger lassies in the village felt skittish they'd tell him: 'Ye look a real smasher!' But Maggie aye kept wearing her old brown hat, though by this time she'd sewn some feathers on to it that she'd got from the minister's wife.

Well, the years went by, and still the villagers were speculating about orange blossom—though fine they kenned this wouldn't be likely at Maggie's age—and a slap-bang tea and drinks in the Women's Rural Institute, which was the place most weddings were held. But the only thing that happened was that Tam got rid of his old motor-bike and bought a new one with a side-car. And so he and Maggie now looked quite genteel going about the country, with Maggie sitting fair jecko in the side-car and giving Tam directions occasionally. 'She's gettin' a bit long in the tooth to ride pillion, onyway,' folk said, and it aye gave them something to natter about before some sat down to listen to the Saturday night play and the lucky ones watched the telly. They never went out on the bike on Sundays, for Tam said the minister wouldn't like it, him being the Beadle and near enough to being an Elder of the Kirk, and he must set a good example to the gormless young men of the village, some of whom were little better than these terrible teddy boys you read about in the papers.

But although there was no great change in the way they'd been going on for years, there was a change in Maggie.

When the Welfare State started in 1947, Maggie, like a lot of folk, was quite unaware that it had come into being. She hardly ever read the newspapers and she had no wireless.

'What would I be wantin' wi' a wireless for?' she had said to Tam when he'd urged her to be modern and upsides with everybody else. 'I havenie time to listen til't.' And so it was quite a whilie before Maggie learned how kind Mr Bevan and other big bugs like him had been to poor folk like herself. It was the minister who eventually explained to her all about the National Health Insurance Act. She couldn't take it all in, but she took in enough to understand that from now on she wouldn't need to pay for the doctor or the dentist, that she could get spectacles for nothing, she could even get an artificial limb free, if necessary, and she could get a wig.

'And what would I be wantin' a wig for?' Maggie said.

The minister looked gey taken aback, but he gave a bit laugh and said: 'Well, it happens to all of us in time, Mrs Logie. Nature, you know! The flow of oil to our roots gets clogged and we all—men *and* women—tend to get a little thin on top. Some more than others, of course,' he added quickly.

This talk garred Maggie think a lot more than usual. She hardly ever needed the doctor and she'd never been to a dentist in her life. She knew that she had an insurance card which the schoolmistress kept, for every now and again she'd have to wash her hands and sign it. But she'd never thought anything about it, not missing the ninepence or whatever it was a week that came off her school wages. But she thought about it all right when she found one week that her wages were less than they should have been. 'It's the new insurance stamps, Mrs Logie,' the schoolmistress explained. 'We've all got to pay more now—but look at the *wonderful* benefits we get!'

The schoolmissy was Labour and some folk said she put a lot of tosh into the bairns' heads. She explained all about the virtues of the National Health Insurance Act to Maggie, stressing what a good thing it was for the likes of her. But Maggie wasn't much wiser than she'd been when the minister explained it. One thing she did understand, however, and that was: that every week she was to pay more money to the Government and that for it she would get free medicine, free teeth, free operations, free specs and free hair.

And so, after chewing it over, Maggie made up her mind that she must get her money's worth. She started to go to the doctor's regularly, and it wasn't long before other folk that had aye been considered the standbys of his Panel were fair put in the shade. They got tired of saying: 'What's wrong wi' ye this time, Maggie?' when they went into the waiting-room and found her sitting first in the queue. And they were gey ill-pleased when she began to outdo them with her ailments, for Maggie got hold of a medical book in the minister's library and studied it that well that it wasn't long before even the poor old doctor got a bit flummoxed. But he soon discovered that it didn't really matter whether he was able to diagnose the odd complaints or not—though Maggie was aye willing to give him the benefit of what she'd read about them in the medical book—so long as she got a prescription to take away with her. Whenever the doctor was in doubt, Maggie would say: 'What aboot a nice tonic, doctor? As well as everythin' else, I feel a wee thing run doon.' And so it wasn't long before the cupboard in Maggie's back bedroom was filled to overflowing with full, near-full and half-empty bottles of coloured water, as well as with boxes of pills of all shapes and colours.

But being the doctor's star patient wasn't enough. Maggie paid a visit to the dentist and had her teeth seen to. The dentist told her they weren't at all bad considering her age and that all that was necessary was a filling here and there, as well as 'a scrape and a polish'. All of which he did, and all of which meant that Maggie traipsed out and in to his surgery once a fortnight for two or three months. But not long after the final polish, Maggie found that the price of insurance stamps was going up and that another shilling or two would be coming off her wages. And so she decided to get her money's worth and have all her teeth out.

The dentist pleaded with her till he was near black in the face, but Maggie wouldn't take 'No' for an answer. 'Out they come,' she said. 'It'll save me a lot o' trouble in the long run.'

Well, after being toothless for a wheen weeks and having trouble when she masticated, Maggie got her brand new upper and lower sets. But even then she wasn't pleased. She didn't think they fitted her just right, and she was in and out the dentist's for a good while having them filed here and filed there. And then when the poor man, near demented, told her that was the best he could do, she decided that really the teeth were ower valuable to wear, except on special occasions. So she kept them in a box on her chiffonier and only popped them in her mouth when she went to the kirk on Sundays. She didn't dare wear them when she was out on the bike with Tam for fear a sudden bump would make her swallow them, so she got into the habit of winding a white woollen scarf round her face. It was a gey wide scarf, and only Maggie's eyes could be seen between it and the rim of her brown hat, and it made an impudent village bairn ask if she had joined the Ku Klux Klan.

Insurance stamps went up again, so Maggie decided she'd have her appendix out. The doctor told her it was worse than idiotic, for the truth of the matter was that the poor old man didn't think that Maggie had such an organ in her body. But she insisted on her rights, and the upshot was that she spent a fortnight in hospital and—although she didn't care for it over much, thinking the nurses were flibbertigibbets and a bit uppish—she wondered what other operations she could have.

Now Maggie wasn't what you'd call a reader, except for the times when she pored over the minister's medical book. When she did read the papers on a Sunday afternoon she aye fell asleep ower them before she'd read more than some of the headlines. There was nothing wrong with her eyesight. She could thread a needle quicker than most folk, and could aye tell when she looked out her window what was going on at the other end of the village. But she decided that she'd have to get spectacles, and spectacles she got—a brand new National Health pair with light yellow frames and bits of glass sparkling like jewels just above her eyebrows. She didn't wear them in the house, of course; nor could she wear them when she was working, for they hindered her something dreadful. But she aye wore them when she went out on the motor-bike.

At first Tam didn't pay much heed to what he called Maggie's capers, but when she started to flight on him to go to the doctor's he put his foot down. 'Why should I?' he said. 'In the first place, there's nothin' wrang wi' me. And in the second, if there was, I could cure it quicker masel' instead o' wastin' my time sittin' among a' thae hippykondricks. Time was when ye went to the doctor, there was nobody waitin' but folk that were really ill. But now every man, woman and bairn in Cairncolm's sittin' there waitin' for a free dose o' cough-mixture.'

'But ye must get yer money's worth, Tam,' said Maggie.

'Money's worth!' Tam spat. 'That's a' folk think aboot nowadays.'

But Tam had a lot more to say when Maggie decided she must have a wig.

'A wig! Good God, woman!' he cried. 'Dinnie talk such damned nonsense. Ye've a grand head o' hair o' yer ain. I never heard such havers.'

'My hair's gettin' thin,' Maggie said. 'The minister tellt me that when ye get to oor age the flow o' oil to the roots gets clogged. I dinnie see why I shouldnie have a wig. I've paid for it.'

The doctor was as flabbergasted as Tam when she went to him for a certificate. 'Really, Mrs Logie,' he said, 'this is something I just can't do for you. There's no sign of baldness on your scalp.'

Maggie pled and pled with him, but he wouldn't budge. He even went the length of saying that he'd be more likely to sign a certificate consigning her to the loony bin if she didn't get away home and stop wasting his time.

But Maggie wasn't to be beat. Her mind was made up. The price of the Health Stamps was still rising, and she saw no reason why she shouldn't get all she could while the going was good. So she did a bit of experimenting with the scissors, and finally she cut off nearly all her hair, even going the length of shaving her head in places. By the time she'd finished plowtering about, it looked as if she'd had a bad case of ringworm. And so she popped on an old dust-cap that had belonged to her mother and wore that for a few days so that folk couldn't but see and ask what was wrong. And, of course, they were all that sorry to hear her health was so bad that her hair was falling out, and one and all said: 'Why don't ye see Dr Crombie aboot it?'

That was what Maggie was waiting for, but she didn't go right there and then. She waited for a week so that the doctor would be deeved by other folk saying: 'Isn't it terrible aboot puir Maggie Logie losin' her hair? She's run doon, puir soul, and nae wonder wi' a' the hard work she has to do. It's high time auld Tam Dodds popped the question and took some o' the burden off her. No' that he's likely to dae that now wi' her lookin' like a witch in a mutch. Puir cratur', what she's needin' is a wig.'

Maggie's own hair had been black, though lately it had got gey streaked with grey. But the wig she chose was a bright ginger one. When Tam saw it he was that dumbfounded that all he could say was: 'What next? Dinnie tell me ye're hankerin' after a gammy leg now!'

But Tam had more on his mind than Maggie's wig. His motor-bike and side-car were ten years old and had seen their day and generation. He thought about it for a long time—the better part of a year—and then plucked up his courage and sold them in part exchange for a new bike and side-car, what the smart-alec in the garage called an up-to-date combination. 'Though I'm thinkin' maybe I should ha'e bocht new combinations for ma auld legs,' Tam said. 'I whiles doot I'm gettin' ower auld for dug-dancin' aboot the countryside on a bike. Especially wi' the traffic bein' so bad and me not bein' able to take the risks a' these young flibbertigibbets take.'

Maggie had been thinking about this, too. And after she read in the papers (for she'd taken to reading the papers to get full use of her new specs) that crash-helmets were necessary and should be made compulsory, she got another bee in her bonnet. If the National Health could give free wigs and free specs and free operations, why could they not give free crash-helmets? And so she paid a visit to the Insurance folk and the upshot was that after she had fair worn them out, so that extra cups of tea had to be made, and there was quite a lot of jookerypawkery, she came away with a certificate.

The following Saturday, when Tam came to the door and shouted 'Keeky-bo!' as he aye did to show Maggie that he was ready, it was a whilie before she appeared. And when she did, Tam stood like a stooky with his mouth wide open.

'Good God!' he said at last.

Maggie had her white woollen scarf wound round her neck and jaws as usual, and on top of them was sitting a muckle white crash-helmet.

'Good God!' Tam said again. 'The woman from Mars!'

Maggie had to pull down her scarf a bit to say: 'Less o' yer sauce, Tam Dodds. If you want to land a cropper and break yer neck, I dinnie. Crash-helmets are very necessary. The papers say so.'

When Tam had recovered and Maggie was sitting in the side-car, he put his leg ower the bike, and they bugbeetled off through the village. A wheen folk saw them whizz by, and one woman said to another: 'Did ye see that daft auld limmer? What next, I wonder!'

That was what Maggie was thinking herself as she sat in the side-car, bolt upright for fear she'd miss anything. She had one cup-board full of medicine, and another cupboard half-full, she had specs, she had teeth, she had a wig and she had a crash-helmet. What could she get next? There must be something. She didn't fancy another operation—though it would aye be a rest. But she was near sixty now, and there seemed to be little else to look forward to but the old age pension. For by now she kenned full well that Tam would never take the plunge and ask her to move into the old cottage behind the smiddy. Not that she wanted to do that, anyway. She was gey content with her own wee house.

There must be something, she thought, as they sped through Stranraer and down the road to Portpatrick. 'Mind that car in front, Tam!' she shouted, for the big black Zodiac was going at a fair lick and it looked as if Tam was ettling to pass it. She was going to add something else, but she jaloused that Tam couldn't hear her for the wind. And just at that moment she had a sudden thought. She'd minded what Tam had once said to her about a gammy leg.

A gammy leg! Now, that was something she'd never managed to get. And it was something she was entitled to, especially with the way these Health stamps kept rising in price. But what would ye do with a gammy leg, Maggie Logie, she asked herself. It would be no good to ye, for ye've got two good pins of your own. Mind you, what with your bunions and sore feet in general, it might be not a bad idea to have a leg sawn off and an artificial one from the Health folk in its place. It would maybe save the wear and tear on stockings. . . .

Maggie was that pleased with the idea that she half-raised herself out her seat and leaned towards Tam to tell him. 'What would ye say if I appeared wi' a gammy leg, auld yin?' she shouted.

But what Tam would say, Maggie never knew. For when she raised herself, Tam was trying to pass the black Zodiac, and what with the wind and the speed, Maggie lost her balance and lurched against him. The next minute the motor-bike-combination had skidded across the road and landed tapsalteerie in the ditch.

When the folk from the black Zodiac came back, they found Tam pinned under the motor-bike. All that was wrong with him was a broken leg, a dislocated shoulder and some scratches. Maggie was lying about five yards away. Her wig and her crash-helmet had come off, and the driver of the Zodiac stared with open mouth at Maggie's cropped head before he bent down to see what was wrong with her. It only needed a bit glance to see she was dead.

Puir Tam. Maggie had never bothered to make a will, so the seven hundred pounds she had in the Post Office and in Savings Certificates all went to her second cousin, who soon made short shrift of all the medicine in the house by filling the ash-bucket with bottles and boxes. Forby taking puir Tibby to the vet to be put to sleep.

ELSPETH DAVIE

Allergy

The new lodger glanced down briefly at the plate which had just been put in front of him and turned towards the window with a faint smile, as though acknowledging that the day was fair enough outside, even if there was something foul within.

'I can't take egg. Sorry.'

'Can't take?' Mrs Ella MacLean still kept her thumb on the oozy edge of a heap of scrambled yellow.

'No. It's an allergy.'

'It doesn't agree?'

'No. It's an allergy.'

'Oh, one of those. That's interesting! But you could take a lightly-boiled egg, couldn't you?'

'No, it's an allergy to egg.'

'You mean *any* egg?'

'Any and every egg, Mrs MacLean. In all forms. Egg is poison to me.' Harry Veitch did not raise his voice at all, but this time his land-lady withdrew the plate rather quickly. She put it on one side and sat down at the other end of the table.

'Yes, that *is* interesting,' she said. 'I've known the strawberries and the shellfish and the cat's fur. And of course I've heard of the egg, though I've never met it.' Veitch said nothing. He broke a piece of toast. 'No, I've never met it. Though I've met eggs disagreeing. I mean really disagreeing!'

Veitch was pressing his lips with a napkin. 'Not the same thing,' he said. 'When I say poison I mean poison. Pains. Vomiting. And I wouldn't like to say what else. Violent! Not many people under-stand just *how* violent!'

Flickers of curiosity alternated with prim blankness in Mrs MacLean's eyes. 'And aren't there dusts and pollens—horse's hair and that sort of thing?'

'All kinds. I don't even know the lot. But they're not all as *violent*.'

There was a silence while Mrs MacLean with a soft white napkin gently, gently brushed away the scratchy toast-crumbs which lay between them in the centre of the table.

'Do you find people sympathetic then?' she enquired at last.

Veitch gave a short laugh. 'Mrs MacLean—when, may I ask, have people ever been sympathetic to anything out of the ordinary?'

'I suppose that's true.'

They both turned their heads to look out onto the Edinburgh street, already crowded with people going to work. There was a stiffish breeze—visitors from the south, like Veitch, used the word 'gale'—and those going eastwards had their teeth bared against it and their eyes screwed up in a grimace which made them appear very unsympathetic indeed. On the pavement below their window, a well-dressed man stooped in the swirling dust to unwind a strip of paper which had wrapped itself round his ankle like a dirty bandage. They heard his curse even with the window shut. This sudden glimpse of the cruelly grimacing human beings, separated from them only by glass, gave them a stronger sense of the warmth within. Human sympathy too. Mrs MacLean was a widow. It was a street of widows—some of them old and grim, living at street level between lace curtains and brown pots of creeping plants, some of them young and gay behind high window boxes where the hardiest flowers survived the Scottish summer. Mrs MacLean was neither of these. She was an amiable woman in her middle years, and lately she had begun to wonder whether sympathy was not her strongest point.

In the weeks that followed Veitch's status changed from lodger to paying guest, from paying guest, by a more subtle transformation shown only in Mrs MacLean's softer expression and tone of voice, to a guest who, in the long run, paid. They talked together in the mornings and evenings. Sometimes they talked about his work which was in the refrigerating business. But as often as not the conversation veered round to eggs. As a subject the egg had everything. It was brilliantly self-contained and clean, light but meaty, delicate yet full of complex far-reaching associations—psychological, sexual, physiological, philosophical. There was almost nothing on earth that did not start off with an egg in some shape or form. And when they had discussed eggs in the abstract Veitch would tell her about all those persons who had tried their best to poison him, coming after him with their great home-made cakes rich with egg, boggy egg puddings nourishing to the death, or the stiff drifts of meringue topping custards yellow as cowslip. It was all meant kindly, no doubt, yet how could one be sure? After all, he'd never made any secret of it. But people who called themselves human were continually dropping eggs here and there into his life as deliberately as anarchists depositing eggs of explosive into unsuspecting communities.

'You'd be amazed,' he said. 'Even persons who profess to love one aren't above mixing in the odd egg—just to test, just to make absolutely certain one isn't trying it on.'

'Oh heavens—Oh no!' cried Mrs MacLean. 'Love! Love in one hand and poison in the other!'

'That's just about it,' Veitch agreed. 'With my chemical make-up you get to know a lot about human nature, and sometimes the things you learn you'd far, far rather never have known.'

By early spring Mrs MacLean and her lodger were going out together in his car on a Saturday, sometimes to a quiet tea-room on the outskirts of the city or further out into the country where they would stretch their legs for a bit before having a leisurely high tea in some small hotel where, as often as not, Mrs MacLean would inform waitress and sometimes waiters about Harry Veitch's egg allergy. Then Veitch would sit back and watch the dishes beckoned or waved away, would hear with an impassive face the detailed discussions of what had gone into the make-up of certain pies and rissoles, and would occasionally see Mrs MacLean reject a bare-faced egg outright. He never entered into such discussions. It almost seemed as though he had let her take over the entire poisonous side of his life. On the whole, he seemed to enjoy the dining-room dramas when all heads would turn and silence fall at the sound of Mrs MacLean's voice rising above the rest: 'No, no, it's poison to him! Not at all—boiled, scrambled, poached—it's all the same. Poison!' But once in a while the merest shadow of irritation would cross his face, and on some evenings he drove home almost in silence, a petulant droop to his lips.

'But you did enjoy your supper, didn't you?'

'Quite.'

'And you didn't mind me saying that about the egg?'

'Why should I?'

'You see, I actually saw them through the door—whipping it up—even after I'd warned them. Even after I'd told them it was actual poison to you. They were whipping it up in a bowl—with a fork.'

'Exactly.'

'What do you mean—"exactly"?'

'I mean your description is obviously correct.'

'How stilted you make it sound. Why don't you relax—make yourself comfy?'

'While I'm driving? You want me to relax into this ditch for instance?' Very touchy he could be, almost disagreeable at times. But then he was allergic, wasn't he? A sensitive type.

Before long Mrs MacLean had given up eating eggs herself. She wouldn't actually say they disagreed with her nowadays. That would be carrying it too far. But how could what was poison to him be nourishment to her? She hardly noticed when the usual invitations to suppers with neighbours began to dwindle under her too vivid descriptions of eggs and their wicked ways. She was too busy devising new, eggless dishes for Veitch. By early summer she and her guest had explored the surrounding countryside and every out-of-the-way restaurant in the city. Mrs MacLean gave him a great deal. It was not only his stomach she tended. She gave him bit by bit, but steadily and systematically, the history of Edinburgh as they went about. 'You're standing on History!' she would exclaim, nudging him off a piece of paving-stone. Or, as he stood wedged momentarily in the archway of a close on a wild afternoon, her voice would rise triumphantly above the howlings and whistlings around him: 'You're breathing in History! Look at that inscription above your head!' He would step up cautiously onto slabs of wintry stone from which famous clerics had declaimed, sit in deep seats where queens had sat, while Mrs MacLean held forth herself. All the teaching experience of her younger days came back to her as she talked, and often when tourists were around a small crowd would gather and ask questions. One or two Americans might jot down her answers in notebooks and occasionally a photo was taken of her standing in the doorway of St Giles or with one elbow laid nonchalantly on the parapet of the Castle Esplanade. Sometimes Veitch got lost. He got lost for hours and hours, and after much searching Mrs MacLean would have to return home alone. It took a lot out of her. At times History really hurt.

By late autumn Veitch had got his job well in hand. It was expanding, he said. Really bursting its bounds. Mrs MacLean knew little about his job, but she identified with it and she was not one to stand in the way of his work. When he spoke of expansion and bursting bounds, however, refrigeration was the last thing she had in mind, but rather some mature and still seductive woman bursting through all the freezing restrictions into a boundless new life. But she felt a difference. He was not so available now. He worked late and had little appetite for the original eggless dishes she set before him at supper. Worst of all, when a few days of unexpected Indian Summer began, a sudden spate of work took him away from her for longer and longer sessions. He began to be busy on Saturday afternoons, and even on Sundays he found he must use the car to make certain contacts he'd had no time for during the week. Reluctantly, Mrs MacLean decided that until the pressure of work slackened she would simply take a few bus trips on her own while the weather lasted. She set off, good-naturedly enough, on solitary sprees at the weekends —as often as not ending up with tea alone in some country hotel or seaside café where they had been earlier in the year. She still had supper and breakfast talks with her lodger, but mostly it was herself talking to keep her spirits up. She never mentioned History now. Egg-talk was also out. In the bleak evenings she secretly yearned for the buttery omelettes and feathery soufflés she had whipped up in the old days.

One Saturday afternoon she took the bus right out into the country to an old farmhouse where they had been a couple of months ago. It stood well back from the road amongst low, gorse-covered hills, and winding through these were deep paths where you could walk for miles in a wide circle, eventually coming out again near the house. Mrs MacLean decided to take her walk after tea. There was nobody in the place but her spirits were rather higher than usual. She ate haddocks in egg sauce, pancakes, scones and plum jam and as she ate she talked on and off to the friendly girl who served it. She even managed to bring in a reference to a great friend of hers who was unable to eat egg in any shape or form, and for a while they discussed the peculiarities of people and their eating habits. Then she set off for her walk.

It was one of the last warm days of the year—so warm that after half an hour or so she had to remove her coat, and a mile further on uphill she was glad to lean on a gate and look down to where, far off, she could just see the line of the Crags and Arthur's Seat with the blue haze of the city beneath. Near at hand the weeds of the fields and ditches were a bright yellow, yet creamed here and there in the hollows with low swathes of ground-mist. But something jerked her from her trance. She realised with a shock that she was not the only person enjoying the surroundings. Unseen, yet close to her behind the hedge, there were human rustlings and murmurings. She bent further over the gate and craned her head sideways to look. Seated on a tartan rug which came from the back of her own drawing-room sofa was Harry Veitch, his arm round the waist of a young woman whose hair was yellow as egg yolk. Their legs lay together, the toes of their shoes pointed towards one another, and Mrs MacLean noted that under a dusting of seeds and straws Veitch's shoes still bore traces of the very shine she had put there the night before. For a few seconds longer she stood staring. From the distance of a field or two away it would have seemed to any onlooker that these three persons were peacefully enjoying the last moments of an idyllic afternoon together. Then, Mrs MacLean suddenly lifted her hands from the top of the gate as though it had been electrically wired, turned swiftly and silently down the way she had come and made for the bus route back to the city.

Sunday breakfast had always been a more prolonged affair than on other days, and the next morning Harry Veitch came downstairs late in green and white striped pyjamas under a maroon dressing-gown. He looked at ease, and on his forehead was a faint glow which was nothing more nor less than the beginning and end of a Scottish sunburn. For the weather had broken. Mrs MacLean greeted him, seated sideways at the table as usual to show that she had already eaten. But now Veitch was showing a strange hesitation in lowering himself into his seat. For some moments he seemed to find extra-ordinary difficulty in removing his gaze from the circumference of the plate before him, as though its rim were magnetic to the eyes which, try as they might to burst aside, were kept painfully riveted down dead on its centre. But at last, with tremendous effort, he man-aged to remove them. Casually, smiling, he looked round the room at curtains, pot-plant, firescreen, sideboard—greeting them first before he spoke. And when he spoke it was in an equable voice, polite and low-pitched.

'Mrs MacLean, I can't take egg. Sorry.'

'Can't take?' There was a cold surprise in her voice. Veitch allowed himself one darting glance at the smooth boiled egg on his plate and another at the mottled oval of his landlady's face, and again let his eyes roam easily about the room.

'No, it's an allergy,' he said.

Mrs MacLean now got up with the teapot in her hand and poured out a cup for her lodger. 'I don't quite catch your meaning, Mr Veitch,' she said, coming round and standing with the spout cocked at his ear as though she would pour the brown brew into his skull.

'An allergy, Mrs MacLean,' said Veitch, speaking with the distinct enunciation and glassy gaze of one practising his vocabulary in a foreign tongue. 'I have an allergy to egg.'

'Do you mean you want special treatment here, Mr Veitch?'

'Mrs MacLean, I am allergic to egg. Egg is poison to me. Deadly poison!'

Mrs MacLean's face was blank, her voice flat as she answered:

'Then why should you stay here? In an egg-house.'

'An egg-house!' The vision of a monstrous six-compartment egg-box had flashed before Veitch's eyes.

'Yes, I love eggs,' she replied simply. 'Eggs are my favourite. I shall order two dozen eggs tomorrow. There will be eggs, fresh eggs, for breakfast, for lunch, for supper. Did you know there are ways of drinking eggs? One can even break an egg into the soup for extra nourishment. I have books crammed with recipes specifically for the egg. There are a thousand and one ways. . . .'

'Poison!' cried Harry Veitch on a fainter note.

'Yes, indeed . . . if you stay. A thousand and one ways . . .' she agreed. And for a start—with the expression of an irate conjurer—she produced a second boiled egg out of a bowl and nimbly bowled it across the table towards her shrinking lodger.

ROBIN JENKINS

Exile

About half-past twelve with a glass of sherry in her hand she went up on to the roof for, as she told herself, another stimulating look at the magnificent vista but really, as she knew, to watch out for the postman on his red motor-cycle.

Though it was mid-February the sun was warm and the sky blue. To the north soared the great pink lump of Montgo, reminding her a little of Suilven. To the east, bluer than the sky, stretched the Mediterranean all the way past the Balearics and Sardinia to Italy. Westward, beyond the groves of oranges and almonds, rose fold upon fold of hazy hills. Immediately below, to the south, lay the great plain of wild grass, small ploughed patches, and abandoned groves, frequented by flocks of small birds. Since this was Saturday she ought that afternoon to walk there calling on the birds to hide in holes or fly off to the hills, for tomorrow many Spaniards would come, after church, and shoot with alien zest every little living creature. She had come upon three murdered hedgehogs.

All round were blocks of flats gleaming in the sun. Like her own they were almost empty in winter. Except for the young Englishman and his Spanish girl friend she was alone in a building with twenty-six apartments. In every block, and most were much bigger than hers, were two or three British people, retired, come to live longer in the sunshine. In her wanderings whenever she met any of them she always found that, instead of having a great deal to say to them, as fellow castaways, no, as fellow adventurers, she had very little. They all seemed anxious, unsure, and even morose. A Tory all her life, she had nevertheless been shocked when the man next to her at the ghastly Christmas party at the restaurant *Casa Luis* had remarked that what Britain needed was a Franco to make the workers work harder and strike less.

All the time she was on the look-out for the postman. Suddenly her hand was shaking so much that she had to put down the glass. Her eyes filled with tears. Angry with herself, she twittered back at the house martins which came flitting over her head.

Unfortunately they reminded her of other birds in another place. In spite of her resolution not to let herself be seduced and tormented by nostalgic memories, she remembered the pigeons that used to fly down from the roofs to the playground after the children had gone in, and help themselves to the crusts, crisps, sticky papers, and 'douts' of apples left behind. She had stood in the doorway with the whistle in her hand and, though she had not known it at the time and therefore could not have shown it on her face, had loved those pigeons dearly.

Mr Proudfoot, the janitor, had apologised. 'I ken they're messy things. Miss Kilsyth was complaining the ither day aboot splashes on her windaes. But to tell you the truth, Miss Struthers, I like them. So do the weans.'

She had thought him a surly, discontented man, always grumbling about his union rights being infringed.

She remembered him too now with love.

A year or so ago, when she still got letters, she had been told in at least three that he had died suddenly of a stroke.

At last she heard and saw the postman. Yonder he was, a glitter of sunshine, speeding past the parador with its big palm trees, and past the beach deserted now except for some stray dogs. He stopped at the block of flats where the couple from Peterborough waited, often in vain, for a letter from their daughter in America or their son in Felixstowe. Soon he was on his way again, making brief stops at other blocks of flats, among them the one in which the woman from Yorkshire and her eight-year-old daughter were living. They had arrived only three weeks ago. Miss Struthers had met them in the supermarket. The woman had complained about the apartment she had rented: it faced the north and got no sun. The silent pale-faced child seemed to be no company for her.

The postman was chatting with the portero beside a big bougainvillea. They were in no hurry. They were at ease in their native sunshine. The many connections that anchored them so safely to their native place were unbroken.

Miss Struthers remembered the shops under those roofs where the pigeons had waited. Doig the butcher's. Jamieson the licensed grocer's. McKail the confectioner's. McAdam the baker's. Meikle the fruiterer's. And all the others, including the two public houses. She could picture in her mind the men and women who served in them. It was as if she had seen them just yesterday and not three years ago.

They had all said how lucky she was and how they envied her. Who with any sense would want to stay in dull, rainy, cold Scotland when there was the chance to live in sunny Spain? Those who knew her well, or rather those close to her, for nobody had known her all that well, had pointed out that the arthritis which had begun to make walking a bit painful would be cured or alleviated in the warmth.

Only one person had expressed misgivings. That was Mr Leitch, who had done odd jobs in her garden. In his brusque way he had said she was daft to go and bury herself among folk she didn't know, whose language three-year-olds could speak better than she. How was she going to pass the time, for God's sake? 'Well, for one thing, I could get to know Spaniards.' 'Not at your age, Miss Struthers. Nae disrespect meant. If onything I'm aulder than you. At oor age it's hard enough getting to ken folk that speak the same language as oorselves. Tak my advice. Bide here where you've spent maist o' your life and where you're kent.'

In spite of his pessimism he had wished her good luck.

As she watched the postman climb on to his motor-cycle again she wondered desperately who might have written to her. When she first came here she had had a letter almost every week. Colleagues, members of the Women's Business Club, neighbours, and acquaintances had written. She had eagerly and promptly answered every letter. As time had passed, though, her having exiled herself was no longer a novelty, letters had become scarcer and scarcer. Those that did come were brief and casual. She had become aware that people whose lives had seemed dull and who indeed had often grumbled about that dullness were really so engrossed in their own affairs that it was easy for them to forget her.

Still, three weeks ago she had written to Margaret Lennox inviting her to spend her Easter holidays in Javea. Of all her colleagues she had liked Margaret best. In her invitation she had tried hard not to appear to be begging for an acceptance. Margaret too had never married. As the saying went, she had no ties. It should be easy for her to uproot herself for ten days.

Leaning over the parapet she watched the postman roar up the steep drive. She had learned to tell from the sound of the engine whether or not he was getting ready to stop.

She realised she was sobbing with anxiety.

'Don't be a wean, Jean Struthers,' she said sternly. 'If he goes by what of it? Some other day he'll stop.'

Yet, still silly as a wean, she was almost dizzy with hope and expectation when he stopped, climbed off, and took from his pannier bag an envelope. It was larger than the usual airmail letter, and it was brown, not blue. More than likely it was a circular for one of the absentee owners.

Without glancing up—why should it occur to him that he could be relieving a siege of loneliness that had lasted over six weeks?—the postman, whistling cheerfully, disappeared into the building.

Since there was no resident portero he had to put letters in the pigeon holes in the entrance hall. It had been peeping into Mr Williams' pigeon hole, and worse still by reading a postcard there, that Miss Struthers had discovered that his lady friend with the brown gypsy eyes and long earrings was known as Señorita Puig and not Mrs Williams.

The postman reappeared, climbed on his motor-cycle again, and shot off.

She did not rush downstairs. Drawing deep breaths, she forced herself to enjoy once again the sunlit view. Anyone who had known her would have thought that she was still the same Miss Struthers, calm, dignified, and self-possessed. They would never have guessed how her heart was racing, and how close to weeping she was.

Taking time to pick up the sherry glass and to drink what was left in it she went down to her flat. It was furnished in bright colours. The only piece of furniture that she had brought from home was an oak writing-desk that had belonged to her father. In it she kept all the letters she had received. They did not make a fat bundle.

She poured herself more sherry and slowly drank it, tapping with her fingers on the writing-desk. This was, she reflected, her third sherry of the morning. At lunch she would drink two, perhaps three, glasses of wine. In the evening, listening to the BBC or trying to for often reception was bad, she would have at least one brandy and water. She was drinking far too much. Her memories of home were most poignant when she was befuddled.

There was no lift, since there were only four storeys. Her flat was on the top. She went down the stairs not particularly slowly, for excessive slowness would itself have been a sign of impatience, but at a normal pace as if she was going to the supermarket. Her arthritic knee hurt, but she was used to that now.

Great joy, the big brown envelope was in her pigeon hole. But sometimes the postman in his hurry made mistakes. She had been disappointed more than once.

Wonder of wonders, the name on the envelope was hers. She did not recognise the handwriting but that did not matter. It was not as legible handwriting as it should have been but that did not matter either. The postmark was blurred but she thought it was her home town's. The envelope was quite bulky. Perhaps it was full of cuttings from the *Observer*, her home town's local newspaper. When she had been asked if she would like a copy sent to her every week she had, too curtly, refused. Where was the sense, she had thought, of beginning a new life hampered by intrusions from the old.

Up in her flat again, on the balcony that faced the Mediterranean, she slit open the envelope with a paper-knife made in Toledo. Inside was another envelope, and a letter so short that she almost whimpered with disappointment.

The address at the top was that of her school.

'Dear Miss Struthers,

I hope you'll excuse me writing to you. I'm a newcomer to the staff. The class I've been given was the one you had when you left. So they're eight-year-olds now. The other day they asked me if they could write a letter to you. So I said they could. Not all of them did. Some changed their minds and wanted to write to Dougal of the *Magic Roundabout* instead. I'm sure you'll understand. I thought you might like to see those that were written to you. I've not corrected the grammar or spelling. Some of what they say may look as if it has nothing to do with you, Miss Struthers, but I think that in everything young children do and say there is a lovely relevance.

Yours sincerely,
Alison Graham.'

Perhaps it was not Alison but Aileen. The writing hardly deserved four out of ten. The grammar too wasn't impeccable.

' "Lovely relevance", indeed!' murmured Miss Struthers, remembering many infantile stupidities. Then in a moment the phrase struck her as beautifully apposite. No doubt Miss Graham had untidy hair and skirts too short, but she certainly understood children.

Miss Struthers took out one of the letters. It was written on the page of a school jotter.

Dear Miss Struthers,

I think you would like to no that I don't pick my nose any more you used to check me We have a new kitten called Snowy.

Jhon Garvie.'

She remembered him well, a nervous inattentive sandy-haired boy, son of a builder's labourer. God help her, she had made him sit with his hands behind his back.

She had not cherished him as much as she should.

She took out another. The writing was much neater.

'Dear Miss Struthers,

My big sister was in Spain and saw a boolfight. There was lots of blood. Oranges come from Spain. I hope your leg is better. I think you are lucky to be in Spain for its raining today and we wont get our game of rounders in the playground.

Mavis Hunter.'

She remembered Mavis too, very pert, plump-cheeked, always with a fresh ribbon in her black hair. Her father was the town chamberlain. He wanted her to go to University one day.

There were at least twenty more. A gift of inexhaustible riches. Reading them, and re-reading them, would make exile no matter how long it lasted not only worth-while but also far easier to thole.

ALAN SPENCE

Sailmaker

It was a fine poem my father told me, a poem about a yacht.

> Ah had a *yacht*
> Y'*ought* tae see it
> Put it in the *canal*
> Ye *can all* see it

I thought he had written the poem himself, but he had learned it from his own father. He was simply passing it on.

The poem had a special meaning for me because I did have a yacht. As yet it had no mast, no rigging, no sails, but my father had promised to set that right.

My father was a Sailmaker. The fact that he was working as a credit-collector instead made no difference to that. To others he might be no more than The Tick Man, a knock at the door on a Friday night, someone to be avoided when money was short. But that was no part of my reality. He was My Father, and if anyone asked me what he did, I would tell them proudly that he was a Sailmaker, in much the same way I would have answered if he had been a Pirate or an Explorer. The word itself rang, in a way that 'Tick Man' never could. It echoed back across time. For as long as there had been ships there must have been Sailmakers.

My father had inherited a craft, an ancient art. His sailmaking tools were kept in a canvas bag that he had made himself. There were marlinspikes, some of hard polished wood, and some, wooden-handled, of shining steel; there was a set of thick heavy needles, and for pushing them through, a leather palm with a hole for the thumb. Often I would play with them, wielding the spikes as dagger, sword and club, pretending the needles were arrowheads and the palm some primitive glove worn only by hunters or warriors. In quieter moods I might even pretend to be a Sailmaker myself.

I never played at being a Tick Man. That was a different kind of job altogether. Sailmaking was a trade, and to have a trade was something special. It was to be an initiate, a master of secrets and skills.

To be a Tick Man was to be up and down stairs all day, covering close after close, trying to collect payments on clothes and furniture bought long ago on credit, trying to sell more to keep the whole process going. The never-never.

There was nothing in my father's battered briefcase—a set of ledgers, some leaflets, a pen—to compare with those sailmaker's tools; except perhaps for his torch, heavy and balanced with a shiny metal barrel. My father needed it to find his way up some of the darker, more dismal closes where the stairhead lights were always smashed. And more than once he'd been grateful just for the weight of it when he'd been attacked for the money he was carrying, the little he'd managed to collect. So far he had been lucky, and the worst he had got out of it was a bloody nose. At one end of the torch was a dent where he'd connected with some thick skull in fighting his way clear.

I sometimes used the torch to help me explore the bed-recess in our room. That was where I had found the sailmaking tools. The recess was a clutter of old junk, piled to the ceiling with furniture and clothes, cardboard boxes full of books and toys, the residue and jetsam of years. My mother called it the Glory Hole. I liked nothing better than to wriggle my way in through a tunnel of chairlegs to the very centre of the recess where there was space enough to stand upright. And from there I could climb and rummage and ransack, forever unearthing something new, or something old and long forgotten —an old comic I hadn't read in years, a toy I'd thought was lost. It was the one place that was mine. Once I'd burrowed in there I was safe, I was hidden. I could look out as from deep in the heart of a cave. The Glory Hole.

It was in the Glory Hole too that I found the yacht, wedged under a sideboard. Triumphant, I dragged it out into the light. It was just a hulk, three feet long with an iron keel. The varnished surface was chipped and scraped and scarred. But already I could see it, fresh-painted, with a new set of sails, scudding across the pond at Elder Park. I carried it carefully through to the kitchen, lovingly cleaned it with a wet rag.

'What ye doin wi that auld thing?' asked my mother.

'Ah'm gonnae get ma Daddy tae fix it up.'

'Then we can all sail away in it,' she said, laughing. 'Away tae Never Never Land!'

Never Never Land was where my father was going to take us when he won a lot of money, from the football pools, or from betting on horses and dogs. He had always been trying, as long as I could remember. 'Trying the Pools' was a magical game that in some mysterious way could make us rich. It had once conjured an image of my father fishing in deep pools of water. And although I had later been told that this had no reality, the image, at some level, had remained.

The other betting had less of a magic. Sometimes I would take my father's line to the back-close bookie. And the bookie scared me. His pitch was in a close that was dark and smelly, and there I would have to queue, everybody furtive, looking out for the police. In my young head, bookie was an echo of bogey. He was the back-close bogeyman, sinister and mean. And somehow this bogey could keep our money or give us back more. He had the power. For writing out his lines, my father used a secret name, a nom de plume, because the whole game was illegal. The name he used was Mainsail, carried over from his sailmaking days.

He still had faith that he would one day win a fortune. Then that mainsail would be set, and away we would sail.

There was a song I liked in those days; I used to hear it on the radio:

> Red sails in the sunset
> Way out on the sea . . .

That was the way I could see my yacht. Red sails.

When I asked my father to fix it up for me, he was tired after work. But he said he would rig it out whenever he had time and they could spare the money for materials. I asked him when that would be and he said 'Wait and see'.

My mother told me the yacht had belonged to my cousin Jacky. His family had emigrated to America years before and all the toys he couldn't take with him had been shared out among his cousins. The yacht had been passed on to me, only to lie forgotten until now.

Because the yacht had been Jacky's, I felt that now it was a link with America, where he had gone. And that pleased me. America was a fabled place, like Never Never Land, a place of cowboys and gangsters, prairies and canyons, skyscraper cities and giant cars. From America, at Christmas, I had been sent a parcel, a fat bundle of comics. They were all in colour, not black-and-white like the ones I could buy here. Superman and Blackhawk, Donald Duck and Mickey Mouse. America was colour.

One Saturday afternoon, my Uncle Billy was visiting and I had the yacht out on the floor. Overturned, with the deck face down, the hulk could be a submarine, or a hill for toy soldiers to climb, or a giant shark, the keel its back fin.

'Where d'ye get the boat?' asked Uncle Billy.

'Used tae be Jacky's,' I said.

'He dragged it out that Glory Hole,' said my mother.

'Ah'm gonnae fix it up,' said my father, 'when ah've got the time.'

'Ah could paint it if ye like,' said Uncle Billy. He worked as a painter's labourer.

He took it away with him that night and brought it back a week or so later. The hull was painted a pure shining white, the deck a light brown, the keel royal blue. I held it, amazed and unbelieving. It was like a whole new boat, unrecognisable, reborn.

After that I must have pestered my father, kept at him to get down to rigging out the yacht. I was aching to see it sail.

But always he was tired from work. Fixing the yacht, he said, was a difficult job. It would take time. Materials were expensive. He didn't have the right tools. But someday he would do it.

'When?' I would ask.

'Wait and see.'

That went on for weeks. And months. And gradually I stopped asking. The yacht went back to being a hulk. A hill for toy soldiers, a submarine, a shark.

In the end I forgot about making it sail, and it found its way back into the Glory Hole.

*

The next time I saw the yacht was long years later.

It was a hard time then. My mother had died. My father had no job. A dark time. Across the road from us was a pub on the corner, and next door to that was a betting shop. The street bookie was no longer outlawed and had opened up a place of his own. Between the betting shop and the pub, my father passed most of his days. Afternoons in the shop, mornings and evenings in the pub. Often enough, though, he had no money for either.

This night I remember, the last of our coal had run out. My father's dole money wasn't due till the next day. It must have been January, the bleakest part of winter, miserable and dank, wind shaking the panes, a damp patch spreading on the ceiling.

And there we sat, freezing, wrapped up in coats and scarves, trying to keep warm. We had nothing much to say to each other in those days. He was a middle-aged man, unable to cope with the death of his wife. I was in the first wretched throes of adolescence. We might have come from different universes. We sat facing each other, separate, at either side of the empty hearth, letting the blare of the radio fill the silence between us.

Then my father had an idea. He thought we could dig out some of the old sticks of furniture packed away in the room, break it up and make a fire.

That meant going in again to the Glory Hole. I hadn't been in there in years. I had grown too big to crawl in and under and through. It was more chaotic than ever, darker, more crammed with junk. The dust had settled thicker. I took down the curtain that hung over the doorway and I eased my way in. The front of the recess was blocked with two old kitchen chairs. Piled on top of them were a few tatty cushions, a cardboard box and a stack of old magazines called *Enquire Within*. The chairs and the magazines would burn so I passed them out to my father. The cushions could be thrown out another time. The cardboard box I brought out, to investigate in the light.

My father had the fire going quickly. He tore up a few of the magazines, scrumpled up the pages in the grate. He smashed up the chairs with a cleaver, placed some splintered bits on top of the paper; then he lit it, and we watched it catch and flare and roar; and we grinned at each other as we warmed ourselves.

'That's more like it,' he said. 'That's the stuff!'

In the cardboard box were more old papers, a tartan biscuit-tin full of buttons and elastic bands, a few toy soldiers and cars, and my father's old torch. The surface of the torch was dull, had lost its shine. The button was stiff and it wouldn't light.

'Batteries'll be dead,' said my father.

'Pity,' I said. 'Could've used it tae see intae the recess.'

I unscrewed the end of the torch and looked in. The inside had rusted and the batteries were stuck, rotted, covered with pale stuff like green mould.

'What makes it go like that?' I asked.

'Don't know,' said my father. 'Just time. Just . . . time.'

The fire blazed and crackled, but the wood burned quick. So back I went into the recess to bring out more.

This time I took a candle, to see further in. I shifted a mattress and the dust I stirred up made me choke and cough. I passed out a wooden stool, a bagatelle board and the headboard from a bed. And I brought back out with me a little canvas bag.

Again my father set to breaking the wood and stoking the fire.

In the canvas bag were his sailmaking tools, the marlinspikes, the needles, the palm. He looked at them long and he started reminiscing, going back. He had worked on the *Queen Mary*, made awnings and tarpaulins, made gun-covers for destroyers during the war. He told me of his apprenticeship when he was my age, how hard those days had been. He looked at the tools and it came back to him. Then he put the wooden marlinspikes on the fire. They were made from lignum vitae, the hardest wood. They were solid and they burned slow.

'Thae other tools can go in the midden sometime,' he said. I put them away and went back once more into the recess. Most of the space was taken up by a sideboard. I tried to shift it and managed to dislodge a mirror that shattered to pieces on the floor.

'Seven years' bad luck,' said my father, then, 'Still. Cannae get much worse than it's been, eh!'

He took the frame from the broken mirror, shook the last bits of

F

glass from it. 'This'll burn,' he said. Then together we struggled and heaved out the sideboard. It was too old to sell, he said, or to be of any use, so it might as well go in the fire with the rest.

As he set to with the cleaver once more, chopping and splitting, he started again to remember back. The sideboard was all that was left of the furniture they'd bought when they were married.

'Got it in Galpern's,' he said. 'That's him that was the Lord Provost . . . Solid stuff it is too.'

He fingered the carved handle on a door, the fancy beading round the edge. 'Nobody takes the care any more,' he said. 'Nobody's interested in this old stuff.'

He was talking himself back into being sad.

'Seems a shame tae break it up,' he said. 'Still. It's a shame tae freeze as well, isn't it!' He split the door into strips, broke the strips in half to fit the fire.

'Ah remember when we bought this,' he said, his eyes glazing over as he watched it burn. His voice was growing maudlin again, drifting into sentimentality. I couldn't take it, and went back into the room.

All the wood was gone now from the recess. We had stripped it bare. But there on the floor, behind where the sideboard had been, was the hull of that old yacht. I picked it up and dusted it off, carried it through to the kitchen.

'Remember this?' I asked my father.

'Oh aye,' he said. 'Yer uncle Billy painted it.'

'You were always gonnae fix it up for me,' I said. 'Ah could always imagine it. Like that song. Red sails in the sunset.'

'Ah always meant to,' said my father. 'Just . . .'

'Just never did,' I said.

'Story a ma life,' he said.

Then I wedged the yacht into the grate. The flames licked round it. The paint began to blister and bubble. Then the wood of the hull caught and burned. And the yacht had a sail of flame. And it sailed in the fire, like a Viking longboat, out to sea in a blaze with the body of a dead chief. Off to Valhalla. Up Helly-A!

And the wood burned to embers, and the iron keel clattered on to the hearth.

DOROTHY K. HAYNES

Changeling

The witch had been sitting on the gargoyle all day. Moreen had watched, saying nothing, while mother combed her hair and tied the ribbon and said, 'There! Now stand quiet at the window till mummy gets ready.' She had kept quite still, crushing flies under the curtain, and sometimes looking at the people in the street; but always she looked again at the gargoyle where the witch sat drowsing, with her hair like nettle blossom, and her shoulders hunched high like wings.

'What are you always looking at?' said her mother, abstract in a haze of face powder and two kinds of perfume.

'That gargoyle,' said Moreen, and her voice caught with a sound like a sob. 'Isn't it funny?'

Her mother went over. 'Oh, that one? Can you see its face from here, darling? Your eyes must be better than mine. I'll borrow daddy's opera glasses and look some time.'

Moreen knew that there was something queer about her. Her mother had never mentioned the witch, and yet there it was, a black hump arching out into the sky. And it was nonsense not to be able to see the gargoyle's face. It was grinning, with whiskers parallel to the wide lips. It had a face like a door knocker, and round ears. The witch was even clearer. Moreen knew that the eyes were looking at her, even though they were shut, and that the hands were green as verdigris, and crippled with warts. Moreen did not like the thought of the witch being feminine. You could not think of it. Undressing a witch, there would be nothing under the black clothes, nothing but a broomstick, and a short stalk for the head to go on.

In the afternoon, at tea in Mrs Black's house, she sometimes forgot. There was a bronze canopy over the fire, and it was nice to see the fire, even though it was too warm. The carpet at Mrs Black's was fawn, and everything else was fawn and new, and not used very much. Mrs Black had only been in her bungalow a little while. The bungalow was different from Moreen's house, new and uncracked, but not nearly so solid.

Biting her chocolate biscuit at tea, or whispering to her mother, and being led to the bathroom, Moreen had quick, sickening memories of what might be waiting on top of the gargoyle when she saw it again, but she put the thought away from her. At five o'clock, Mrs Black said goodbye to them at the gate. After the quiet of the new road, with its villas and rockeries, the High Street was bedlam with red buses and red freestone houses and the sun soon to be red with setting. Moreen looked up at the church clock. 'Half past five,' she said, but what she wanted to say was, 'Oh, mother, the witch is still there!' Her mother could not see the witch. She had shifted a little, but was still asleep, like a lump of carrion festering on a rock.

Moreen wanted her mother to sit with her at bedtime. She looked so feverish that she got her own way. Mother spoke about sending for the doctor. 'I don't like it,' she kept saying. 'Can't you tell mummy what's wrong? Is your head aching? Your eyes are far too bright, dear.' At last sleep came, breathing in from the open window in dark sighs. The child looked very young and babyish. The woman put the night-light on the table and stood still, watching the dull orange tongue lapping up the gloom. Ten o'clock. Moreen should have been asleep hours ago. One had to be firm with children. The woman yawned. Ten o'clock.

The moon was a thin rind curled low in the sky. The spire was squint on the church, and all the houses were leaning backwards. The lighted windows were at all angles, like red postage stamps. Smoke went sideways, a dim black flag in the night.

'I'm seeing things as if my eyes were crossed,' thought Moreen. The bare cliff of the steeple shot out the gargoyle like a dangerous ledge. There was no witch, nothing but space, and a sky the deep colour of bluebells. But below the window came a scrabbling like knives scratching along a plate, and a green hand like verdigris clutched at the sill. It was a palsied hand crippled with warts, but it clung with nail and sinew, and raised the witch's head over the sill. Moreen choked into a little whimper, because the witch's eyes were open now, and looking at her.

'I'm old,' said the witch, getting her knee over the sill. 'I'm nearly done. I had to climb that last bit.'

'Yes,' said Moreen, but she wanted to scream for her mother.

The wind clutched the candlewick, and tweaked off the waving tongue. 'You were watching me,' said the witch. 'You looked up at me at half past five.'

'Yes,' said Moreen. Her hands and feet were cold under the covers.

'I've come for you,' said the witch. 'I don't want to frighten you. It's not me that wants you, it's the little people.'

'No. I don't want to go! I'll scream!' The witch was horrible with the many horrors of the old, the shawlies who swear at Moses and smell of gin, the cretins who gape and do not understand, and the fusty poor who never wash. 'I'll scream for my mother, and she'll push you out into the street, you nasty old pig!'

The witch stepped back and did not fall. Solid pillars of air held her level in space. 'You'll have to come,' she said. 'Your mother can't help. I thought all little girls wanted to go to fairyland!'

'I want my mother!'

'Your mother won't wake till morning.'

'I don't want to go!'

'No, dearie, and the changeling they've put in your little bed doesn't want to come here, either. She'll have to, though, like it or not. Your mother won't know the difference, but she won't love her the same. It's not me that says it has to be, it's the little people.'

'I want my mother. Go *away*, you dirty witch! I don't like you!'

'It's not my fault. See, the changeling's there already. She doesn't want to come here, but she's taking it better than you.'

There was a head on the pillow, a strange, fair head like her own reflection. She hated it. The face smiled from the frills, pale and stupid, the kind of face that always did as it was told. A heavy body was beside her in bed, seeming to sweat, suety. There was no room for her. She edged away, and the cold blue linoleum pressed her bare feet. The window swung towards her; the floor dropped away. The moon, curled low in the sky, dangled over the chequered tiles, and all the dogs in the street seemed to be howling. She screamed, 'Mother, mother, I don't want to go! Oh mother!' But the witch was the person who caught her hand. 'All right, dearie, I'm rested now. I won't let you fall. You won't need to see me again, unless you want to, after we get to the little people.'

She screamed. Nobody listened.

*

She had resisted the witch? 'Yes,' she said. They did not scold her, but she felt afraid of the way they talked. She hated the little people, sharp as thorns and shrill as treble chanters. She was afraid when they said she would forget. 'I don't want to forget!' she screamed. 'I want my mother! I want my mother!' She was very brave for seven years old, but she was afraid.

'You will forget your mother!' they said, chirping and dancing round about, and clapping their hands on the soles of their feet.

'You will forget your mother! You'll forget everything, you'll forget your house, you'll forget everything. You'll forget everything. But you'll always try to remember, and never quite find out what you want to remember. Serves you right!'

They were cruel and slight, nipping her on the arms out of curiosity. 'Why does it serve me right?' she sobbed. 'I want to go home! I haven't done any harm. I didn't want to come here. It was the witch brought me.'

'We sent for you, and you struggled with the witch! You struggled! You should have come when you were told!'

'I didn't want to. I didn't want to leave my mother.'

'You'll forget your mother! You'll forget everything, but you'll never stop trying to remember. Serves you right!' They were hostile, these dark little red and brown people, hostile and far too old for her. The youngest had age written on their faces; the oldest were spry and dreadful. They resented her, resented her youth and her strangeness, and the way she did not want to stay. They tormented her in little stabs of spite. She wept, and they gathered round in squeaking wonder. None of them understood how much she wanted her mother, none of them liked her.

She forgot. She forgot about everything. She sat beside a lake, thinking of summer, and the work they had made her do. She had had heavy labour among the spiked petals and the drugging scent of flowers, and she had had unpleasant tasks with bees, whose legs were clogged and clarted with pollen. It was a lifeless, hot summer, a season in a sealed sphere of glass. Beyond the glass was something she could not call to mind, and round the sphere mist was quiet and thick. She lived in a land of twilight, of low stars and dim green woods. Everything was low. Sometimes, she felt as if the sky was no higher than a ceiling.

Once the sphere had cracked and the mist had thinned. It had been on the brightest day of summer, when the sky was the colour of stone, and the sun a dull lamp burning in one corner. The sky gradually turned white. She heard a shaking rumble and a pounding regular thud which jarred her body. Shadows sketched lightly on the mist-pall, moving large like ferns magnified to fern trees. Something flickered. She was in a green and yellow landscape, with strong white light glaring on grass. Pink flowers stared at her from a bush, laughing above a collar of green leaves on thorns. She was choking as thoughts rushed over her like water.

The rumbling and pounding passed. A huge animal with a cart had gone by; its shadow inked over the view, and for a moment, very dimly, superimposed on the air and the ground, she could see the lake, and the wee people scurrying along, all unconscious. They were frail and transparent, and vanished again as the sun shone on them. She did not know which world was real.

Dog-roses and vetch bloomed bright among the green, and the road smelt of nettles and cow-dung and honeysuckle. These were strange things to her, but safe and comforting. She wanted to sob. She was very near to what she wanted to remember. Then a little boy in blue trousers tumbled through the hedge, stared at her, and said 'Ooh!' His fat hand, with black-rimmed nails, bulged above her in fleshy pillows, his fingers cut the light into four sections. The light strips grew narrower as the sound of the cart faded into flat air. It seemed as if the sky was closing with his fingers. She was sitting by the lake, with the waves like grey syrup under the mist, and the sun sinking into the crawl of the tide, to sizzle like a black ember.

*

It was autumn. Yellow leaves soaked sodden into the lake, and rain and frost raced each other over the brilliant berries. She would not work. She felt sick when she moved from the lake, and her head was a hollow iron ball, with words rolling round and knocking into each other. What the words were she did not know. She sat by the lake and poked her fingers between the pebbles, waiting for the mist to break again. The little pixie things were angry with her because she sat and dreamed all day. They grumbled. She watched them frisking and cheeping as they worked, and turned her back on them till they were tired of her sulking, and then they tried to be kind. They had wanted her to come to them, and during the long winter she would have to play with them. She would have to. Sad or dull, she would have to sing and play and be lively.

'The harvest's in!' they screamed, when the wind crisped and freshened over the gathered grain. 'The harvest's in, and you never helped us! You never helped! If you were afraid of work, it's all done now, and all we have to do in the winter is to have fun. Oh, we'll have jolly fun, when the snow comes! There won't be any flowers left, and we'll hang icicles on the branches, and sweep the snow away from under the trees, and dance mad on the bare ground. Dance like this, like this, like this!' They stamped about in front of her, clapping their hands on the soles of their feet. She turned away from them. 'I don't want to dance. I want—' She had nearly said it that time, the words that were knocking in her head. 'What—what do you want?' piped the little people, tweaking their fingers at her, deeving her. 'Oh, I hate it here! I *hate* it!' she sobbed, and they all ran away.

She went with them into the forest, the dark forest where they danced. It was blue midnight, but the frost shone white. They swept up the hoar with twigs and bristles, and danced to the snap of dry branches, clapping their hands on the soles of their feet. They danced fast and jerky, and the Northern lights swept fans and floods of mauve and crimson above the pines. Everything outside the dance was silent, except when a fircone trembled and dropped, or the lush firs lifted bloomy layers and sighed. They dragged her into the circle and spun her round. She felt cold. Her feet went heavy with desire for rest, and she tripped clumsily. They pushed her on and on; she sank to the ground and screamed at them. 'She is no good to us,' they muttered among themselves. 'She is no good. We'd be better without her.' They turned to her and scolded. 'You could have been happy here, but you'll never be happy now. It's your own fault; you struggled with the witch. You struggled too much!'

'What witch?' she said. 'I don't remember a witch. There's something—I don't know.'

'She's no good,' said the little people. 'She won't play. She won't work, and she won't play. We will send her back again.'

So they let her sit by the lake a while longer. One day the witch appeared, older and a little more weary. The nettle blossom of her hair had blight on it, and the warts on her fingers were mildewed. She grinned, lolling her tongue about like lard in a hot pan. 'Moreen!' she crooned. 'It has been a long, long time, Moreen!'

The child did not know her name. The witch snatched her by the wrist and circled her in the air above the excited fairies. The little red and brown people threw stones after them, and bits of gravel pinging and stinging at their legs. Moreen wept. She hated them.

They flew through grey, choking tunnels of cloud, where the thunderclaps sulked and rested. Moreen was tired, too tired to see where she was going.

*

Where—what place? There was an emptiness, a shabbiness about it, but the line of the houses was the same. She felt inside as if she ought to know where she was, but she could not remember. The house at the corner had its windows misted over with damp, and there were lace curtains, and geraniums gasping for air against the panes. She did not want to go to that house, but there was a bell pull at the door, and letters on a brass plate, and she knew she would have to put her hands on the bell and tug it a little sideways. She knew how her fingers would grip on the black handle, but she did not understand or wonder what made her know.

She rang the bell, and her eyes went squinting over the curlicues on the stained name plate. A shadow moved behind the curtain of the glass door. When the door opened, there was an old woman standing in a long skirt, a fat, square-looking woman, with her hair piled grey over her head, all knobs and pins and the concealed teeth of combs. Her blouse was frilled, high at the neck so that it should have choked her, but it only made her sweat. The child could smell the dirty scent of her and the shut-in smell of the house. There seemed to be mice there.

'Well,' snapped the woman, 'what do you want!'

'I—I don't know.'

'Come, come; don't be silly. You wouldn't have rung the bell if you hadn't wanted something. Are you a new pupil?'

'Pupil . . .?'

'Yes. A music pupil. Do you want to learn the piano?'

'No. I don't know.'

'Tut-tut! Who sent you? What's your name?'

'I don't remember.'

'Oh dear, tiresome child! You'd better come in till I find out what you want. Wipe your feet, now!'

It was a sad, dark house. Somebody in a room was playing a monotonous little jig on a piano. The woman opened the door and leaned in, pressing her weight on the handle, and the child knew without seeing that the piano was black with a musty smell, and a girl in a pink dress sitting at it.

'Clara! You are not yet ready for the jig. Get on with your scales, as I ordered you.'

A flat, sunless voice said, 'Yes, Miss Moreen.'

They went upstairs, on a red and blue carpet. On the landing a she-dog dragged her tired body to a basket. The woman opened a door to a room where there was a big bed and a desk. It was a dirty room, full of furniture. 'Now!' she said, sitting down and wiping her moist hands. 'I suppose you *have* come for music lessons. Did your mother send you?'

'No.' She began to cry. 'I was away. They took me to a place where there was a lake, and woods, and—'

'Oh, you've been on holiday? Well, don't waste all the afternoon. If you don't want lessons, what do you want? What's your name? Where do you come from?'

The piano was faint behind the closed door, doh me soh doh soh me doh, arpeggios crawling like the fat she-dog. The child did not know what to say. She looked at the closed, steamy window. There was a dead fly on the sill, but beyond was the sky, like blue enamel, with a steeple stretching towards it. High in the stonework was a clock, and above that a gargoyle, jutting out as if it wanted to be sick. Astride its back was a witch, loose and insecure as a piece of burnt paper. The child opened her mouth and screamed.

'This is my house! I remember it by the witch sitting on the gargoyle! It's my house.'

The woman's face was like dirty suet. 'Here, that's enough! You're not well. This isn't your house. I've lived here all my life, and my mother lived here before she died. You sit quiet and I'll get you a drink of water. It's that hot—I thought there was something not quite right about you. . . .'

'But it's my house. I know it by the witch. Don't you see it?'

'No. There's no witch, dearie, it's just in your own mind you're

F*

seeing it. You sit quiet and I'll see what I can do for you. Oh dear, such a bother. . . .'

She went out of the room, leaving the door open, and the old dog waddled in. The piano was still tumbling out notes,—doh me soh doh, soh me doh—but it stopped on a black key, and the door banged. The child was watching the witch, but she could see things happening in the street. A little girl in a pink frock ran over to the doctor at the corner. Soon the window was too steamy to see any more.

MORLEY JAMIESON

Moon and the Merry Widow

'It comes on you like a dose of salts.'

So Moon Mackintosh was apt to describe his own reactions to the combination of women and moonlight. It was good for a laugh, as he would say himself, but one winter he found the process less easily explained and perfunctory, if somewhat more mysterious, than usual. This was when he met the Merry Widow.

The Flower Show Dance usually began the winter's round in Boddlehall of kirns, balls and dances on every conceivable occasion. They were genuine social events bringing together large gatherings of the young of the neighbourhood, and sometimes the not-so-young. But for Moon Mackintosh and his companions the dance was simply an opportunity for the grosser pleasure of drinking and indulging other country matters. They would spend a lot of time sitting in corners with bored expressions on their faces, and screw-top beer bottles sticking out of their pockets. A 'good bucket' of beer was what they most obviously enjoyed since it did not entail on them any further obligations. There they lolled like the lords of creation, surrounded, not by Olympian vistas, but by a fug of cigarette smoke.

It was through such a haze of bemused semi-intoxication and smoke that Moon caught sight of the Merry Widow. His reflexes had him on the floor almost before he was aware of it and he had asked her to dance with him. He knew her very slightly and mostly by hearsay. Since her man Angus had been killed eighteen months before she had been making the round of the dances apparently intent on enjoyment.

Despite his loud voice and coarse manners Moon had spells of excessive shyness and, waiting for the band to strike up, he rubbed his large hands with his handkerchief, without even a commonplace to his partner. The introductory bars of the waltz began and he put his arm round her: just then she took a deep breath and her breast swelled up against him. The effect of this contact on Moon was one of exhilaration: he almost felt himself raised on the air she had drawn into her lungs and this brief happiness never quite faded from his mind. As they went round the floor, he traced the pattern of the dance carefully, wanting it to last, holding her closer than was perhaps necessary and hoping for a repetition of what must have been unintentional.

That was the beginning: it was only incidental that there was a fine harvest moon that night. When he got home, late as it was, he sat a long time by the kitchen fire reviewing in his mind the day's events and especially taking the Merry Widow home. To his surprise and intense regret she had refused to be kissed goodnight. Now he was sweir to admit he was being attracted by a skirt. With the persistence of his own desires his mind went over her remarks, her way of talking and the sudden way her face would light up with laughter. To be attracted and held like a beetle in a web he never wished for: all the women he had known he had kept at a mental and emotional arms-length: they were the easier discarded. He always worked on the idea that every woman was the same, as he would voice to all, 'with their skirts ower their heids.' His thoughts of Jean excited memories of former lovers and he got into bed drowsily tabulating their charms, forming a mental cradle for himself which presently set him asleep.

After that dances and dancing were only an excuse for meeting and a kind of rhythmic aperitif or titillation for their love. Leaving the dance hall, their feelings already heightened and excited by the dancing, the music and the noise, they were overwhelmed by the contrast of the dark and quiet night. They could get no further than the Glebe where they would lie down behind the hawthorns and listen to the stragglers coming up the brae. Now and then there was an antrin scream and a cackle of laughter that made the lovers smile at each other. Across the Glebe the huge elms and beeches came down almost to the burn side, moving luxuriant boughs in the gloom, suggesting joy. In the end they stopped going to dances altogether, having, as it were, discovered each other.

Abandoned to passion and the influence of the widow a change came over him, her mildness and good nature won him over to kindness. He courted her shyly like a boy and whenever he said anything that pleased her she would put up her face to his and kiss him. He felt that she was vying with him in making love and the first time they lay together he was as embarrassed as a virgin, though he did his best to conceal his feeling in unconcern as if the whole thing was an everyday job like shawing turnips. He wondered with vague pessimism how long it would last and how it would end. Some of his previous affairs had frittered out sordidly, some had ended in the Sheriff Court. But he had never known a woman like this; she held him in a skein more durable than physical desire while that in itself seemed inexhaustible.

He remembered when he was a halflin his father's brother Geordie, a lazy sodden patch of a man, had initiated him into the ways of women and had left Moon the axiom:

'Love them all until you find one you never tire of having and marry that one.'

His uncle had never married.

The more Moon thought on these words the more reason they seemed to have because it pleased him to think so. No woman had ever given him the same pleasure as Jean; and it appeared to him that his bastards were not only mistakes but were the results of an itch created by a make-believe of enjoyment.

'Ach, to hell,' he said to himself, 'I'm not going back.'

But he was like the pigs in Fife, he flew backwards: and he did go back to her, waiting on her like a halflin.

The widow excited him in a strange way and seemed to draw his scattered thoughts together, to fasten them on one object, herself. At the same time she claimed him, making him feel that nothing mattered so much as sitting beside her on the bank of the glen and listening to her talking though he seldom remembered anything she said there in the green aqueous shade of the trees: it was as if the magic were too much for him and kept escaping him. He never saw a blossom until she looked at one, and her body held him in thrall long after he had enjoyed her. Looking on her half-uncovered breast white in a blade of sunlight he thought her paps were still unknown to him: that behind them was some dignified mystery and that he was only on the threshold of it. She was like a flower unfolding in the sunshine of love and he melted into a fondness for her which for a time made him half-ashamed because fondness had not entered his previous attachments.

The act of loving became a power outside them; and though they made love often it never became stale or an accepted thing: or something to be seized whenever the chance presented itself, irrespective of mood or humour. Each time he was impressed by her freshness and the glowing urgency she lent to each occasion.

In the midst of an adventure he said:

'Jean will you marry me?'

Moon had come a long way from telling his father's serving girls, 'I'll marry you,' to asking Jean, 'will you marry me?' It took some great emotional strain to overcome his pride and the calculated cynicism of deliberate cruelty and callous unthinking. The tears came to her eyes.

'Oh Jim, Jim.' Lying in her arms among the bracken he found the pleasure of having asked her to marry him outlived the words themselves.

'Well Jean?'

She said nothing but continued to caress and embrace him as if about to part with him.

'No Jim we'd only spoil it.'

The possibility of such an answer hadn't occurred to him: he thought the chief end of every woman was to get herself a man; and she wouldn't have him. He was intensely jealous; and unsure of his possession without being aware of it. Though she gave herself freely and joyed in doing so, she was not like a young girl returning always to the man who had taken her and her maidenhood. For a long time Moon had a great hatred of the dead Angus as if he were still flesh and blood. He tortured himself imagining their loves of the past, and badgered Jean with questions about their relationship, only partly mollified by her assurances that she had only been happy with himself. That Angus had enjoyed her undermined his peace. A neighbouring farmer spoke to her once at a sale and Moon was furious. Jean said, 'He is a nice man.' The words made Moon think her lost to him. There was a married woman at the Barony with whom he had been intimate and since he had broken with her he knew that she always referred to him as a 'nice man.' He therefore looked suspiciously on Jean's remark as if it were prophetic of her conduct.

Once in the glen he seized her and shouted at her regardless of people passing on the road.

'This is damnable, the one woman I want won't have me.'

'Ssh, Jim, she does want you, oh heavens how I want you,' and she showed him she had left off some of her clothes.

'Yes honey, but marry me.'

He who had spent the last ten years of his life avoiding women desperate to marry him now found himself frantic to be married.

And they were married.

He became sensible of a serenity in the old farm-house which had been hitherto dominated by the girning and grumbling of the first ploughman's wife who pulled the furniture about noisily in an inexplicable and ineffective rage. The quiet uninhabited rooms, filled with their ponderous antique pieces, drew him back along the passages to look in as if he expected to see someone sitting there enjoying the tranquillity.

Jean in turn had fallen in love with her new home: she had a guileless art of being pleased: not that false humour which sees assets in everything new, delighted and pleased because already determined to be so. The evening he brought her home she gazed blissfully on the expanse of grey-white moors where the sheep moved like toys living all the time on the edge of their appetites; and she felt her happiness stretching on the ridges before her towards the sunset, renewing itself like a pain as she turned to watch. A few sad brown fields where Moon expected crops did not dismay her. Behind the house was a group of green mounds, the remains of an old keep, then suddenly the ground fell away into a deep strath in the folds of which were Moon's cattle; and at the far end could be seen the blue surface of the water reserve. Over by the stackyard a number of sparse Douglas firs shuddered in the gale that struck them from the Moorfoots. As they held out their half-stripped arms to the wind and the pale sky Jean's eyes glistened.

'What,' said Moon, 'are you greeting already?'

'It's only the wind.'

And now it was all hers, the rock-fast double-storied house, the barns, the bothy with its pasteboarded windows, and even the firs, even Moon himself. She lived her happiness, milking, feeding the hens, cleaning the house; and the unthinking Moon was compelled to share her mood.

But one evening he stopped reading an advertisement for a milking-machine and said to her:

'We're married eighteen months now, do you not think it's time we had a youngster? I want a son.' He said it as if he were still thinking of the milking-machine and ordering the kind he wanted.

'My dear I should love that so much.'

Her habit of addressing endearments to him at table or even when some neighbour was in, embarrassed him and filled him with a shame-faced apprehension as to what other people would think to hear the like of that in his house. Yet he realised that he wanted to hear her call him so, to hear her heart flow out at her mouth in the soft voice she had. In return a timid tenderness made him address her as 'honey' twice in the same day.

A few months later he was telling about a cow that had wakened them in the night with her bawling: she had had a bull calf. Moon looked at Jean slyly.

'I see no sign of you calving.'

She blushed and immediately he was sorry but instead of retreating under an apology and a kiss he blundered on.

'I'm no at fault anyway.'

He got up in confusion, muttered about the work he had to get through and hadn't the time to sit gaping, and went out the back door into the sunlit yard.

Jean forgot her breakfast: she only enjoyed it so long as Moon sat at the table wolfing the buttered toast, and eating with a slight air of annoyance because he had to eat: he was always anxious to get it over. She began slowly to clear the table and suddenly became chilled and she ran outside not knowing properly what she was about. Moon had gone to the field. A cart of dung trundled from the close, and the second man sitting on the front of the cart looked at her with grey inquisitive eyes, his toothbrush moustache twitching as he chirped to the horse. She winced under his gaze and could barely answer his greeting.

'It's a fine day mistress.'

On the first Wednesday of the month Moon occasionally took her to the market. He had no scruples now: she was his wife: she was handsome and he was proud of her. They were driving past a few old houses one day where some ragged children were playing and shouting among the ruins of a cottage. The children stopped their game and stared insolently as he drew the car to a stop. He indicated one of the girls, a red-haired unpleasant-looking ten year old.

'What do you think of that one!'

Jean looked at the child for a moment and smiled faintly.

'She's quite nice—if she were clean.'

'She's anything but nice the brat, she's like her mother.' A few yards down the road a woman was bent over her doorstop pipe-claying it. Her broad hips hid the rest of her save for the dirty-grey laddered stockings and the wasted once tricksy shoes. She raised herself stiffly from the doorstep and turned her red head towards them. Immediately her mouth sprang open.

'Lizzie come in here at onc't.'

Lizzie came girning and reluctant and was pushed into the house followed by her mother who slammed the door with a bang.

'That's Teen Briggs isn't it?'

'It is.'

Moon had seen each of his former lovers turn from overdressed proud women to quarrelsome hard-faced sluts, grim with their grievances. Despite this experience he had expected them to retain their freshness and the allure of novelty. Yet only the idea of youth remained and he was obsessed by a fashion-plate notion of woman-kind: as if a woman could for ever remain twenty-two. Instead of seeing that woman must blossom like a flower he now saw her fading and short-lived which made him pine the more for his lustful mind picture of the ever-youthful. Though a vigorous man himself he knew that youth had gone from him and he looked about him with consummate vanity in order to revive it. So he had settled Jean in on the farm on the uplands to be his permanent fashion plate. Yet when he and Jean did go to bed he would take her in his arms thank-fully and say, consoling himself:

'You are my ain, my ain, my ain.'

She was the only thing he was sure of, and the words created in her a passion her body couldn't express: she would willingly have been crucified for him.

But Moon's mental insecurity became evident one day when at table he deliberately eased himself and farted. The sound distended itself about the room. He was half ashamed.

'Let your wind blow free where e'er you be. I can't help it, it's
in me and it's got to come out.'

'Have you left your manners in the byre?'

Moon couldn't quite make out whether she was cross or only
amused: anyway he had to fart though it was the first occasion he
had allowed himself to do it at the table. Jean repented saying anything when he had left the house. It was the first time she had said
anything about his personal habits: his deliberate act had surprised
her into a momentary distaste. He went off in a mood of petulance
but the incident was so insignificant that by dinner time his gusty
mind had forgotten it. To Jean her mild reproof magnified itself into
an enormity as if she had quarrelled violently with him. That she
had even for a moment rejected him wrought a discord in her generally
harmonious thought. A terror of having offended him spoilt the day
for her. In the evening he simply laughed in her face when she
apologised for her ill-nature earlier in the day.

He was going down the steps in the passage out to the byres when
she came out of the kitchen.

'Oh Jim will you—'

'What is it now?'

The irritable sound in his voice stopped her request in her throat:
she wanted him to shut the hens in as she was busy with the supper.
A coarseness had come into his voice; and she saw a glimpse of him
that filled her with an uneasy fear. She stared at him as if she had
only just seen him. He stood on the steps looking up at her, his mouth
a little open and the baldness of his wide forehead accentuated by
his greasy cap turned back to front: he was suddenly alien and
unknown to her and she felt she had slept with one of the ploughmen.

Then Moon went to the sales alone and stood at the Ring side
and watched the animals with what was now a habitual savage gloominess. As the day wore on and he took a dram his sullen stare was
directed at the people around him. He would set out for a sale filled
with a strange importance enhanced by weeks of comparative isolation
in the farm on the moorland, but when he reached the market town
his importance dwindled amid the noise, the boisterous voices of
the other farmers and he became only another figure. Here and
there he met acquaintances, but their commonplaces filled the day
with a noisy boredom, so that he was pleased to settle about his
animals and get back home. He usually came back as cross as two
sticks and Jean could do little to relieve his fuddled ill-temper.

One day he was walking along the streets of the market town
where the crowded little shops shouldered the people off the cobbled
causeways, when his thoughts were startled by a loud coarse laugh.
He hated ridicule and imagined that all laughter was aimed at himself so that he turned sharply. The laughter came in great gusts from

an out-by worker called Ag Macag who was with one or two other girls chaffing two ploughmen. At the moment when Moon caught sight of her, her big wide mouth was open in a throaty enjoyment of some smut that Johnny Sods was telling them: not her laugh only but the vulgarity of her person screamed at the passerby.

'The gallus bitch,' said Moon to himself, 'just like a bag of tatties tied in the middle.'

Later in the day he was sitting in the Black Bull drinking heavy beer and eating bread and cheese when Ag Macag with Fanny Fatlips and a local butcher and a man Moon didn't know came in and sat down near him. The butcher nodded knowingly to Moon, half in greeting, half leering at him, then he went to the bar and got the drinks. Moon watched the group in cynical amusement, and recalling the laugh regarded Ag speculatively. He fell into an absent stare at the blousy creature when in the course of their noisy conversation she glanced round and caught his eye. She stared at him boldly until he feigned to pull his dog to order. Then she stretched her fat legs in their pale skins of silk under the table where he could see them.

Moon reached his third whisky and as he looked at Ag Macag sideways the muscles of his body began to tauten as if he were preparing to fight. Just then the two men went off to the lavatory and Moon leaned across his table and spoke to Ag.

'When are you going home I can give you a lift?' She answered with a promptness that startled him into a consideration of what he was doing.

'I'm going home now.'

The men came back and seeing Moon had joined the party the butcher spoke to him.

'Are you not married now to the Merry Widow her that was Angus Henderson's wife?'

'That's so.'

'I ken her fine, well every man to his ain hirsel.' Anger suffused Moon's mind at the mention of his wife: not anger at the butcher's familiarity but because he was called on to destroy the thought of her as he was about to break up their relationship.

'Ach to hell with her, I'm tired knocking on that door and getting no answer, you try her.'

'No thanks I'd rather a pund o' steak.'

The butcher was then unwillingly dragged into an argument about prices at the other end of the bar and Ag Macag went home with Moon. Now that he almost possessed her, his mental and physical tension began to abate giving place to a mood of high good humour: a prelude to exhaustion. His love affairs had always wrought in him this tide of nervous and physical effort and as they progressed towards surfeit the storm died away leaving him limp like a wet seaweed among the boulders. Before they reached Carronford he stopped at the Three-cornered Wood and as he turned in the rustling dead leaves to enjoy her the great limbs took possession of him and the monstrous body, 'like a horse,' he thought, absorbed him.

Even afterwards while her sour smell still disgusted him he felt elated, naively feeling like a youth after his first assignation. He was glad that he was at last breaking the spell Jean had over him. He never thought he had just committed adultery but had merely asserted his rights. He refused to be bound and Ag was the right stuff too, no damn nonsense, knew what she wanted as well as he did, off with her bloomers and there you are, as nice as ninepence.

Jean noticed a change in Moon: his face lost its ruddiness and became an unhealthy lard-like colour. He came and went about the house with an arrogance which was more painful to her than his sullen rages. In his fits of gloom he would say nothing at all: then she suffered the pain of loneliness shut out from the one person whose thoughts and feelings she wanted to share. But she would have preferred that solitude which with patience would resolve itself into a joyous reunion: she disliked the gloominess but did not despair of it. But now his arrogance dominated the house. He went out a lot in the evenings with his dogs up the Carronford direction presumably to look at some sheep he had there.

She didn't know what was wrong or what to do. Time and again she was on the point of dropping into a whine of where are the days gone by, but she knew that was useless; and she instinctively turned away from quarrelling or fighting with him when he provoked her. The days that had seemed so bright on the farm, even in the winter, were now wearisome to her. Winter came again to Howburn and the snow lay a long time on the limestone ridges.

About half-past four one day she went into the stable on the chance of finding a hen's nest and at the far end were two of the men lowsing their horses. They didn't hear her come in.

'There's some queer folk in the shaws richt enough.'

'He's been going his dinger again they tell me.'

'Aye Ag Macag's away with it.'

'Is that so, I'm sorry for the mistress she's a decent enough wummin.'

'Ah he'll never rest until he's out o' house and hald.'

Without thinking Jean called out gaily:

'What unfortunate are you scandalising now Geordie?' Geordie didn't answer and after a moment's silence went on fumbling with the hames. Then she realised that she was the mistress: a decent enough wummin. The men's voices speaking to their horses sounded hollow, and presently they rattled the harness on to the pegs and shuffled outside.

She leant against the corn-kist and at first a physical weakness destroyed her calm; and the sense of ineffectiveness which overcame her brought tears. She was incapable of rage; only a thin fount of pride within her formed the thought of leaving him. But the farm drew her, and even the dim stable with the scraping heavy-breathed beasts, the harness, the smell of soiled straw and the old bare stones of the building surrounded her and comforted her. There was nowhere nor anyone she could go to. Angus's sister Nora whom she had stayed with refused to have anything to do with her when she married Moon. Jean thought of her thin mouth and flat chest as of a funeral shroud, a skeleton comfort. She had an ache in her breast that bereavement creates and she stood crying in a premature mourning for her husband.

'What the hell's wrong with you standing there, do you want your death of cold?'

It was Moon standing in the doorway: he couldn't see she was crying. She made one feeble bid for his tenderness and a moment later her pride reproached her.

'I don't feel too well Jim.'

'Ah it's indigestion, indigestion, you're all the same, aye ailing and wailing.'

'I've had bad news.'

'What news?'

'Oh news.'

He didn't bother any further about her bad news.

'Where's Mick McCoggin?'

'In the bothy I think.'

And away he went to give Mick a tongueing for coming off the field five minutes too early.

Jean went soon to her bed and when Moon went upstairs she wasn't to be seen. Finally he found her in the spare bedroom apparently asleep. 'Funny bitch,' he thought, 'has she got the wind of it at last?' The following night she slept in his bed and the silent resolute act struck him at the time by its deliberation.

Had Moon discovered Jean to be unfaithful he would have been profoundly shocked, not because of the act itself, but because she could dare to discard him. The possibility of her ever having a fancy man was terrible to him because he knew the end of it would be terrible. Jean resembled him in this apparently easy temperament which would find itself disturbed and hurt by any impropriety. But in this instance it was the act which appalled her. The agony of her wounded pride, of being scorned and only desired for an animal necessity filled her waking hours with shame and grief, and penetrated her dreams with poignant insistence. She felt more sorrow for herself than jealous hatred of Ag Macag; and she kept trying to convince herself that she was mistaken but the certain knowledge smashed her wilful fantasies and horrified her senses. She noticed one day the patch of sunburnt skin on his chest and the strong brown arms he had and she imagined how that skin may have touched that of Ag Macag and the arms embrace her. The thought made her physically sick and she had to hold on to the table until she recovered.

Her quiet behaviour puzzled Moon because it didn't seem natural and he imagined the lid would blow off her feelings when he was least prepared. He didn't see her when she flung the handle of the kirn from her and ran to the bathroom to cry her heart out in its privacy. He would leave her in the morning when her day's misery was only mounting in her breast; and by noon her mind was so full of madness that she could barely eat her food. Though neither spoke of it Moon's infidelity became an accepted fact and hung over them like a common topic of conversation.

One day about the beginning of March he came in for his dinner. He had a restless puzzled air, but Jean knew she would share his mind presently and waited as if for an explosion. At last he said:

'Well I've got a son now.'

'I'm glad Jim you'll be pleased.'

He looked at her sharply wondering if she was having him on but her face had a calm expression and her teeth showed a little, in that artless manner that had so charmed him in the past. She put out his food and he shuffled as he ate.

'The thing is she's blamed the butcher McUdder and he owns it, but it's my image, it's my very image.' Jean was silent thinking over what she had to say.

'I wanted it here in the house.'

'But you have your image here in the house, it's here.' And she put her hand on her belly.

'What,' he shouted, getting up and taking hold of her arms 'that's the limit, that's the bluidy limit.' He squeezed her gently. She felt no repulsion or attraction, only the nearness of his large face and wrinkles on his bald brow made her feel somehow faint. She put him away.

He was unable to face a situation of delicacy and generally something that merely called for good manners resulted with him in bad manners. But this surprise froze his reactions and in his embarrassment he spoke loosely and with a pretended indifference. 'Ah well,' he said, 'I suppose there's nothing for it but hard work.' He took his jacket off the back of the chair and went outside pulling at the awkward sleeve linings.

Left alone Jean could not look at the forgotten meal. She tried to think clearly of his news but it seemed unimportant, and overshadowed. Her misery had touched bottom: but like a balloon that falls slowly and relentlessly to the ground her spirit was unable to resist the deflection upwards. Happiness crowded her thoughts like a melody until, though conscious of her own natural grace, her body seemed clumsy and unequal to it. She went to the back door and saw Moon across the yard at the pig-sty.

'Jim,' she called and he looked round at her good-humouredly, the wind ate up her words.

'It doesn't matter.'

'What?'

'It doesn't matter, nothing matters.'

'What's that?'

'I love you.'

'I can't hear you for the wind, go into the house there's snow coming.' And he pointed to the grey hills. She stood still in the wet yard oblivious of the cold, feeling the wind only as a caress. She saw the storm driving across the moor but her thought was for what lay behind it, the spring and its promise. The first snowflakes decorated her hair. Moon kept shouting, 'Go in, go in.' She heard him faintly and he began walking towards her. She saw him as part of her elation, that he was still her lover. She turned and went indoors filled with an inexplicable joy.

JEREMY BRUCE-WATT

Father to a Monster

She was a scrawny, leggy tinker girl—one of the travelling people. She was brown as an oak apple and as full of wily movement as a trout in a Highland burn. Her hair hung black and ragged to her shoulders as though her mother had seized it and roughcut it with blunt scissors or an open razor. Her eyes were the darkest he had ever seen. Usually their expression was of wild animation, or contemptuous disbelief, but at other times whoever looked into them encountered only the un-answering mystery of an alien race.

He was fascinated by her, and she was in some way interested in him, for she came every day to the beach in front of the house and loitered there on the deserted sand.

The summer holiday was being spent as usual in the North, in a remote crofting township where always he felt himself marooned with elderly parents on the edge of a cold North Sea. Every day he went out—a pale uncertain child wandering over the windy dunes and among the dank boulders at the cliff bottom. Whenever he came across the crofters going about their slow timeless routines he would hang about, watching. They looked back at him in keen-eyed, non-committal silence.

Then one morning she appeared. He had been squatting among the dunes—hot, silent dunes overgrown in places by yellow trefoil and purple thyme—examining swarms of green-and-red moths which hung drying their wings on the stems of the marram grass. He had found a jam jar and was cramming the struggling insects into it, deciding that he wanted to collect them but having no knowledge of how to go about it.

He didn't see her until she was suddenly there at his elbow, and she gave him a considerable fright. He twisted himself away and gaped up at her, leaning back on his hands. Her old brown dress seemed too big for her, and the front was stained and torn. He noticed with disdain that her toenails were rimmed with black.

'What you wanting with them things?' Her voice was queer and guttural, not at all like the local people.

'I'm collecting them,' he said haughtily.

She squatted down to look at the jar of six-spot burnets, now fully alive and active, crawling over each other, spreading their sinister bottle green forewings and scarlet underwings.

'How?'

'I don't know. Well, because I want to, I suppose.'

She took the jar and held it up. He noticed her fingers like twigs against the shining glass, the nails bitten down to the quick. She screwed up her face. Then, without a word, she suddenly flung the jar from her, over the rim of the hollow and out of sight.

The wanton, deliberate act threw the boy into utter confusion. He was also furious at the loss of his precious insects. He got up and gave a shout of indignation. In answer the girl put out a hand, thin brown fingers extended, and prodded him on the cheek. He was aware of a rank smell, like the last of the hay at the end of winter, and of dark eyes scanning him without telling him anything at all.

Then she was gone. He climbed the dune and saw her running back along the track to the village, her feet sending up little spurts of sand. He watched her out of sight and then retrieved the jar of insects. He unscrewed the lid and tipped them out. They zig-zagged crazily away over the waving grass.

Something urged him to go and look for her, so he set off towards the village and the sea, planning to observe from some concealed place, find out where she lived, what her people did. He hid in some gorse and looked down on the village, but there was no life among the cottages except for an old man carefully lifting early potatoes. Beyond the last house, right on the edge of the sea, he noticed a parked lorry and a group of small black huts, and a movement of men and dogs. These were tinkers, and it occurred to him that perhaps she might have come from there.

His father had told him he was never to talk to tinkers.

At the end of the morning he walked slowly back to the holiday bungalow and told his parents he had been to the headland to watch the seals.

The next day he wandered off farther than ever before. He went up to the clifftop and walked in the din of sea birds feeding their young. He had been sternly told not to go here alone. He descended inland across a great waste of heather and bog myrtle to the old church set in a huddle of tabletop tombstones. A blackbird gave an alarm call, but otherwise there was no sound. He returned by the shore and came upon a group of men putting out in a boat. Again he hid among the gorse and watched, but still she was not there.

Day after day he went looking for her. He even plucked up courage and spoke to the driver of the baker's van.

'You don't happen to have seen a girl, do you? A girl with—er—black hair and sort of torn clothes. With bare feet. She just—walks about.' He couldn't think how to go on.

The vanman looked away. 'Well. Unless she would be one of the tinkers. They were up the road last week but now they're off towards Tain and Dornoch. They'll likely be back in a few days. It depends where the haymaking is, you see. You never know with the travelling folk. It's a case of here today and gone tomorrow. Just like the wind!'

The van drove off, trailing a skein of white dust.

Two mornings later he ran out of the bungalow and down the road to the old pier and saw, far along the beach to the west, a thin wild figure running by the edge of the sea.

He rushed after her.

The tinker girl saw him coming and dawdled until he caught up. He went close to her. She put up a hand like she had before and this time she pushed the side of his neck with a lightly closed fist. There was nobody else in sight.

'Hullo,' he said, his smile twisted with shyness. 'Where have you been?'

After that he met her every day. He would eat breakfast with one eye on the window until he saw her down at the sea's edge, skiffing her feet in the wavelets or swinging a long frond of seaweed like a whip. He gulped his milk and pushed back his chair.

Once his mother enquired who was the girl he seemed to be walking about with so much.

'She's from the village,' he said. 'She's sort of interested in what I'm interested in.' He flushed. 'It's all right. She's a very nice girl. Really!'

His mother smiled and changed the subject.

Instead of returning home for lunch he took to asking for sandwiches and a bottle of lemonade. They had picnics on a flat rock at the cliff bottom or on a tussock where a burn ran out to the sea. They tried to catch flounders with their hands. He was fearful that one day it would rain.

His parents, involved in endless golf with another couple, remained incurious. Their child was not obviously in trouble and seemed content.

For the first time the holiday came to an end far too soon. After breakfast on the last day he ran out of the house to the clump of withered pine trees—the place he had decided was a better place to meet.

Against his mother's instructions he was chewing gum, bought in the village shop. He put out his tongue briefly with the lump of chewing gum on the end, to show her.

As they idled along the shore he said: 'I'm going home tomorrow.'

She did not seem to hear him.

'What you eating?' she asked in her guttural way.

'Chewing gum,' he said, feeling superior. Probably she wouldn't be able to afford even the penny it had cost him.

'Here,' she said, turning so that he almost bumped into her. She was wearing an old black cardigan, very frayed and worn, with a safety pin in place of the top button. Under it was a thin dress, yellowish and badly creased. Her face came close to his. The full intensity of her strange eyes played on his face. He was suddenly disturbed and fearful.

'Let's see your chewing gum.'

He made a movement with his hand, as though to pick it out of his mouth and hold it up.

'Go on! Let's see it on your tongue. Open up your mouth!'

He obeyed. He opened his mouth and put his tongue right out, as for the doctor. The chewing gum lay on the end of it.

With a quick darting movement she put her own face forward. He had a fleeting glimpse of dark lips and a flash of white. It was like a trout rising or a bird taking a worm. Then she was away, her brown legs and feet leaping the tufts of wiry grass. She tossed her head with its mane of hair, and laughed.

Alone in the hollow he stood rigid with disgust and fear. He was only a little boy on holiday, but now of course his whole life was changed, changed in an instant by this alien, perplexing mesmerising creature. Everyone in the playground of his small school in another part of the Highlands knew what happened if you passed something from your mouth into the mouth of a female. The terrible truth was that something passed with it—and the girl, sooner or later, would have a baby! Terrified, he watched this female child throw herself on a distant mound of thyme and lie there, looking up at the blue vault of the sky. His chewing gum was still in her mouth.

The next realisation struck him like a thunderbolt. Everyone also knew that if the man and the woman were not married to each other the baby would be a monster. It was true. He had noticed such beings on visits to the big towns.

Seeing him standing there petrified, white-faced and staring the girl raised a thin brown arm—and thumbed her nose at him.

He turned and fled. He ran panic-stricken over the desert of dunes where flies rose from the warm sand and the green-and-red six spot burnet moths clung to the stems of the marram grass, exhausted. He ran through air perfumed by the flowering gorse and seaweed left by the last tide and tar on the roadway melting in the sun—the sun that shone so constantly throughout that last fateful summer before the war.

The child headed straight for the dull security of the holiday bungalow on the edge of the golf course, with its protecting fringe of blackthorn hedge. In the last hundred yards he caught up with his mother returning from the village shop and was disappointed because her baskets of groceries prevented him from taking her hand. Had he done so she would have been surprised. She would have known that something had upset him, but never would she have guessed that in a few weeks, or months—he had no idea how long it took—he was to become a father.

He—her little boy. Father to a monster.

*

The tall man in the white safety helmet and the collar and tie showing neatly under his blue donkey jacket stood on the edge of the same northern sea and smiled as he recalled those distant but well-remembered days. Of all the development sites he could have been sent to, it had to be this one—this emotive place in the far north-east, scene of the furious embarrassment of his solitary youth.

'I used to be taken there on holiday every year up to the war,' he remarked to his general manager at head office as they took a first look at maps and plans.

'Splendid,' the executive had said. 'Local knowledge is always advantageous. Good for public relations. Helps to smooth things out with the natives and all that.'

'Yes, of course.'

He had spent so much time in the Middle East, Nigeria and Brazil that there never had been time to drive North again, just for a laugh, to see what was doing up the road. Now they were sending him anyway. A new site. A temporary appointment.

In the late afternoon he came to the place where the track led off towards the sea. He saw with a pang that it was still edged with wild thyme and yellow trefoil and, with a sharper pang, that here again by the roadside were tinkers. In place of rounded huts made with old tarpaulins they now had battered lorries and peeling caravans. He scanned their faces as he edged past in a car that suddenly seemed absurdly large and pretentious.

The sullen faced men did not respond to his nod. Good public relations? When he came to the site, established by the sea where the bungalow had been, he thought it might be rather late for that.

The old road suddenly became lost in churned up mud. Beyond a fifteen foot barbed wire fence the landscape had been laid open like a carcase gutted in a butcher's shop. The marram grass and wild flowers had been flayed from the dunes, the dunes stripped from the rock, the rock itself gouged, transported and dispersed. Where once his parents had played their golf now yawned one of the largest, deepest man-made holes in Europe.

As time went on he met most of the local people and recognised some of them from over thirty years back. Grown old and taciturn, numbed by what was happening, they wobbled to and fro on their heavy bicycles. Sometimes they would say: 'Fine night!' or 'The wind iss getting up!' More often they passed on by, looking nowhere.

On summer evenings before tea he would occasionally make a point of standing outside the main gate in case any of them wanted to have a direct word with him. Few did.

As he lingered there now, conspicuous in his white helmet and unsoiled donkey jacket and feeling unusually pensive and mellow because of the stirred memories, he became aware of an old crofter coming straight for him, pushing his bicycle over the deep ruts.

The man was wearing the usual dark clothes and an old bonnet whose stud fastening had rusted away, making of it a comic cloth crown. Bleary and red-veined, he approached warily, like a bull investigating a strange bullock in his field.

'One of your dumper trucks took away my garden gate!' There was none of the Highland preamble about the weather or the state of the fishing. 'You'll need to get a new one to me. It wass quite a good gate! It wass up since before the war. Indeed, it wass my brother made it before he went away to enlist. That wass the summer of 1939, but still it wass a good gate!'

The engineer studied the face, groping for recognition. Could he have been one of the salmon fishermen, emptying the nets of great silver fish?

'Were you here yourself in the summer of 1939?'

The old eyes peered back at him. They were full of suspicion.

'Yass. What interest is it to you?'

The sunburn of Africa was fast wearing off but he must still have looked and sounded entirely a foreigner to the local man—the penalty which tends to await the returning cosmopolitan Scot. For a moment they studied each other, the veteran resident with the outmoded bicycle and the transitory technocrat whose prematurely grey hair showed beneath his official helmet. Then the engineer raised an arm and pointed.

'Go to the office over there and leave your name with them. Say you've had a word with the resident engineer—that's who I am—and we'll get a new gate to you. In a few days.'

He smiled and spoke kindly, but the old man was not impressed.

'I haff been to quite a few offices already and I can tell you I obtained no satisfaction whateffer!'

The RE smiled again. 'Just mention the resident engineer. This time it will be all right.'

Nonplussed, the man began to move off.

'It iss just the wood I am wanting,' he flung back over his shoulder. 'I will be making the gate myself!'

Something in the elusive Highland defiance pressed a button in the console of memory. There she was again, a scrawny tinker girl, brown as an oak apple and full of wily movement as a trout in a burn. Inscrutable eyes and dark lips, and a traumatic snatch of a sticky sweet from a protruding tongue.

High above the roar of machinery a siren wailed. He turned on his heel and walked towards the sound, towards his office perched on the edge of a vibrating abyss.

The security man at the gate shifted a two-way radio to his other hand and saluted.

'Good evening, sir.'

The resident engineer smiled absently and passed inside the barbed wire to commune with the monster he had fathered.

DOUGLAS DUNN

The Blue Gallery

Inside the Blue Gallery, each room is a different shade of blue. Blue graduates from the palest of washes to a blue so dark it is the colour of naval uniforms, of nights at sea with the North Atlantic Fleet.

All the paintings were specially commissioned from the most famous of living artists. 'Paint me a picture that is predominantly blue according to the shade on the card enclosed.' No one could afford to ignore such an eccentric commission; the fee was enormous.

Because it is situated in a remote part of the country, there are few visitors. Those who come have to make a special journey. A few items have appeared about it in the papers, but publicity is completely unwanted by the proprietor. On several occasions he has firmly turned down requests by editors of arts features, specialised art magazines, and producers of television programmes. The last thing the proprietor wants is for the Blue Gallery to catch on.

The proprietor is never seen. He watches the approach of any visitor from his apartments above the Gallery, and opens the door with a push of a button. There are no catalogues or postcards in the foyer, no chairs to sit on, no uniformed guards. Even the most famous people—even artists the proprietor admires—are left entirely to themselves. When he recognises a face, he feels the desire to go down and welcome them, to talk to someone. He resists this urge, and when one of the few people who know he's there call out for him, his resistance is so painful he has to tighten his hands into fists. He gets no pleasure from watching them depart. To see them walk along the narrow path towards the road and the small car park is anguish.

The blues of the Blue Gallery are irresistible. They have the effect of brainwashing, so much of one thing, one blue question, room after room of blue variations. Dimensions people had known of themselves fall away like clothes. You can almost see their departures. Familiar identities are teased into internal laughter, into what seems like internal laughter, as if preconceptions were laughing at the preconceiver. Promises become lies. Loves become, in the memory, no more than brutalities; tender aerial blues become aquatic blues and then nocturnal blues that hurt. No one wins in the Blue Gallery. It is the same for everyone and the Blue Gallery is dead against them. It has comprehensive guile but attacks head on. It has no instruments, is just itself. So clever is the Blue Gallery that you forget it at the same time as it does its blue work on your nerves. It makes your eyes naked.

For all the savagery of it, it has killed no one; the Blue Gallery is benign. The proprietor has a hard time of it convincing himself of that. There is only one way to put his mind at rest, and he walks daily in the Blue Gallery, hoping that one day it will stop. 'One day,' he hopes, 'I'll sort out how it is that it works so strongly. Why did I build it? Was my dream a good one? Is my invention for the good? Why do visitors never return? Do they die of it?'

He is afraid to ask visitors as they re-emerge what they think of it. 'It is beauty,' he repeats to himself, 'and I have given it, I have made it, a strong beauty.' But he has watched visitors leaving. They rush along the path, very few of them ever look back. Sea-sounds follow them, coughs of the sea as it breaks down the cliffs. Do they really gulp down air as they seem to, or are they just in a hurry? And that way they look at the sky; is it meaningful? Do they realise they will never escape blue, that there are hidden vastnesses everywhere to remind them?

The proprietor guards his Gallery and cannot leave it. For him, it is punishment one day, reward the next; he cannot make his mind up. He is the curator of the Blue Gallery. He made it, but it does not belong to him. One day, he feels, it will slip loose and escape him. Or year after year, it will exhaust him, the blue will blur on his eyes, the world will be blue wool. Sleep often eludes him; its thin blue threads fail to hold him down. Then he listens to the vibrating of the delicate burglar alarms, taut, invisible beams that protect the rooms of blue paintings. The proprietor feels himself possessed by these private electronics. Some nights he switches them off, but he can still hear them, polite, like considerate musicians at practice in the next room.

When he does sleep, he dreams his paintings go back to the various depths of the sea, the atmospherical ranges of the sky. He forgets they came from tubes of paint. One of these nights they are not going to come back. He is prepared for that. Already he has plans for a Green Gallery, a White Gallery, a Red Gallery . . . he would just like to see what they'd do, how they'd behave. He dreams of them with the sad smile of a man who knows what he is fated to dream of forever. But secretly he believes art is just not worth the candle. 'Ah!' he says. 'A Gallery of candles!'

IAIN CRICHTON SMITH

Timoshenko

When I went into the thatched house as I always did at nine o'clock at night, he was lying on the floor stabbed with a bread knife, his usually brick-red face pale and his ginger moustache a dark wedge under his nose. His eyes were wide open like blue marbles. I wondered where she was. The radio was still on and I went over and switched it off. At the moment she came down from the other room and sat on the bench. There was no point in going for a doctor; he was obviously dead: even I could tell that. She sat like a child, her knees close together, her hands folded in her lap.

I had regarded the two of them as children. He had a very bad limp and sat day after day at the earthen wall which bordered the road, his glassy hands resting on his stick, talking to the passers-by. Sometimes he would blow on his fingers, his cheeks red and globular. She on the other hand sat in the house most of the time, perhaps cooking a meal or washing clothes. Of the two I considered her the simpler, though she had been away from the island a few times, in her youth, at the fishing, but had to be looked after by the other girls in case she did something silly.

'Did you do that?' I said, pointing to the body which seemed more eloquent than either of us. She nodded wordlessly. As a matter of fact I hadn't liked him very much. He was always asking me riddles to which I did not know the answer, and when I was bewildered he would nod his head and say, 'I don't understand what they are teaching at these schools nowadays.' He had an absolutely bald head which shone in the light and a sarcastic way of speaking. He would call his sister Timoshenko or Voroshilov, because the Russians at that time were driving the Germans out of their country and these generals were always in the news. 'Timoshenko will know about it,' he would say and she would stand there smiling, a teapot in her hands.

But of course I never thought what it was like for the two of them when I wasn't there. Perhaps he persecuted her. Perhaps his sarcasm was a perpetual wound. Perhaps, lame as he was, sitting at the wall all day, he was petrified by boredom and his tiny mind squirmed like the snail-like meat inside a whelk. He had never left the island in his whole life and I didn't know what had caused his limp which

was so serious that he had to drag himself along by means of two
sticks.

The blood had stopped flowing and the body lay on the floor like
a log. The fire was out and the dishes on the dresser were clean and
colourful rising in tier after tier. The floor which was made of clay
seemed to undulate slightly. I felt unreal as if at any moment the
body would rise from the floor like a question mark and ask me
another riddle, the moustache twitching like an antenna. But this
didn't happen. It stayed there solid and heavy, the knife sticking from
its breast.

I knew that soon I would have to get someone, perhaps the policeman or a doctor or perhaps a neighbour. But I was so fascinated
by the woman that I stayed, wondering why she had done it. Girlishly
she sat on the bench, her hands in her lap, not even twisting them
nervously.

Suddenly she said, 'I don't know why but I took the knife and
I . . . I don't know why.'

She looked past me, then added, 'I can't remember why I did it.
I don't understand.'

I waited for her to talk and after a while she went on.

'Many years ago,' she said, 'I was going to be married. He made
fun of me when Norman came into the house. He said I couldn't
cook and I couldn't wash, and that was wrong. That must have been
twenty years ago. He was limping then too. He told Norman I was
a bit daft. That was many years ago. But that wasn't it. Anyway, he
told Norman I was silly. Norman had put on his best suit when he
came to the house. He wasn't rich or anything like that. You don't
know him. Anyway he's dead now. He died last week in the next
village. He was on his own and they found him in the house dead.
He had been dead for a week; of course he was quite old. He was
older than me then. Anyway he came into the house and he was wearing his best suit and he had polished his shoes and I thought that he
looked very handsome. Well, Donald said that I wasn't any good at
cooking and that I was silly. He made fun of me and all the time he
made fun of me Norman looked at me, as if he wanted me to say
something. I remember he had a white handkerchief in his pocket
and it looked very clean. Norman didn't have much to say for himself. In those days he worked a croft and he was building a house.
I was thirty years old then and he was forty-two. I was wearing a long
brown skirt which I had got at the fishing and I was sitting as I
am sitting now with my hands in my lap as my mother taught me.
Donald said that I smoked when I was away from home. That was
wicked of him. Of course to him it was a joke but it wasn't true. I think
Norman believed him and he didn't like women smoking. My brother,
you see, would make jokes all the time, they were like knives in my

body, and my mind wasn't quick enough to say something back to him. Norman maybe didn't love me but we would have been happy together. Donald believed that his jokes were very funny, that people looked up to him, and that he was a clever man. But of course he . . . Maybe if it hadn't been for his limp he might have carried on in school, so he said anyway. I left school at twelve. I had to look after him even when my parents were alive.

'It didn't matter what I did, it was wrong. The tea was too hot or too cold. The potatoes weren't cooked right or the herring wasn't salt enough. "Who would marry you?" he would say to me. But I think Norman would have married me. Norman was a big man but he was slow and honest. He wasn't sarcastic at all and he couldn't think like my brother. "She was in Yarmouth," Donald told him, "but they won't have her back, she's too stupid. Aren't you, Mary?" he asked me. That wasn't true. The reason I couldn't go to Yarmouth was because I had to stay at home and look after him. I was going to go but he made me stop. He got very ill the night before I was due to leave and I had to stay behind. Anyway Norman went away that night and he never came back. I can still see him going out the door in his new suit back to the new house he was building. I found out afterwards that my brother had seen him and told him that I used to have fits at the time of the new moon, and that wasn't true.

'So I never married, and Donald would say to me, if I did something that he didn't like, "That's why Norman never married you, you're too stupid. And you shouldn't be going about with your stockings hanging down to your ankles. It doesn't look ladylike." '

I remembered how I used to come and listen to the News in this very house and it would tell of the German armies being inexorably strangled by the Russians. I would have visions of myself like Timoshenko standing up in my tank with dark goggles over my eyes as the Germans cowered in the snow and the rope of cold was drawn tighter and tighter. And he would say to me, 'Now then, tell me how many mackerel there are in a barrel. Go on now, tell me that.' And he would put his bald head on one side and look at me, his ginger moustache bristling. Or he would say, 'Tell me, then, what is the Gaelic for a compass. Eh? The proper Gaelic, I mean. Timoshenko will tell you that. Won't you, Timoshenko? She was at the fishing, weren't you, Timoshenko?'

And he would shift his aching legs, sighing heavily, his face becoming redder and redder.

'He thought I knew nothing,' she said. 'Other times he would threaten to put me out of the house because it belongs to him, you see.' She looked down at the body as if he were still alive and he were liable to stand up and throw her out of the house, crowing like a cockerel, his red cheeks inflated, and his red wings beating.

'He would say, "I'll get a housekeeper in. There's plenty who would make a good housekeeper. You're so stupid you don't know anything. And you leave everything so dirty. Look at this shirt you're supposed to have washed!"'

Was all this really true, I wondered. Had this woman lived in this village for so many years without anyone knowing anything about her suffering? It seemed so strange and unreal. All the time we had thought of the two as likeable comedians and one was cruel and vicious and the other was tormented and resentful. We had thought of them as nice, pleasant people, characters in the village. We didn't think of them as people at all, human beings who were locked in a death struggle. When people talked about her she became a sunny figure out of a comic, blundering about in a strange English world when she left the island, but happy all the same. We hadn't imagined that she was suffering like this in her dim world. And when we saw him sitting by the wall we thought of him as a fixture and we would shout greetings to him and he would shout back some quaint witticism. How odd it all was.

'But I knew what was going on all the time,' she continued. 'I could follow the news too. I knew what the Germans were doing, and the Russians. But he made me out to be a fool. And the thing was even after I heard of Norman's death I didn't say anything, though he said a few things himself. He told me one day, "You should have been his housekeeper and he wouldn't have been found dead like that on his own. But you weren't good enough for him. Poor man." And he would look at me with those small eyes of his. They had found Norman, you see, by the fire. He had fallen into it, he was ill and old. He hadn't been well for years. I often thought of taking him food but Donald wouldn't let me. After all we're all human and a little food wouldn't have been missed. I used to think of when we were young so many years ago. And when I was young I wasn't ugly. I wasn't beautiful but I wasn't ugly. I used to go to the dances when I was young, like the others. And of course I was at Yarmouth. He had never been out of the island though he was a man and I was only a woman and we used to bring presents home at the end of the season. I bought him a pipe once and another time I got him a melodeon but he wouldn't play it. So you see, there was that.'

There was another longish silence. Outside, it was pitch black and there was ice on the roads. In fact coming over from my own house I nearly slipped and fell but I had a torch so that was all right.

I wasn't at all afraid of her. I was in a strange way enjoying our conversation or rather her monologue. It was as if I was listening to an important story about life, a warning and a disaster. I remembered how as children we would be frightened by her brother waving his sticks from the wall where he was sitting. And we would run away full tilt as if we were running away from a monster. Our parents would say, 'It's only his joking,' and think how kind he was to go out of his way to entertain the children, but I wondered now whether in fact it might not be that he hated children and it wasn't acting at all, that cockerel clapping his sticks at us as we scattered across the moor.

Maybe too he had been more in pain than we had thought.

The trouble was that we didn't visit the two of them much at all. I did so, but only because I wished to listen to their radio to hear the news. Also, I was a quiet, reserved person who was happier in the company of people older than myself. But I hadn't actually looked at either of them with a clear hard look. To me she was a simple creature who smiled when her brother made some joke about Timoshenko, for his jokes tended to be remorselessly repetitive. It didn't occur to me that she was perhaps being pierced to the core by his primitive witticisms and it didn't occur to me either that they were meant to be cruel and were in fact outcrops from a perpetual war.

Suddenly she said to me, 'Would you like a cup of tea?' Without thinking I said 'Yes,' as if it was the most natural remark in the world while the body lay on the floor between us. I was amazed at how calmly I had accepted the presence of the body, though I had always thought of myself as sensitive and delicate. But on the other hand it was as if the body was not real, as if, as I have said, it would get to its feet, place its sticks under its arms, and walk towards me asking me riddles. Naturally however this didn't happen. And so we drank the tea out of neat cups with thin blue stripes at the rim.

'I had to give him all my saccharins,' she said, 'because he liked sweet things. It's a long time since I've had such a sweet cup of tea.' I noticed then that she had put saccharins in my tea and I realised that this was the first time that I had had tea in her house. She was in a strange way savouring her transient freedom.

'I remember now,' she said. 'It was the Germans and Timoshenko. The Germans had been trying to destroy Russia. I knew that, I'm not daft. And now the Russians were killing them. I heard that on the six o'clock news. And Timoshenko, he was doing that, he was winning. It was then that I . . .' She stopped then, the cup at her lips. 'I remember now. It was when it said about Timoshenko and he said the tea wasn't sweet enough. That was when I . . . I must have been cutting bread. I must . . .'

She looked at me in amazement as if it was just at that moment that she realised she had killed him. As she began to tremble I took the cup from her hands—it was spilling over—and put my arm around her and comforted her while she cried.

ALLAN MASSIE

In the Bare Lands

'No, you most certainly can't see him.'

Giles was accustomed to flat refusals. They didn't faze him.

'I don't want to intrude,' he said. 'I did write, you know, and I've come a long way.'

It was cold on the steps of the seedy-looking house which had certainly seen better days.

The woman—you could imagine from her cheek-bones she had once been beautiful—didn't seem impressed.

'You didn't get a reply, did you?'

Giles nodded.

'I know he's very old,' he said. 'I would have telephoned but you're not in the book.'

'Are you surprised?' she said.

'I'm a perfectly respectable person. I'm not a journalist if that's what you're afraid of.'

'I don't care who you are. Can't you see that?'

'I'm afraid it's beginning to rain.'

The wind which had been blowing for the last two days was now swirling heavy gouts of rain with it. The house—why had it been built facing north—lay or, rather, crouched directly in its path. Further up the mountain it might be snowing.

'Couldn't you just let me in to explain myself. It reminds me of trying to sell encyclopaedias, standing here.'

He turned up the collar of his Donegal tweed coat.

'That couldn't do any harm, could it, Miss Urquhart? You are Miss Urquhart, aren't you, his daughter, I mean?'

When she didn't reply, he turned for a moment and looked back down the valley. There were meadows a couple of hundred feet below and a sort of byre or bothy standing alone. It was limestone country.

'I've got very respectable credentials,' he said, 'even a letter of introduction. Mr Alkins said he would write too.'

'Henry Alkins?'

'Yes, of course.'

It was the first sign that she might relent and he followed it up, though he knew well that what would really count was his docile dejection—his air of a spaniel that isn't being taken for a promised walk.

'I know there's been a postal strike,' he said, 'perhaps both our letters got lost that way.'

'I don't know what you want,' she said. 'You can't have sold encyclopaedias.'

'Not very successfully, I'm afraid.'

There was no point in telling her that he'd never come near to needing to do anything like that; friends' accounts had only established it in his mind as the most pathetic of imaginable holiday jobs.

'Well,' she said, 'he's out just now.'

'In this weather?'

'It's the lambing season.'

She pointed to the byre below.

'You can come in and talk to me if you like. I'll give you some tea. It's English.'

They entered a narrow hall. There was a heavy oak chest and the walls were painted white. The painting had been done a long time ago.

Miss Urquhart said,

'We'll go in here. There are no comfortable rooms in this house. I sometimes think that's why my father chose it.'

'The bare lands the surgeon's scalpel,' said Giles.

'Oh,' she looked at him with surprise, 'you do know a little then. I promised you tea. Or would you rather have kirsch? It's local.'

'I'd love both. I'm afraid that's very greedy.'

Giles gave her his little boy smile—he had been brought up by a maiden aunt while his parents were on a tea-plantation in Assam.

'There is whisky,' she said, 'but that's his.'

She went out through a door at the back of the small room to make the tea. Giles stood by the fire and looked around. It was like a Victorian art photograph—'Cottage in the Hebrides,' perhaps. There should be an old woman with a shawl round her head sitting at her spinning-wheel by the fire. The only thing that spoiled the effect was the book-case which ran along the wall beside the door they had come in by. Giles examined it. There were two shelves of Urquhart's books—poetry, history (damned tendentious history he could imagine), political philosophy, social studies, six volumes of autobiography—Christ, he hadn't realised he'd written so much, and most of it crap. He pulled one out, not bothering to choose.

'The warder had knowledge of which my fellow-prisoners were ignorant. He knew he was a prisoner more closely confined than they.'

What bloody arrogant nonsense. He put the book back.

He had a feeling, rare to him, of being out of place. If Judkins thought up any more of these bright assignments he could bloody well follow them up himself.

He sat down—the chair had a straight back and the seat was too short—and pulled out Simon Lumsden's letter. It was brief and badly typed, the signature barely legible. He supposed it might do, though he, remembering Lumsden's animosity, could read reluctance between the lines.

'Simon Lumsden's the man to go to,' Judkins had said.

'Isn't he dead?'—his memory of Lumsden was very vague—his name surely hadn't appeared in the papers for at least a decade.

'No, he lives in Gravesend, but he isn't dead.'

It was the nearest approach to a joke Judkins could assemble from his card-index mind.

'And what if he won't see me?'

The whole project was unattractive—he would far rather stay in Venice instead of having to drive into the mountains above Bolzano. It was typical of Judkins to come up with something like this—'we've got the unit there, kill two birds with one stone,' he could just hear him say it, even though Judkins was more the type of sentimental moron who would put out a bird table in his suburban garden.

'Lumsden'll see you,' he had snickered. 'All you need do is go along with a bottle of brandy in one hand and a bottle of Scotch in the other.'

'But I thought they quarrelled. Will Lumsden's letter do any good?'

'You can get off your arse and try.'

Miss Urquhart came back into the room and set a tray down. She poured two cups of very dark tea.

'Milk and sugar?'

'Both, please.'

She handed him the cup and a small glass of kirsch and passed a plate with caraway-seed cake on it.

'It's a little stale, I'm afraid. He's finished with politics. You know that? That's why we live out here. He doesn't even like to talk about them. I don't know when he last wrote to the newspapers.'

'Well, he's eighty-five, isn't he?'

'The last visitor we had, sometime back in the autumn, didn't realise that. He was still looking for a lead from him. He was a boy from Glasgow University. I'm Edinburgh myself.'

'I'd better explain why I've come.'

'There's no point in that. I only asked you in because it's pleasant to talk English now and then.'

She must have seen surprise on Giles's face.

'He'll only talk Gaelic to me. That shows what he feels.'

'I didn't realise . . .'

'He only learned it in prison, you know. In the second war, not the first.'

'I thought,' Giles had done his homework, 'he belonged to the Lallans school at one time.'

'That was before the working-man let him down.'

'You sound bitter.'

'Bitter? You're quite a wit, aren't you?'

Giles began to feel his resentment deepen.

'I've a letter from Simon Lumsden,' he said, handing it over.

'Poor Simon,' she replied. She only just glanced at the letter and laid it aside. 'How is he?'

It wasn't really a question to be answered.

'We haven't seen him for years. Simon had no ideas, you know. He just wanted a cause to attach himself to. Don't look at me like that, please. What do you imagine I think about when I'm sitting here? What have I to think about? The Workers' Republic of Scotland or the Union of Celtic Commonwealths?'

'I haven't said anything. I thought you said he was finished with politics'—if you call that sort of nonsense politics, he nearly added.

'Precisely.'

'Look,' said Giles, 'I didn't want to come here.'

'I used to think I was in love with Simon,' she said. 'I wanted to be. He did too. Oh well, do you know my fate? I chose the wrong man to save.'

She started to try to laugh and then to light a cigarette and then to cry—she stopped frozen between the attitudes.

Giles said,

'It's a television programme. My boss thought of calling it "A Leader in Search of a Party". It's his notion of Pirandello, half-baked, you know, but that's his style, it needn't be as awful as it sounds . . .'
—he was speaking too fast, almost unaware of what he was saying and at any moment the ice would break and she would cry.

But instead the door opened and a very tall old man came in. He walked very erect, no suggestion of a stoop. He was wearing a plaid and looked . . . Giles had once spent a wet afternoon in Aberdeen and between closing and opening time gone into the Municipal Art Gallery (it was a choice between that and 'Sex—Swedish-Style', and though he detested great Galleries and would run a mile rather than visit the Uffizi or the Prado, he had in certain moods a weakness for provincial ones) and there seen a Landseer of truly impressive ineptitude entitled 'Flood in the Highlands', depicting what he took to be a Laird surrounded by family and retainers with assorted livestock perched on cliffs or struggling in the flood-waters . . . yes, Urquhart looked exactly like Landseer's conception of a Highland chief. He might even have modelled for the painting, or, more probably, based his conception of himself on it.

He didn't look at Giles but said something in what was presumably Gaelic to his daughter. She replied in the same language. Giles couldn't avoid the impression that hers sounded more fluent, even more natural.

Urquhart's hand disappeared somewhere under his plaid and emerged with a key. He unlocked a heavy deal cabinet, took out a bottle of whisky (Talisker, Giles enviously observed) and poured himself a half-tumbler which he swallowed at one gulp. He made another brief remark to his daughter, filled his glass, replaced the bottle, locked the cabinet and marched out of the room.

'Well?'

'I told you it was pointless.'

'What in fact did he say?'

'He told me to tell you to get the hell out of here. That's a paraphrase. It's more vivid in the Gaelic.'

'I see.'

They could hear footsteps overhead.

'Well, I never really thought anything would . . .' He tried to think of just what he'd like to do to Judkins. 'Do you think I could have another drop of kirsch before I go. It's really rather good.'

The footsteps marched up and down like a man pacing his cell.

'He'll live to be a hundred, I know he will,' she said, but she filled his glass. 'You can buy it in the village below.'

Giles drank it quickly and shrugged himself into his overcoat. Or something in a cage.

'Thanks, I will, I certainly will.'

He might as well get something out of the trip. Mind you, for the first time he conceded that Judkins had a point. Visually it would be damned good, but, still, if the old loony would only speak Gaelic—well, there were bloody few Gaelic speakers and most of them probably had no TV reception. He'd tell Judkins he'd sent him on a two hundred mile round trip to interview a monoglot Gael—that'd puzzle him.

'And give my love to Simon. For what it's worth.'

'He won't live to be a hundred, that's for sure. I'm not likely to see him again. He didn't like me much.'

'No,' she said.

It was sleet that was being blown on a diagonal by the wind now. He got into the hired Fiat, and turned, surprising himself, to say something, he didn't quite know what, something to bring life to her, even perhaps just thank you, but the door was already shut, and he drove down into the valley, the sleet changing to a thin rain as he descended.

G*

DEIRDRE CHAPMAN

Into Europe

'Sharl. . . .'

'Oui p'tit chou?'

'Arrêtez immedibloodyatement.'

'Patience my dove. It is but two hours less a quarter.'

'You keep going on and on. I've seen at least six places and you keep going on.'

The Clarks were one and a half days from Boulogne, heading into the interior. Their Scottish-built Imp said 'Ecosse' on the back and 'It's Scotland's Oil' on the windscreen. As it juddered past a dawdling Mercedes, their sleeping sons Callum and Rory collided on the back seat and sat up blinking in a flurry of crumbs and Kleenex.

'Is this still France, Daddy?'

Callum was wrestling with the concept of roads. It seemed an endless strip of tarmac circled the world carrying through traffic. To get to proper places like the Eiffel Tower or the Leaning Tower of Pisa you had to get off the road and in behind those hedges. He wished they'd get off the road.

'When are we having our picnic?'

He'd had nothing for breakfast but a bent roll that tasted more like a cookie.

'Say it louder, darling. Daddy's a bit blocked. Things aren't getting through. You too, Rory. All together now. "WHEN ARE WE HAVING OUR PICNIC, DADDY?" Very good. Now naughty Daddy will have to stop going on and on.'

Charles, who liked going on and on, felt pressured to invent a destination.

'I'm looking for a river,' he said. 'Déjeuner sur l'herbe. Près de l'eau. Sous les arbres.'

'Avec les midges.'

'Bugger the midges. I'm looking for a river to cool the wine.'

And, now that he'd said it, it seemed the idea had been germinating pleasantly in his head all morning.

Spotting a likely sign he spun the wheel and the Imp nipped under the nose of a family Peugeot and scuttled off down a slip road. Behind them the Peugeot howled with outrage and the Mercedes flowed past unchecked. 'Curses,' said Charles, who'd worked for half an hour to overtake it.

They were in a narrow twisting road dropping away from the route nationale between shaggy verges and straggling cottages. Hens scattered round a blind bend and a man in faded denim leant on a spade and watched them go.

'Which river are we looking for, Daddy: the River Clyde, the River Nile, the River Rhine . . ?'

'The River Allier. What did that sign say, Helen?'

'Pont de something. Keep going. I bet it's a foul trickle full of old prams.'

'The route map says "A straight and level road through agricultural country becoming sinuous through the more picturesque scenery beside the broad River Allier".'

'What's sinuous, Daddy?'

'Twisty, Callum. But not *just* twisty. There's a suggestion of movement too. You wouldn't call a liquorice stick sinuous, for example. It's twisty, all right, but it's twisty in a rigid sort of way.'

'Daddy . . .'

'Quiet, Callum. When you ask a question you listen to the answer. Let's see if we can think of anything else that's sinuous. We've got a road and a river. What else moves in a twisty sort of way?'

'A snake. '

'Well done, Mummy. Mummy says a snake.'

'Daddy . . .'

'I've told you not to interrupt. Now we've got a snake. A snake stationary is straight. But when it moves it doesn't go along all in one piece like you do or Spotty does. . . .'

'I want Spotty. I *want* Spotty.'

'Spotty's very happy with the nice lady in the kennels, Rory, playing with all the other doggies.'

'Daddy. . . .'

'I wish you'd be quiet, Callum. I can't concentrate on driving and explain things to you and have you interrupting all the time. Now a snake is sinuous when it moves because. . . .'

'But Daddy we've passed the river.'

'Where?'

'Back where the trees were.'

'Nonsense.'

'I can see something glinting through the trees, Charles.'

'Well I wish you'd said so before. I can't do all the driving *and* the navigating *and* watch out for bloody rivers.'

The road had carried them into a skeletal village, two sides of a funnel, a short funnel.

'God, what a nowhere place,' Helen said.

The church was big enough, though, to cast a black shadow outside the café. In the shadow the population sat.

Callum wondered where all the children were. Maybe they had died, in the heat. And the mummies, too, where were the mummies? The busy mummies in their light coats and red clacky shoes pushing their shopping trolleys, racing one another to the shops, looking in the windows, looking at nothing but stacks of canned peaches and tea bags with 2p off. Where were the windows? Where were the shops?

Something dreadful had happened here. Only the grannies were left.

Charles pulled up at the café and took off his dark glasses so they could see his eyes were friendly.

He shouted, 'Pardonnez moi, où est la rivière?'

The population went into a huddle. Charles revved tetchily. 'You'd think they'd remember where their bloody river was.'

'It's your accent, darling. They're interpreting.'

A small fierce man, bristly, with little eyes like a wild boar, approached the car. His wrinkled fingers were indented with gold rings. All the grannies watched him. One of them was knitting without looking at the pins. Callum thought maybe he was going to shoot them.

'Anglais?'

'Écossais.'

'Huh. The river is là-bas. You go bac bac bac. Always bac.'

'Merci.'

'M'sieur.'

'You see,' Charles said, reversing, 'it always does the trick. As soon as they know you're Scottish they can't do enough to help you.'

Rory said nothing. In a dark doorway he'd seen a witch, all in black, leaning on a broomstick.

Back amongst the trees they turned left over a broad stone bridge, and pulled up in a half-cleared bramble patch. Charles killed the engine. The radiator boiled painfully to a standstill. In the silence the river could be heard, moving.

'The car,' said Helen, 'is an international zone. When the engine stops we're suddenly in France.'

Charles unsprang the safety catch and the children, released, tumbled out and slithered off into the undergrowth to catch up on the day.

Helen peeled her thighs off the hot Rexine and hobbled out into France. Charles was throwing the picnic things out of the boot into the long grass. Grasshoppers started up angrily where they fell.

'Écoutez les fourmis!'

'Don't be ridiculous, Helen, ants don't make a noise.'

'Fourmi is grasshopper. We had a poem at school, "La Cigale et le Fourmi." The ant and the grasshopper.'

'The grasshopper and the ant.'

'Are you sure?'

'Sure I'm sure. Fourmi is ant. Formic acid is derived from it.'

'From an ant? What do they use it for?'

'How do I know what they use it for? It's from an ant, though.'

'You'd wonder how they ever discovered it, wouldn't you?'

With holdall, basket and carrier the Clarks advanced into the undergrowth. Helen's sling-backs scooped up mud like a bottom-grubbing duck and fed it up between her toes. Cold leaves stroked her bare arms and thorns picked at her dress.

When they came out into the sunshine they were in a fairy ring of cropped grass, open at one side to the river. Behind them the bushes closed up against the shoulder of the bridge. Their eyes scaled its height to the parapet, toppling against a moving sky, and, under the pale curve of its armpit, trembling water patterns.

Helen spread her arms prettily to embrace it all, their bridge, their river, their clearing.

'It's all ours, not a soul in sight.'

'I told you I'd fix it, didn't I?'

They kissed then, still holding the baskets, in a spotlight of slanting sun. Like a pair of Peynet lovers, Helen thought. Then Charles went off with the boys to relieve himself and cool the wine in the river.

Helen spread the red checked cloth in full sunlight where the grass was flattened. The French were odd the way they hugged the shade.

The pâté was rather warm and bitty, the Camembert moulded to the shape of the wine bottle. And the plastic plates were hot and smelly with echoes of past picnics. She picked some broad leaves and used them as doylies. She hoped they weren't poisonous. She felt quite paysanne and provident.

When Charles came back she was pouring liquid butter out of a hot plastic box into a nettle patch. He picked up the long loaf and began to slice it in his hand in the French way. When he nicked his finger he said 'sacré bleu' and wrapped it in a red paper napkin. It was so quiet they could hear the crumbs drop.

Helen wriggled out of the top half of her dress and sat there in her bra. 'Let's buy a cottage in France, darling.'

'What's wrong with the Highlands?'

'Too farouche. Nothing but sliced bread and you can't take children in the pubs. No. France is for me. I'll bottle fruit and preserve goose and you'll wear a funny straw hat and hoe the field. And we'll keep a goat called Clothilde.'

'What field?'

'We'll need a field for you to play with. Like those peasants in the north. All in funny hats and hoeing. With their children too. It looked fun. We could cash in an insurance policy or sell our Scotbits. I bet you can buy a cottage here for peanuts.'

With wild warcries the children came bounding out of the nettles, leaving footprints of molten butter all over the tablecloth.

Charles slapped Callum and Helen smacked Rory, quite hard, out of fright, and he sat down suddenly on the tablecloth and howled.

'All right, Rory, all right, darling. Mummy didn't hurt you. Mummy has to smack Rory sometimes so that he'll look where he's going the next time.'

'Shut up, Helen, and find some bloody dockens. Can't you see the child's covered with nettle stings.'

Charles snatched all Helen's doylies off the plates and scrubbed at Rory's legs, green spinachy lumps among the red blotches. Callum was suddenly sick in a bush.

'I'm car sick, Mummy.'

'Nonsense, darling, no one's car sick after the car has stopped.'

'I am, Mummy.'

Helen picked the pâté and the Camembert out of the grass and wiped them off with a Kleenex. Charles took it from her and wiped Rory's eyes.

'Now watch you don't go near that bush. I'll put a newspaper over it just in case. And stay out of nettles in future.'

'What's nettles, Daddy?'

'Good God, Helen, haven't you even taught the child what a nettle looks like?'

They ate, then, in four degrees of silence. Helen fantasised a French lover smouldering beside her in the grass, eating a peach. What a pity he was such a noisy eater.

Rory was an ant, hacking his way through the impenetrable grass, watching out for the dread sinuous caterpillar.

Callum swam powerfully across the river to rescue a dog, no, two dogs, cheered on by the staff and pupils of Greenside Primary.

Charles had a Citroen up there in the clearing and a mistress in Neuilly. The responsibility of it cast a tiny grey cloud over his happiness.

All the time little grass creatures came and bit their legs, and the river passed quietly towards a meaningless sea.

The silence cracked suddenly like an empty glass. Particles of sound fell down to them from the bridge and as the bushes began to shake and crackle Rory sat bolt upright and proclaimed in a sonorous voice, 'Here Comes The Sinuous Snake.'

But it was only some children. Callum was glad they weren't dead, though they didn't look like real boys either. They were all dressed in

blue, the colour of deckchairs that get left out all summer in the sun
and rain. And their arms and legs were greyish-brown.

Helen thought they were beautiful. Their heads were neat and
woolly like field mice. Her fingertips tingled with wanting to pat
them. Only then she remembered about her dress and tried to get
back into it.

The leader nodded. 'M'sieur dame.' He stepped off the path into
the long wet grass, making a display of it, taking a wide berth round
them, and emerging back onto the path with his espadrilles sodden.

'M'sieur dame.'

'M'sieur dame.'

'M'sieur dame.'

'What did he *say*, Daddy? What did it mean?'

'Mr and Mrs. French children are very polite.'

'So are we,' said Callum sullenly.

'So am I,' said Rory.

'YOU told ME,' said Callum, 'it was rude to call people mister or
missus.'

'It's different in France.'

'M'sieur dame.'

'M'sieur dame.'

'It's like the Champs Elysées in rush hour.'

'You've set the table right in the middle of their bloody thorough-
fare.'

'How would you like to be a little French boy, Callum, and come
here every day?'

'I'm a Scottish boy,' said Callum.

'Me Scottish boy too,' said Rory.

How pink they are, Helen thought, how pink and squat and stocky.
They'll never tan with that carroty hair. They'll just go to freckles.

Charles said, 'When you're big boys Mummy and Daddy will send
you to stay with a French family. And then we'll have their boys to
stay with us.'

And what will their boys think of that, Helen wondered. Our boys
are children. French boys are men, waiting for their turn.

'You see, Cally, the French people and the Scottish people are
special friends. They used to get together to fight the English people.'

They would look much better if they didn't wear those awful
green tee shirts, Helen thought. Green is such an industrial colour.
Northern and industrial. They wear them because of Celtic and then
everyone thinks we're Catholics. Of course it's all right being a
Catholic if you're a French Catholic. It's different in France.

'Do the boys know we're friends?'

'How do you mean?'

'Do they know we're Scottish boys?'

'We-ell, probably not. You see the Scottish people and the English people speak the same language. Of course when you learn to speak French they'll know you're Scottish because Scottish people speak French much better than English people. If Mummy hadn't packed so many clothes for herself we'd have brought your kilts and then everybody would have known you were Scottish boys.'

'If you learn to speak French very well and practise your manners, some day they might even think you're French boys.'

'My juice is sour,' said Callum, truculent with his failure to be French.

'Nonsense, it's lovely French apple juice.'

'My duce sour too.'

'Don't be a copy-cat, Rory.'

'Mummy's duce sour?'

'Mummy isn't drinking apple juice, Mummy's drinking grape juice. Special grape juice for grown-ups. They've done special things to it. Like they do special things to apple juice to make—here, Rory, let Mummy taste your juice. Good God. It's cider. It had an apple on the label. I didn't think . . . no, Rory, you mustn't drink any more. It's not little boys' apple juice. I don't care if you *are* thirsty, give me that cup . . . you little brat!'

Helen stood up, dripping. Rory hurled the cup at her and lay back, roaring. One Startrite sandal flew off and landed on the pâté. Callum moved cautiously out of range of the flailing feet and began to giggle. He giggled till his chest ached, rolling in the grass, cool and tickly on his tingling face, laughing his defiance at them, hearing his own voice laughing and laughing back at it.

'They're stoned out of their minds,' said Charles.

'French children drink wine from the cradle,' said Helen.

It was Charles who picked them up and straightened their tee shirts and took them off to sober up in the river.

Helen lay back to sunbathe with her dress top off. Resting her eyes amongst the murky underpinnings of the bridge she saw a movement. A pair of eyes met hers. A boy was sitting astride a girder directly overhead.

Helen shrugged back into her dress and glared. The boy shifted position and a piece of grit fell into her eye. She sat up angrily. A Peeping French bloody Tom and not even out of short pants. And she had to get behind a bush soon or burst.

On the fringe of the bushes she looked up again. He was still there. Casually she began to pick sprays of blossom, arranging them fussily as if she had all the time in the world. Her dress kept snagging on the thorns as she worked her way farther into the bushes. When she seemed to be well screened she looked back. The boy was still on her skyline, smiling now.

Furiously tearing off any branch that would come away she hacked on into the thicket. Every time she looked back the eyes were following her, obscene adult's eyes in a child's face.

Charles and his sons laid their six sensible brown sandals in a row and stood hand and hand in the shallows, watching their white feet turn scarlet.

The French boys were on a concrete island where the bridge touched down in midstream. Seeing them, they began to display to the foreigners, pushing one another off and swimming splashily back to the island.

'They can swim, Daddy,' Callum whispered, 'swim proply. I can just pretend.'

'Let's show them a thing or two, shall we?'

Charles picked up a flat stone.

'Watch this.'

His arm described a perfect curve and at just the right second his fingers opened and flicked. Slap slap plop.

The French boys stopped splashing and watched. Rory jumped up and down and tugged at his father's shirt tail.

'Me try, Daddy, me try.'

Charles slotted a stone into Rory's small palm and worked his arm from behind. Slap plop.

'Again, Daddy.'

'No, it's Cally's turn.' Plop. 'Hard luck, Cally, try again.' Plop. 'Look, Daddy will show you how.'

This stone was a beaut. Five times it skimmed and hopped before it disappeared. Rory was wild with pride and the French boys gave up their game and started swimming towards them.

'Me try again Daddy.'

Rory snatched the stone from his father's hand, a thin sharp-edged one like a flake of slate, and flung it wildly, straight at the oncoming boys.

Charles closed his eyes. He wondered if French boys were too God-fearing to swear. Hopelessly he started batting around in his brain for the French for 'sorry'. 'Dommage'—that rang a bell.

'Quel dommage!' he said out loud.

As the leading swimmer stepped out on to the bank, bleeding profusely from the forehead, he realised he had said 'What a pity.' A mad snigger escaped him. He looked at the boy helplessly and the boy looked at him. Between them incomprehension settled like slow sediment.

It was Rory who broke silence. Staring at the boy and trembling all over with excitement, he pointed at the blood snaking from drop to drop down his wet cheek.

'Look look,' he shouted. 'SIN' he yelled, 'SIN YOU', he was ecstatic, 'SIN YOU US!'

Slowly the boy bent to pick up a stone. Charles noted miserably that it wasn't flat.

In desperation Helen had dropped to her knees and crawled under a dense bush. Cider had cemented her skirt to her legs and bits of tree jabbed her shoulders and fell down her neck as she struggled.

When she crawled out again the boy was still there. She should have thrown something at him, words even. But she stood there, weakly, pinned by the skirt, the hair, the buttonhole.

From the direction of the river a child's scream came to her. Then she saw the top of Charles's head moving quickly above the bushes.

It seemed to her they would pass her by, get into the car, and drive off while she struggled here alone in the thorns beneath the laughing boy. Pushing, tearing and calling she charged through the bushes and fell out bloodstained at Charles's bare feet.

Rory was in his arms, blood trickling from a cut across his cheekbone. Callum came behind with all the sandals.

'For Christ's sake what *happened*?'

'He was stoned.'

'You mean it was an accident?'

'No accident.'

'But surely . . . well if it wasn't an accident hadn't you better do something about it?'

Charles looked back. Boys stood where the path met the river, waiting. Helen looked up. A solitary boy sat on a girder, watching.

The Clarks gathered the plastic plates into their tartan holdall and collected the rubbish carefully into a polythene peddle-bin liner. Turning their backs on the river they tramped back through the bushes to the car.

Rory sat on Helen's knee and Callum squeezed on to the front seat beside her so that it was hard for Charles to engage second gear.

As the car turned back across the bridge towards the main road he said 'Daddy. . . .'

'Yes, Callum?'

'We should have weared our kilts.'

Biographical and Bibliographical Notes
on the contributors

Most of the material in these notes has been supplied by the contributors themselves, or by their executors. Where an author's reticence seemed to the editors to be excessive, the information provided has been added to. Under each entry a brief biography appears first, followed by a list of publications. In the case of the more prolific authors, only the most important titles are given. Where authors have published collections of their own stories, these are given first, followed by novels, then by other publications. The publishers' names and dates of publication apply to first British volume publication (except in one instance where a book was published only in the USA). Further details about many of the authors may be found in *Scottish Writing and Writers* (Ramsay Head Press, 1977).

GEORGE MACKAY BROWN was born in Stromness, Orkney in 1921. He went to school there, and later attended Newbattle Abbey College when the poet Edwin Muir was warden. He received much encouragement and help from Edwin and Willa Muir in his writing. After Newbattle he read English at Edinburgh University, where he later did some post-graduate work on Gerard Manley Hopkins.

Discovering no vocation in himself for teaching, he tried to make his living as a writer and eventually succeeded in a modest way. Some of his stories have been televised, and some of his books published in USA, Sweden and Norway. The composer Peter Maxwell Davies has put music to several of his texts. Davies's opera *The Martyrdom of Saint Magnus* is based on the novel *Magnus,* and the children's opera *The Two Fiddlers* on the short story of the same name.

He still lives and works in Stromness. Being an unenthusiastic traveller, he has only once been out of Scotland to Ireland (1968) on a Society of Authors Travel Award.

Unsought honours have come his way: OBE in 1974; MA (Open University) in 1976; LL.D. (Dundee University) in 1977; and he was elected FRSL in 1977.

Short Stories: *A Calendar of Love* (1967); *A Time to Keep* (1969); *Hawkfall* (1974); *The Sun's Net* (1976).
Novels: *Greenvoe* (1972); *Magnus* (1973).
Poetry: *Winterfold* (1976); *Selected Poems* (1977).
Play: *A Spell for Green Corn* (1970).
Essays: *An Orkney Tapestry* (Gollancz, 1969); *Letters from Hamnavoe* (Gordon Wright Publishing, 1975).
Children's books: *The Two Fiddlers* (1974); *Pictures in the Cave* (1977).
Except where otherwise indicated all these books are published by The Hogarth Press/Chatto & Windus.

JEREMY BRUCE-WATT was born in 1929, in Calcutta, where his father was manager of a jute mill. He was brought up in Inverness and East Lothian, and left school at sixteen to become a copy boy for the *Scotsman* in Edinburgh. National Service (1948-50) was spent as a corporal in The East Surrey Regiment in Salonika and Athens. Later he became in turn assistant editor of *Scotland's Magazine,* an interviewer for BBC television in Glasgow, and a feature writer with the *Scotsman.* In between times he worked in a London factory, on a Scottish hill farm and in the West Indies. A full time writer since 1973, he won a Scottish Arts Council bursary in 1976. His first novel *The Captive Summer* is set in Edinburgh, where he has lived for the past fifteen years. He often feels compelled to get away from the place, he says, only to find himself equally pleased to return.

He has had broadcast a number of radio plays, and one television play, *The Grill,* the stage version of which was put on at the Traverse Theatre, Edinburgh in 1976. He is a frequent contributor to BBC Scotland Radio 4, with short stories, feature programmes and talks. *The Captive Summer* was winner of the Chambers Award for Fiction, 1977.

Novel: *The Captive Summer* (Chambers, 1978).

JANET CAIRD was born in Nyasaland (now Malawi) in 1913 where her father was an educational missionary. She was educated at Dollar Academy and Edinburgh University where she took a degree in English. After a postgraduate year in France at the Sorbonne and Grenoble University, she trained as a teacher. She married James B. Caird, H.M. Inspector of Schools, and has two daughters. She has lived in different areas of Scotland, from Dumfries to Wick and is now settled in Inverness. She began writing seriously when housebound with the cares of a young family. Her main interests, apart from writing and omnivorous reading are art, travel and archaeology. Her stories have been published in various periodicals and anthologies.

Thrillers: *Murder Reflected* (Bles, 1965); *Perturbing Spirit* (Bles, 1966); *Murder Scholastic* (Bles, 1966); *The Loch* (Bles, 1967); *Murder Remote* (Doubleday, 1973).

Poetry: *Some Walk a Narrow Path* (Ramsay Head Press, 1977).

Children's books: *Angus the Tartan Partan* (Nelson, 1961).

DEIRDRE CHAPMAN was born in Carnoustie, Angus in 1936 and brought up there. She has worked as a feature writer and columnist for various newspapers in Glasgow and, briefly, in London. She is married to fellow journalist Michael Grieve, whose father is Hugh MacDiarmid. They have three sons and live in Glasgow. 'Into Europe' is one of only two or three stories she's written: every other word of her prolific output has been for newspapers, magazines or television.

ELSPETH DAVIE was born in Ayrshire. Her father was Scottish and her mother Canadian, and she spent some early years in the south of England. She went to school in Edinburgh, trained at the University and at Edinburgh College of Art. For some years she taught painting. She is married, and has one daughter. She lived for some time in Ireland before returning to Edinburgh. Her work has appeared in various anthologies including *Scottish Short Stories* 1973, 1974 and 1977 (Collins), and *The Penguin Book of Scottish Short Stories*. In 1971 and 1977 she received Scottish Arts Council Awards.

Short stories: *The Spark* (Calder & Boyars, 1968); *The High Tide Talker* (Hamish Hamilton, 1976).

Novels: *Providings* (Calder & Boyars, 1965); *Creating a Scene* (Calder & Boyars, 1971); *Climbers on a Stair* (Hamish Hamilton, 1978).

DOUGLAS DUNN was born in 1942 in Inchinnan, Renfrewshire and grew up there, educated in the local primary school, Renfrew High School and Camphill School, Paisley. He lived in the United States for a year and since 1966 has lived in Hull where he went to university. A freelance writer since 1971, he has earned his living from journalism, poetry, and other forms of writing including work for radio and television. His books of poems have received the Somerset Maugham Award and the Geoffrey Faber Memorial Prize. Works in progress include a novel, short stories, radio and TV plays and poems.

Poetry: *Terry Street* (Faber & Faber, 1969); *The Happier Life* (Faber & Faber, 1972); *Love or Nothing* (Faber & Faber, 1974); *Barbarians* (Faber & Faber, 1979).

IAN HAMILTON FINLAY was born in 1925, in Nassau, Bahamas,

of Scottish parents. He returned to Scotland at an early age, and now lives in the moorland part of Lanarkshire. During the fifties, he published short stories and had a number of plays performed on radio (and subsequently on foreign television). Thereafter he has concentrated on poetry, from the relatively conventional *The Dancers Inherit The Party* to the 'post-concrete' and neoclassical idioms of his work in the gardens surrounding the Max Planck Institute, Stuttgart. He is represented in the *Oxford Book of Scottish Short Stories,* has had versions of his plays published (in German) in Vienna, and has notable sundials at the University of Kent, (Canterbury), in the Royal Botanic Gardens, Edinburgh, and in the grounds of the new University of Lige, Belgium. In the autumn of 1977 a large exhibition of his collaborations in various mediums was held in the Serpentine Gallery, London.

The Sea-Bed and Other Stories (Alna Press, Edinburgh, 1958); *The Dancers Inherit The Party,* (Migrant Press, 1960); *Und Alles Blieb Wie Es War . . .* plays, (Universal Editions, Vienna, 1965); *Poems to Hear and See,* (Macmillan, New York, 1971); *A Sailor's Calendar,* (Something Else Press, New York, 1973); *Honey By The Water,* (Black Sparrow Press, Los Angeles, 1973); *Selected Ponds,* photographs of the poet's garden, (*West Coast Poetry Review,* 1976); *Heroic Emblems* (Z Press, Vermont, 1977).

JAMES ALLAN FORD was born in Auchtermuchty, Fife, in 1920 and educated at the Royal High School and (inconclusively) the University of Edinburgh. From 1940 to 1946 he served with the Royal Scots, winning a Military Cross in Hong Kong in 1941 and spending the rest of the war years in Japanese prison-camps. Apart from a few brief spells in London, he has lived in Edinburgh since the war, trying to pursue two careers simultaneously, as civil servant and author. At present he is an Under-Secretary in the Scottish Office, and the pressures of official life have diminished his output as author. His writing has consisted mainly of novels, one of which, *Season of Escape,* set in a Japanese prison-camp, won the Frederick Niven Award in 1965. But he has also turned his hand to short stories, articles and reviews and has had one play broadcast. He is married, with a son and daughter.

Novels: *The Brave White Flag* (Hodder & Stoughton, 1961); *Season of Escape* (Hodder & Stoughton, 1963); *A Statue For A Public Place* (Hodder & Stoughton, 1965); *A Judge of Men* (Hodder & Stoughton, 1968); *The Mouth of Truth* (Victor Gollancz, 1972).

GEORGE FRIEL was born in Glasgow in 1910. He was educated at St Mungo's Academy and Glasgow University, where he graduated MA. He edited the university literary magazine at a time when it was criticised for being 'too literary'. He became a teacher and published his 'Plottel' short stories in various pre-war magazines. During the war he served in the RAOC but found on his return to civilian life that there was virtually no market for short stories. In 1959 his first novel was published. Thereafter he continued to write novels as well as short stories and plays for the Scottish BBC, for whom he also scripted the television version of his novel *The Boy Who Wanted Peace*. In a radio appreciation of his work for sixth formers he was described as 'one of the greatest writers about cities'. He read widely and was particularly interested in Proust, Chekhov and, especially, Joyce, whose influence may be seen in much of his writing. He knew only Glasgow, having no interest in 'nature'. He roamed its streets, taught in its 'underprivileged' schools and tried at all times to tell with truth what was happening in, and to, the city. He died on 5 March 1975.

Novels: *The Bank of Time* (Hutchinson, 1959); *The Boy Who Wanted Peace* (Calder, 1964); *Grace and Miss Partridge* (Calder & Boyars, 1969); *Mr Alfred MA* (Calder & Boyars, 1972); *An Empty House* (Calder & Boyars, 1975).

EDWARD GAITENS was born in Glasgow in 1897. Little is known about his life. His literary executor, Charles Turner, says that he put his life into his writings and there is nothing else he would have wanted to be put on record. Although he published only two books, his picture of early twentieth-century Glasgow and his sensitive but unsentimental portraits of its warm-hearted, gregarious, rumbustious people ensure him a lasting place in Scottish literature. He died in 1966.

Short Stories: *Growing Up* (Jonathan Cape, 1942).
Novel: *Dance of the Apprentices*, a novel of Gorbals life (William Maclellan, 1948).

GILES GORDON was born in Edinburgh in 1940, and was educated at the Edinburgh Academy, as were his father (Esme Gordon, the architect) and his father. Upon leaving school he studied typography and book design at Edinburgh College of Art and was trained in publishing at the then indigenous Scottish publishing house of Oliver & Boyd. Since the early sixties he has worked in London, where he lives with his wife—Margaret Gordon, the children's book illustrator —and their three children. His publishing jobs included stints at Secker & Warburg, Hutchinson, being plays editor at Penguin, and five years as editorial director at Victor Gollancz. Since 1972 he has divided his time between working as a literary agent with Anthony Sheil Associates and his own writing.

Short fictions: *Pictures from an exhibition* (Allison & Busby, 1970); *Farewell, Fond Dreams* (Hutchinson, 1975); *The Illusionist* (Harvester Press, 1978).

Novels: *The Umbrella Man* (Allison & Busby, 1971); *About a marriage* (Allison & Busby, 1972); *Girl with red hair* (Hutchinson, 1974); *100 scenes from married life* (Hutchinson, 1976); *Enemies* (Harvester Press, 1977).

Poetry: *Two and Two Make One* (Akros, 1966); *Two Elegies* (Turret Books, 1968); *Twelve Poems for Callum* (Akros, 1972); *One Man, two women* (Sheep Press, 1974); *The Oban Poems* (Sceptre Press, 1977).

As editor: *Factions*, with Alex Hamilton (Michael Joseph, 1974); *Beyond the Words* (Hutchinson, 1975); *Members of the Jury*, with Dulan Barber (Wildwood House, 1976); *Prevailing Spirits*: a book of Scottish ghost stories (Hamish Hamilton, 1976); *A Book of Contemporary Nightmares* (Michael Joseph, 1976).

NEIL MILLER GUNN was born in Caithness, 8th November 1891. He was educated at a Highland school and privately, and became a civil servant in the Customs and Excise department. He resigned from the civil service in 1937. He married Jessie Dallas Frew in 1921. In 1931 he attracted great attention with *Morning Tide,* and soon established himself as one of Scotland's leading writers. Professor Alexander Scott believes that *The Silver Darlings* 'is perhaps the greatest of all modern Scottish novels.' Gunn won the James Tait Black Memorial Prize in 1938 and was given the honorary degree of LL.D. by Edinburgh University. He died in January 1973.

Short stories: *Hidden Doors* (1929); *The White Hour* (1950).

Novels: *The Grey Coast* (1926); *Morning Tide* (1931); *Sun Circle* (1933); *Butcher's Broom* (1934); *Highland River* (1937); *The Silver Darlings* (1941); *Young Art and Old Hector* (1942); *The Well at the World's End* (1951); *The Other Landscape* (1954) and many others.

Autobiography: *The Atom of Delight* (1956).

His first two books were published by the Porpoise Press, Edinburgh. Faber & Faber took over the Porpoise Press and published all Neil M. Gunn's books.

Critical studies of Neil M. Gunn: *The Scottish Tradition in Literature,* by Kurt Wittig (Oliver & Boyd, 1958); *Neil M. Gunn, The Man and the Writer*: essays in tribute to Neil Gunn's 80th birthday (Blackwood, 1973).

MARGARET HAMILTON was born in Glasgow in 1915. She was educated at Hutchesons' Grammar School and then, until her marriage to Robert McIlhone, worked as a local government officer. Her first stories were published and broadcast when she was in her early twenties. Her husband died in 1966 and in her last years she worked as secretary in a school in one of Glasgow's largest housing schemes. She died in 1972, and is survived by her daughter, Nora. Her stories have appeared in literary magazines and anthologies, and have been broadcast. Her novel, *Bull's Penny*, was written in a form of Ayrshire doric. In the two years before her death, she published a number of short poems in the dialect of present-day Glasgow. These verses have been used by teachers in under-privileged areas to demonstrate to their pupils that poetry is not just for other people, but can be about themselves, in their language—an application of her work which delighted her.

Novel: *Bull's Penny* (MacGibbon & Kee, 1950).

DOROTHY K. HAYNES was born in Lanark in 1918. She was educated at Lanark Grammar School and at St Margaret's Episcopal, Aberlour. She is married, with two sons. She lives in Lanark, and was a member of the Town Council, 1972-1975. She won the Tom-Gallon Award in 1947, has had innumerable stories published in magazines and anthologies, and contributes regularly to the *Scots Magazine*. Over fifty of her stories have been broadcast.

Short stories: *Thou Shalt Not Suffer a Witch* (Methuen, 1949).
Novels: *Winter's Traces* (Methuen, 1947); *Robin Ritchie* (Methuen, 1949).
Autobiography: *Haste Ye Back* (Jarrolds, 1973).

J. F. HENDRY was born in Glasgow in 1912. He worked as a translator for various United Nations agencies after the war, in Vienna, Geneva and Africa, translating into English from German, Italian, French and Russian. He has lived in France, Italy, Austria and Belgium but is happiest in Scotland where he is at present living and working as a novelist, though he has now retired. He was editor of the wartime anthologies *The New Apocalypse, White Horsemen,* and *Crown and Sickle,* expressing in essays, poetry and fiction the views of a movement little studied by critics, although including the work of Norman MacCaig, G. S. Fraser and Robert Melville. In 1970 he edited *The Penguin Book of Scottish Short Stories.*

Short stories: *The Blackbird of Ospo* (William Maclellan, 1945).
Novel: *Fernie Brae* (William Maclellan, 1946).
Poems: *Bombed Happiness* (Routledge, 1942); *Marimarusa* (Caithness Books, 1978).
Translations: *Your Career in Translating and Interpreting* (Richard Rosen Press, New York, 1969); *Gnosis* by R. Haardt: translated

from German (Brill, Leiden, 1971); *Russian for Scientists* by Y. Gentilhomme: translated from French (Dunod, Paris, 1970).

ALAN JACKSON was born in 1938 and has lived mainly in Edinburgh. He has declined to provide a biographical note for this book, regarding his life as 'The same as every other soul's: the struggle through ignorance and darkness to light and love.' However, there is a biographical note in *Penguin Modern Poets 12* (1968), which includes a substantial selection of his work.

Poetry: *Underwater Wedding* (self published, 1961); *Sixpenny Poems* (self published, 1962); *Well Ye Ken Noo* (self published, 1963); *All Fall Down* (Kevin Press, 1965); *The Worstest Beast* (Kevin Press, 1967); *The Grim Wayfarer* (Fulcrum Press, 1969); *Idiots Are Freelance* (Rainbow Books, 1973).
Non-Fiction: *The Knitted Claymore*: an essay on culture and Nationalism (Lines Review, 1971).

MORLEY JAMIESON was born in 1917 at Newlandrigg in Borthwick Parish in Midlothian. He left school at the age of twelve and spent three years in a sanatorium. He began his working life in a limestone quarry, which he found uncongenial but remained there for six years. He left the quarry to go to Newbattle Abbey College, and later went to Coleg Harlech, Merioneth. He became a convert to Roman Catholicism, married, and lived for two years in the household of Edwin and Willa Muir. He has been a bookseller for many years now, an occupation which he thinks must be one of the most congenial there is. He has written radio scripts (one on Newbattle Abbey) and short stories, and has recently established a new periodical, *Brunton's Miscellany*, which he edits.

Short stories: *The Old Wife and Other Stories* (M. Macdonald, 1972).
Poetry: *Nine Poems* (Brunton's, 1976); *Ten Poems* (Brunton's, 1978).

ROBIN JENKINS was born in Lanarkshire in 1912 and educated at Hamilton Academy and Glasgow University. He has a home in Dunoon, Argyll, but has spent a good part of the last twenty years abroad, teaching English. He received the Frederick Niven Award in 1956.

Short stories: *A Far Cry From Bowmore* (Gollancz, 1973).
Novels: *Happy for the Child* (John Lehmann, 1953); *The Thistle and The Grail* (Macdonald, 1954); *The Cone-Gatherers* (Macdonald, 1955); *Guests of War* (Macdonald, 1956); *The Changeling* (Macdonald, 1958); *Dust on the Paw* (Macdonald, 1961); *A Would-Be Saint* (Gollancz, 1978), and many others.

JAMES KENNAWAY was born in 1928. His father was a solicitor in Auchterarder, Perthshire and his mother was a doctor. He was educated at Trinity College, Glenalmond. At eighteen he was commissioned into the Cameron Highlanders, though he served with the Gordons in Germany. In 1948 he went to Trinity College, Oxford and read Philosophy, Politics and History. While he was at Oxford he met, and subsequently married, an art student. They had four children. In addition to his novels, he wrote an original filmscript, *Violent Playground* (1958), as well as filmscripts based on his novels *Tunes of Glory* (1960) and *The Mindbenders* (1962). Other filmscripts included the *Battle of Britain*. His play, *Country Dance*, was also filmed (1969) with Peter O'Toole and Susanah York, and published by Elek in *Plays of the Year* 1967 volume 33.

Novels: *Tunes of Glory* (Putnam, 1956); *Household Ghosts* (Longmans Green, 1961); *The Mindmenders* (Longmans Green, 1962); *The Bells of Shoreditch* (Longmans Green, 1965); *Some Gorgeous Accident* (Longmans Green, 1967); *The Cost of Living Like This* (Longmans Green, 1969); *Silence* (Cape, 1970) was put together posthumously from his own notes.

ERIC LINKLATER was born in Penarth in 1899, the son of a sea captain, who several years later took the family back to his native Orkney. An education at Aberdeen's Grammar School and University was broken by two years' service on the Western Front with the Black Watch, during which he was severely wounded. After graduating from university in English Literature, Eric Linklater worked on *The Times of India*, and in 1928 won a Commonwealth Fellowship to the United States. His first novel *White-Maa's Saga* was published in the same year, and his last, *A Terrible Freedom*, almost forty years later. In between came more than twenty other novels, and plays, short stories and histories in unfashionable profusion. The craftsmanship was sure, but it was the language rather than the form which he enjoyed. His writing was marked by an ebullient pleasure in being alive, which showed itself in wit, bawdiness and good humour, and was admirably served by an Elizabethan delight in the sound and sense of words. The greater part of his life was passed in Orkney and the north of Scotland, interspersed by travel, and soldiering in the two World Wars, and his own preferred self-description was 'A peasant with a pen'. He died in Aberdeen in 1974 and was buried in Orkney.

Short stories: *God Likes Them Plain* (Cape, 1935); *Sealskin Trousers* (Rupert Hart-Davis, 1947); *A Sociable Plover* (Rupert Hart-Davis, 1957) and *The Stories of Eric Linklater* (Macmillan, 1968).
Novels include: *White Maa's Saga* (Cape, 1929); *Poet's Pub* (Cape,

1930); *Juan in America* (Cape, 1931); *Magnus Merriman* (Cape, 1934); *Private Angelo* (Cape, 1946); *Mr Byculla* (Rupert Hart-Davis, 1950); *Position at Noon* (Cape, 1958).

Children's Books: *The Wind on the Moon* (Macmillan, 1944); *The Pirates in the Deep Green Sea* (Macmillan, 1949).

History includes: *Mary, Queen of Scots* (Peter Davies, 1933); *The Prince in the Heather* (Hodder & Stoughton, 1965); *The Ultimate Viking* (Macmillan, 1955); *The Conquest of England* (Hodder & Stoughton, 1966).

NEIL McCALLUM was born at Portobello near Edinburgh in 1916. He learned to read at Preston Street Primary School, memorable because the school was built on the site of one of the city's gibbets. He then went to George Watson's College and Edinburgh University. He started to write, and was published regularly in the *Scotsman*, when still a schoolboy. He began work as a newspaper copy boy, then became a reporter. He was a wartime soldier in North Africa and Sicily, then joined the staff of an army newspaper unit in Italy, where he worked on the daily production of newspapers for the troops. After the war he went into the advertising agency business in Edinburgh, where he still lives. He was Scottish feature writer for the *New Statesman* from 1947 to 1952. He served on the governing board of Newbattle Abbey College when Edwin Muir was warden, and was subsequently honorary secretary of the Edwin Muir memorial fund. He is a member of PEN and of the Society of Authors.

Novels: *Half Way House* (Cassell, 1949); *My Enemies Have Sweet Voices* (Cassell, 1951); *Fountainfoot* (Cassell, 1952); *A Scream in the Sky* (Cassell, 1964).
Autobiography: *Journey with a Pistol* (Gollancz, 1959).
Folklore: *It's an Old Scottish Custom* (Dobson, 1951).

EONA MACNICOL was born a member of the Fraser clan in Inverness in 1910. Her parents were both born and brought up in a village set high above Loch Ness; it is her knowledge of this community, where during her early girlhood her grandparents still lived, which provides the background of her collection of short stories, *The Hallowe'en Hero*. Her connection with the town of Inverness, and with that part of Loch Ness-side where there are traces and a tradition of the Columban Church, led her into the research on the life of St Columba which has resulted in two historical novels, *Colum of Derry* and *Lamp in the Night Wind*, as well as a third novel not yet published. Mrs Macnicol has spent part of her life in Madras, South India where both she and her husband lectured in English. They now live in Edinburgh; and have two sons, one daughter, and three grandchildren. Apart from her family and her writing, she is concerned with the World Development Movement and Amnesty International.

Short Stories: *The Hallowe'en Hero* (William Blackwood, 1969); *The Jail Dancing* (Albyn Press, 1978).
Novels: *Colum of Derry* (Sheed & Ward, 1954); *Lamp in the Night Wind* (William Maclellan, 1965).

ALLAN MASSIE was born in Singapore in 1938. He was educated at Glenalmond and Trinity College, Cambridge. He has taught in Scotland and Italy, and lived in Rome from 1972-75: he now lives with his wife and two children and a cat in Edinburgh. He reviews fiction regularly for the *Scotsman,* and has contributed to the *London Magazine,* the *Times Literary Supplement, Punch, Blackwoods, Akros,* the *Scottish Review,* and *Brunton's Miscellany,* and to the Collins *Scottish Short Stories* series. He is working on a new assessment of Muriel Spark for the Ramsay Head Press.

Novel: *Change and Decay in All Around I See* (Bodley Head, 1978).

NAOMI MITCHISON was born in Edinburgh at her grandparents' house in 1897. Her father was Professor J. S. Haldane and as he was working mainly at Oxford she spent most of her young days there, but always came back to Scotland for holidays. In 1937 she and her husband Dick Mitchison bought a house at Carradale on the Kintyre coast, and she has lived there more than anywhere else ever since. She writes: 'I have been much involved with local politics and the problems of the inshore fishing industry; I was a member of the Highland Advisory Panel and got to know every small harbour in the Highlands and Islands. Later I was on the Highland Council. I am not a Gaelic speaker but I realised early that Gaelic grammatical structure underlay west Highland speech—so different from that of the farm servants, mostly from the Mearns, at my Haldane Grandmother's house at Cloan! However, the basis for this story is something which (perhaps) happened in my Skye daughter-in-law's family. I live mostly at Carradale but rush off when I can and usually get involved in the problems of the under-dogs in whatever countries I get to.'

She has written about seventy books including:
Short stories: *When the Bough Breaks* (Cape, 1924); *Black Sparta* (Cape, 1928); *Barbarian Stories* (Cape, 1929); *The Delicate Fire* (Cape, 1933); *The Fourth Pig* (Constable, 1936); *Five Men and a Swan* (Allen & Unwin, 1958).
Novels: *The Conquered* (Cape, 1923); *The Corn King and the Spring Queen* (Cape, 1931); *The Blood of the Martyrs* (Constable,

1939); *The Bull Calves* (Cape, 1947); *The Big House* (Faber, 1950); *Lobsters on the Agenda* (Gollancz, 1952); *To the Chapel Perilous* (Allen & Unwin, 1955); *Memoirs of a Spacewoman* (Gollancz, 1962).

Autobiography: *Small Talk* (Bodley Head, 1973); *All Change Here* (Bodley Head, 1975).

Children's books: *The Land the Ravens Found* (Collins, 1955); *The Rib of the Green Umbrella* (Collins, 1960); *The Family at Ditlabeng* (Collins, 1969); *Snake* (Collins, 1976).

Others: *The Cleansing of the Knife* (Canongate Press, 1978).

ANGUS WOLFE MURRAY was born in Edinburgh, where he now lives, in 1937. He was educated at Eton, and is married to a publisher. He and his wife have four sons. His jobs have included: greensman, bank clerk, surveyor, insurance broker, journalist, critic, publisher, van driver, and owner operator of a transport company. He has published articles in national magazines and stories in anthologies.

Novels: *The End of Something Nice* (Macmillan, 1967); *Resurrection Shuffle* (Peter Owen, 1978).

IAIN CRICHTON SMITH was born in the Isle of Lewis in 1928. He was educated at the Nicolson Institute, Stornoway, then at Aberdeen University where he took an Honours English Degree. During National Service he was a Sergeant in the Education Corps. He taught English for twenty-five years, most of that time in Oban High School. He gave up teaching in 1977 to concentrate exclusively on his writing. He married in the same year.

Short stories: *Survival without Error* (Gollancz, 1970); *The Black and the Red* (Gollancz, 1973); *The Hermit and other stories* (Gollancz, 1977).

Novels: *Consider the Lilies* (Gollancz, 1968); *The Last Summer* (Gollancz, 1969); *Goodbye, Mr Dixon* (Gollancz, 1974).

Poetry: *The Long River* (M. Macdonald, 1955); *Thistles and Roses* (Eyre & Spottiswoode, 1961); *The Law and the Grace* (Eyre & Spottiswoode, 1965); *From Bourgeois Land* (Gollancz, 1969); *Selected Poems* (Gollancz, 1970); *Love Poems and Elegies* (Gollancz, 1972); *Hamlet in Autumn* (M. Macdonald, 1972); *The Notebooks of Robinson Crusoe* (Gollancz, 1975); *In the Middle* (Gollancz, 1977).

MURIEL SPARK was born and educated in Edinburgh, and spent some years in Central Africa. She returned to Britain during the second world war and worked in the Political Intelligence Department of the Foreign Office. She subsequently edited two poetry magazines, and her published works include critical biographies of nineteenth-century figures, and editions of nineteenth-century letters. Since she won an *Observer* short story competition in 1951 her creative writings have achieved international recognition, and are published in twenty different languages. Among many other awards she has received the Italia Prize and the James Tait Black Memorial Prize. She was awarded the OBE in 1967, and is currently living in Rome. Mrs Spark became a Roman Catholic in 1954, and has one son. Her novel *The Prime of Miss Jean Brodie* was dramatised, and enjoyed a long and successful run on the West End stage. It has also been filmed and was recently adapted as a television serial. Her one play, *Doctors of Philosophy*, was first produced in London in 1962.

Short stories: *The Go-Away Bird* (1958); *Voices at Play* (1961); *Collected Stories 1* (1967).

Novels: *The Comforters* (1957); *Robinson* (1958); *Memento Mori* (1959); *The Bachelors* (1960); *The Ballad of Peckham Rye* (1960); *The Prime of Miss Jean Brodie* (1961); *The Girls of Slender Means* (1963); *The Mandelbaum Gate* (1965); *The Public Image* (1968); *The Driver's Seat* (1968); *Not to Disturb* (1971); *The Hothouse by the East River* (1973); *The Abbess of Crewe* (1974); *The Takeover* (1976).

Poetry: *Collected Poems* (1967).

Play: *Doctors of Philosophy* (1963).

Biography: *John Masefield* (Peter Nevill, 1953); *Child of Light* (Mary Shelley); *The Brontë Letters*.

Children's book: *The Very Fine Clock* (1969).

All these books are published by Macmillan.

ALAN SPENCE was born in Glasgow in 1947. He attended Glasgow University 1966-69 and 1973-74. In between times he took various jobs, spent time in Europe and the United States. He received a Scottish Arts Council Bursary in 1971, and was Fellow in Creative Writing at Glasgow University, 1975-77. He is married, and since 1970 he and his wife have been disciples of Sri Chinmoy, the Indian spiritual master. They are at present living in Edinburgh, where they run the Sri Chinmoy Meditation Centre.

Short stories: *Its Colours They Are Fine* (Collins, 1977).

Poetry: *ah!* (50 haiku) (Agni Press, New York, 1975).

FRED URQUHART, born in Edinburgh in 1912, spent most of his childhood in Fife, Perthshire and Wigtownshire. He was educated at Stranraer High School and Broughton Secondary School, Edinburgh. He worked in an Edinburgh bookshop 1927-1935. His first published story was in the *Adelphi* in 1936. After that his stories were printed in most of the leading periodicals of the time. His first novel *Time Will Knit* appeared in 1938, was recommended by the Saltire Society, was reprinted in Penguin and Ace Books, and is still in print in a Portway edition. He worked in a literary agency in London 1947-51, was a reader for MGM 1951-54, and was London 'scout' for Walt Disney Productions 1959-60. From 1951 to 1974 he was a reader and editor for Cassell, and he also read for several other London publishers from time to time. Many of his stories have been broadcast and have appeared in numerous anthologies. He received the Tom-Gallon Trust Award in 1951, and Arts Council bursaries in 1966 and 1975. He has lived in Sussex for nearly twenty-five years.

Short stories: *I Fell For a Sailor* (Duckworth, 1940); *The Clouds Are Big With Mercy* (William Maclellan, 1946); *Selected Stories* (Fridberg, 1946); *The Last G.I. Bride Wore Tartan* (Serif Books, 1948); *The Year of the Short Corn* (Methuen, 1949); *The Last Sister* (Methuen, 1950); *The Laundry Girl and The Pole* (Arco, 1955); *The Dying Stallion* (Rupert Hart-Davis, 1967); *The Ploughing Match* (Rupert Hart-Davis, 1968).

Novels: *Time Will Knit* (Duckworth, 1938); *The Ferret Was Abraham's Daughter* (Methuen, 1949); *Jezebel's Dust* (Methuen, 1951).

Edited: *No Scottish Twilight,* with Maurice Lindsay (William Maclellan, 1947); *W.S.C., A Cartoon Biography of Winston Churchill* (Cassell, 1955); *The Cassell Miscellany* (1958); *Scottish Short Stories* (Faber, 1957).